THE EVANGELICAL ALLIANCE PRIZE ESSAY

ON INFIDELITY.

---

# INFIDELITY DISSECTED.

BY

THE REV. THOMAS PEARSON,

EYEMOUTH, SCOTLAND.

---

CHICAGO:

GEO. MAC DONALD & CO.

KNIGHT & LEONARD, PRINTERS, CHICAGO.

THIS ESSAY

IS RESPECTFULLY DEDICATED

TO THE

EVANGELICAL ALLIANCE

BY THE AUTHOR.

# CONTENTS.

## PART THE FIRST.



## PART THE SECOND.

# INTRODUCTION.

THE answer given by the messengers to the angel of the Lord that stood among the myrtle trees, in the vision of Zechariah the prophet, does not apply to our times: "We have walked to and fro through the earth, and behold all the earth sitteth still and is at rest." Politically and morally, in things sacred and civil, Europe, in the nineteenth century, is a troubled sea. Numerous and mighty agencies, both for good and evil, are abroad and at work. These agencies may embody the same great principles that have been opposing and struggling with each other from the beginning. Light and darkness strove on the face of the deep before this goodly universe rose out of chaos, and they have their strivings still. Error is not of yesterday, any more than truth. They encountered each other in Paradise, they have had many encounters since, and they are yet in the field. But periods arise which become exalted into epochs, when these ancient forces, on the one side or on both, display more than usual vigor,—appear in new or revived forms, change their modes of attack and defense, and come off with honors. Such a period was the beginning of the Gospel, when truth, in her fairest form, descended from heaven, sustained the combined attack of all the powers of evil, and, by her own inherent vigor, spoiled principalities and powers, and went on conquering and to conquer. Such a period was the dark or middle ages, which, like a long and dreary night, succeeded a short but bright day, when it seemed as if truth had been driven from the field, and the world had been given up to the reign of ignorance and error. Such a period was the Reformation of the sixteenth century, which, with a voice whose sound was like the sea, awoke Europe from the sleep of ages, mustered in fierce and vigorous conflict all the powers of good and evil, and sent throughout the heart of ransomed humanity a thrill of joyous liberty that has echoed over the earth and down the stream of time. Such a period (to contract our view within our own England) was that august and earnest century when an oppressed people rose up, resolute and majestic, against their faithless oppressors,—when the Puritans sounded the Gospel trumpet against the formalism and irreligion of the age, and men awoke at once to civil freedom and that yet higher liberty wherewith the truth makes men free. And (to leap over the bridge that spanned the dark and boisterous waters that rolled between,—one of those dreary intervals that ever and anon occur in history,—and which constituted in itself a dark age, when the foe was permitted to advance and stretch his scepter over the church and the world, and, in a great measure, corrupt the form and stifle the voice of truth itself) such a period was the latter half of the last century, when an awakening evangelism, big and feeling-hearted, counteracted the materialistic tendencies which a skeptical, soulless philosophy had given to the age, and blew upon the cold, earthly morality that had usurped the place of the Gospel in the college chair and in the church pulpit.

The fruits of this latter age — fruits both good and evil — we are now reaping. There is more reason, however, to be thankful for its legacy of good, than to deplore the inheritance of its evil. Its shining light has shone more and more unto our own day; but masses of dark cloud, envious and portentous, have followed it. We are not so moodishly disposed as to call to remembrance the former days, and say they were better than the present. No; the age, carrying along with it much of the rich good of the past, is, in spite of many drawbacks, advancing onward in the right path. There is in the heart of humanity a much larger amount of the leaven of heavenly truth than could be found at any preceding period, and, notwithstanding all opposing tendencies, it is spreading, and will spread. Despotism, which robs man of his rights and obstructs the progress of God's truth, is losing its ground, and truth and freedom are advancing. The Bible, the schoolmaster, the evangelist, and the missionary are abroad. The church at home is becoming more and more alive to the call of her Lord, "Arise, shine." Her voice is becoming more loud and earnest in the pulpit, her instruction agencies among our home population are strengthening and thickly multiplying, and she is lengthening her cords so as to embrace within her pale the abundance of the sea and the forces of the Gentiles. But if it is unwise to brood over the maladies of an age, as if it were only evil, and that continually, it is not less so to glory in its fair forms and healthy activities as if oblivious of its wounds and bruises and putrifying sores. The sun is in the heavens bright and beaming, but the clouds have gathered, surcharged with the elements of strife, and they are ever and anon darkening and troubling the sky. Our age is one of intense earnestness and action, both for good and evil. The old truth and the old error, which have struggled throughout the past, are in the field. But neither is slumbering; both are vigilant, extending their lines, increasing their forces, devising and adopting new modes of defense and attack, as if conscious that a blow was about to be struck which would mark another great era in the conflict between the powers of good and evil.

There are giants on the earth in these days, both in the one encampment and in the other. A mighty force is on the side of the friends of truth, but it is sadly divided and scattered What is wanting is the strength of union,— the concentration of those energies, in defending the citadel and making inroads on the enemy, which are spent on the defense of comparatively unimportant posts, or in one detachment of the same corps guarding against the encroachment of another. The champions of error, though not without their discords and divisions, are yet wiser in their generation than the children of light. As of old, they discern the signs of the times, and take counsel together against the Lord and against his anointed. The Press, to which, under God, we owe so much of our light and liberties, wields a mighty influence on the side of evil. The halls of philosophy, hallowed though they be by many a name illustrious for Christian worth as well as intellectual greatness, are often sending forth doctrines as gross as the earth or as vague as the air, but alike adverse to that truth which, coming from above, is above all. Our current literature and works on science, with not a few bright and beneficent exceptions, are hostile, either by their silence in reference to divine truth when their subjects afford them occasions to speak out, or by their avowed opposition to much of what constitutes the essence of true religion. And what is peculiar, in a great measure, to our times, and throws a vast potency into the scale of irreligion, is the unceasing effort of infidels to diffuse their principles among the artisans and laboring classes of the land. The earth is not still and at rest. Men of every class are searching after an unknown good. The demon of infidelity is stalking abroad, knocking at the palaces of the rich and the cottages of the poor,[1] transforming itself into this shape and that, and becoming all things, except an angel of good, to all men. One dreary theory succeeds another, like storm-cloud chasing storm-cloud over the face of the sky, and yet man is not at peace. The cravings of his mind are agonized, not satisfied. It becomes those, then, who know

[1] ——"Aequo pulsat pede pauperum tabernas
Regumque turres."—*Horace.*

the truth, and whom the truth has made free,—those who, having believed, do enter into rest, to arouse themselves for the two-fold object of meeting infidelity at its various points and combating its diversified forms, and of presenting, in every lawful way, that truth which they know only can give rest to a laboring and heavy-laden world. Let the antagonist forces, on the one side as well as on the other, be pressed into the unfettered conflict, and the lovers of God and the friends of man have nothing to fear, but much to hope. "Christianity, like Rome, has had both the Gaul and Hannibal at her gates; but, as the 'Eternal City,' in the latter case, calmly offered for sale, and sold at an undepreciated price, the very ground on which the Carthaginian had fixed his camp, with equal calmness may Christianity imitate her example of magnanimity. She may feel assured that, as in so many past instances of premature triumph on the part of her enemies, the ground they occupy will one day be her own,—that the very discoveries, apparently hostile, of science and philosophy, will be ultimately found elements of her strength."[1] "All flesh is as grass, and all the glory of man as the flower of grass. The grass withereth, and the flower thereof falleth away. But the word of the Lord endureth for ever."

[1] Rogers' Essays, vol. ii, p. 345.

# PART THE FIRST.

## INFIDELITY IN ITS VARIOUS ASPECTS.

ATHEISM—PANTHEISM—NATURALISM—PSEUDO-SPIRITUALISM—INDIFFERENTISM—FORMALISM.

INFIDELITY, though elaborating its own creed, is, properly speaking, a system of negations. It suggests rather what it seeks to demolish than what it attempts to build. In this respect it is like the palmer-worm of the prophet,[1] the mere mention of which leads one to think more of what it has destroyed, than of what it has left to be eaten by the locust. But in the work of demolition, one man or class of men advances farther than another. Some sacred truths which one band of fell destroyers clear away in their march, another band, leagued in the same warfare, leave standing. Just as we may suppose some of the soldiers of Cæsar, in attacking the Massilian grove, went scrupulously and sparingly to work from a superstitious dread of invisible power, while others, less timid and superstitious, leveled to the ground everything that had for ages been counted sacred.[2] Infidelity in one age or country may be much more sweeping than in another, and, as everybody knows, contemporaneous systems of unbelief among the same people may differ widely in the number of things sacred which they proscribe. But there is a clearly

[1] Joel i. 4. [2] Foster's Essays, p. 39, 15th ed.

defined body of religious truth, in reverencing which, people and nations who have had and fairly used the means of judging, however much differing on other points, have generally been agreed. This is the ark of the God of Israel; and however the Philistines may outstrip each other in laying hands upon it, they are yet to be numbered under one genus, on the principle that depredators are but depredators, though some may be braver and more successful in the work of plunder than others. This body of truth comprises all the commonly understood doctrines of natural and revealed religion: such as the independent existence of one absolutely perfect Being, the Creator, Preserver, and Governor of all things; the doctrine of the Trinity, or of three Persons in the Godhead, the Father, the Son, and the Holy Spirit; the Incarnation and Atonement of the Son for human salvation; and the necessity of the Spirit's influences to regenerate the souls of men. This is God's truth, the substance of all that material nature teaches, the purest reason has ever been able to discover, and the Scriptures have revealed. There is room for a diversity of opinion about modes of ecclesiastical government, external rites and ceremonies, and the interpretation of certain Scriptural passages, but no one who has ears to hear, and who humbly listens to the voices of nature and revelation, can fail to discover what God is, and what he has done, what man is, and what he needs. Infidelity, then, is found to manifest itself in such forms as the following: in the denial of the Divine Existence, or absolute Atheism; in the denial of the Divine Personality, or Pantheism; in the denial of the Divine Providential Government, or Naturalism; in the denial of the Divine Redemption (including, as it does, the doctrines of the Trinity, Atonement, and Spirit's influences), or Pseudo-Spiritualism. And to these may be added, what belongs more properly to practical, than to theoretical infidelity, the denial of Man's responsibility, or Indifferentism; and the denial of the Power of Godliness, or Formalism. These forms we shall now develop.

# CHAPTER I.

## THE DENIAL OF THE DIVINE EXISTENCE, OR ATHEISM.

Atheism completes the negation — A somewhat strange phenomenon — Its existence doubted — No man of straw — Processes by which men have become atheists — Prevalent in most depraved times — French atheism — Reign of Terror — An atheistical nation self-destructive — No lack of adverse speculations respecting the Divine Being, but absolute atheism comparatively rare — Development hypothesis not positively atheistical — Atheism, however, a fact — Involves a monstrous assumption — The existence of God an intellectual necessity — Arguments *à priori* and *à posteriori* — Exclusive claim for either disposed of — Inductive proof from matter and mind — Defect of Induction — Bible testimony — Practical proof the real one — Dr. Arnold.

HERE the negation is complete. The work of demolishing things esteemed sacred, has advanced so far as to leave nothing more for the destroyer to do. He has reached the dreary brink from which many destroyers, by no means craven-hearted, have shrunk back. And from that bad pre-eminence he looks upwards to the heavens, vacant at first in his wishes, and now in his creed, and with as much boldness as if he had traveled through the realms of space and beheld all dark and desolate, says, There is there no God. He looks down to the gulf of annihilation, and, amid the troubles of his godless existence, feels something like a morbid satisfaction in the thought that the grave is an eternal sleep and the present scene the whole of man. He looks abroad upon the mass of human society, ill at ease and yearning after an enjoyment that it has never found, and to the question, "Who will shew us any good?" he has only one answer, "Let us eat and drink, for to-morrow we die." No religion is his religion. And he struggles, against the aspirings of his better self, to rest in the dark dogma that the highest being is man.

Atheism in this unqualified sense is, it must be admitted, a somewhat strange and startling phenomenon. People in many parts would turn out and look at a real and avowed atheist, just as they do at some singularly huge foreign animals, with mingled astonishment and alarm. Faith in God is so inherent in the heart of humanity, and so essential to our reason, that many wise and good men have doubted if ever there lived an intelligent mortal so absolutely destitute of religious belief as is implied in atheism. Addison would have told a man who gloried in this distinction, that he was an impudent liar, and that he knew it. Bacon accounted atheism to be rather in the lip than in the heart, and that a contemplative atheist is a prodigy, a thing unusually rare. "I confess," says Dr. Arnold in one of his weighty letters, "that I believe conscientious atheism not to exist." And it does appear an incredible thing, that a man possessed of intelligence and feeling, standing amid this glorious amphitheater of earth and sky, gazing upon its grand and lovely forms, and listening to its thousand voices of rapturous praise, can coolly deny the existence of Him who sits enthroned above the heavens. It does seem hard to be believed that one of our race can retire into the depths of his own inner nature, and familiarize himself with the wondrous phenomena of his mental existence, and yet come out of himself and unhesitatingly say that this great system of animate and inanimate being is without a presiding and independent mind. It does look like a very prodigious thing in the world that men should be found who not only rob God of the attributes that are essential to his nature, and extrude Him from the domain of his own creation, but can frame and assent to the proposition that God is not. But such prodigies have been and are ever and anon recurring. Every one indeed is not an atheist who wishes to be so. And many who would fain persuade the world that they are heroes of this description, are no more to be credited than the coward who, in the absence of the foe, boasts of his bravery. But absolute atheism is no man of straw that controversialists have set up in order that they might knock him down. It is an embodied breathing reality. And however much violence may be implied in freeing the mind of a belief in God, in thwarting and representing those moral instincts which naturally go out thither and rest in that faith, and in falsifying all the signs palpably marked on the shining heavens and the green earth, which have spoken from the beginning to the philosopher and the peasant of a supreme presiding intelligence, the violence in not a few instances has been done.

In some minds of a philosophic cast the work has proceeded with something like system and deliberation. From one or two principles, which in their fondness they no more thought of doubting than axioms in mathematics, they have wrought out, through a series of inevitable developments, an independent universe, governed exclusively by mechanical laws, the lawgiver being fate or necessity, or some other equally vague and unintelligible name. In other minds less accustomed to scale the heavens and traverse the fields of space, the consummation has been reached by a felt necessity of advancing after having thrown off religious restraints; just as some people are necessitated to do a second wrong action because they have done the first, to do a third because they have done the second, and so on until the character for daring has been stereotyped into something like the shape of an indomitable hero. And never but in the whirlpool of revolutionary frenzy, or in such circumstances as to be at once the cause and effect of the corruption of a state, has atheism been boldly adopted and acted upon by the masses of a nation. A Diagoras, a Bion, and a Lucian, are marked out from among the minds of the ancient world as having made this unenviable attainment. The men of Athens were wont to banish from their city the solitary skeptic that now and then appeared and dared even to doubt the existence of a supreme intelligence. Ancient Rome, we know, had passed the climax of her glory before atheism obtained any hold of the public mind, and its prevalence was followed by such a course of degeneracy, oppression and bloodshed, as makes the reader of her history even now tremble; the age of Pericles among the Greeks and the age of Augustus among the Romans had departed, and in the deluge of depravity that in either case set in, the monster abounded. But never was atheism, whether of a philosophical or political kind, more boldly manifested than in the history of modern Europe. During the latter half of the last century, the religious world had to contend not only with a stupid deism, but with the abettors of an undisguised atheism. The very first principle of natural religion was avowedly rejected and stoutly contended for. Sensationalism reached its culminating point. The materialistic school of France sent forth an infidel science and literature of the broadest stamp, and that school had its disciples in many lands. In the "Système de la Nature," the celebrated work of Baron d'Holbach, the most absolute atheism is asserted as openly as the existence of God is maintained in any of our treatises on natural theology. "The grand object of the book," to use the language of Lord Brougham, "being to show that there is no God, the author begins by endeavoring to establish the most rigorous materialism by trying to show that there is no such thing as mind — nothing beyond or different from the material world."[1] This work, full though it be of gratuitous assumptions and in-

[1] Discourse of Natural Theology, p. 172.

conclusive reasoning, was well fitted, as Dr. Chalmers, speaking from his own experience, once remarked, "by its gorgeous generalizations on nature and truth and the universe, to make tremendous impression on the unpracticed reader."[1] The French Encyclopædia of Sciences, which numbered among its contributors some of the most brilliant writers of the age, was avowedly a work of atheism. Matter and its laws became the engrossing subjects of investigation, the existence of God was treated as the fiction of an over-credulous age, and man was regarded as but an organized animal, the offspring of chance, the sport of fate, and whose end is annihilation. The great work of Auguste Comte, which has obtained for him a wide reputation, is the most celebrated of the recent productions of the same school. It is a system of huge materialism, which "records the dread sentiment, that the universe displays no proofs of an all-directing mind, and records it too as the deduction of unbiased reason." Newton, Kepler, and others of the greatest discoverers in science, have risen from nature up to nature's God, and had their minds filled with religious emotion when exploring the earth and the heavens, but the disciples of the school to which we have referred, brilliant though their reputation be in the departments of physical research, have presented to the world productions of their genius which must bear the broad brand of atheism.

What has been too truly called the Reign of Terror, in France, was avowedly the reign of the most absolute atheism. Infidelity then assumed its boldest front and lifted up its loudest voice, and it found an echo in some parts of our own land. "I frankly confess that I am an atheist," said one of the members of the French Convention in a deliberative assembly of his countrymen; and

[1] Hanna's Life of Chalmers, vol. 1, p. 45.

though the declaration startled multitudes by its daring, yet voices were not wanting in that assembly to cry out, "You are an honest man." The Revolutionary leaders, in the height of their impiety, not only sought to destroy every vestige of Christianity by abolishing the Sabbath, altering the calendar, plundering and shutting up, or converting into warehouses, the various churches; but in the climax of their guilt, they brought the Convention to yield to the cry, that the era had come when men should cease to fear the Eternal, and, in the person of a strumpet, enthroned with heathen orgies the goddess of Reason as the object of national worship. France thus presented to the world the singular and appalling spectacle of a refined and civilized nation openly declaring that there is no God, proscribing all the acts of religious homage, and inscribing on the entrance to the sepulcher that death is an eternal sleep. "This," as Robert Hall remarks, "is the first attempt which has ever been witnessed, on an extensive scale, to establish *the principles* of atheism; the first effort which history has recorded to disannul and extinguish the belief of all superior powers." It had been a matter of dispute in former ages whether a community leavened throughout with atheistical principles could possibly subsist. No great powers of reasoning were requisite to show that, abstractedly considered, the thing is impossible. It is not necessary to see the ocean shifting its bed or rapidly advancing beyond its ancient limits, to feel persuaded that were it to do so, it would carry a sweeping devastation into the towns and villages that skirt the shore. Let the throne in the heavens be declared vacant, and proclamation be made throughout the land that there is no God, and society is reft of all its safeguards, crime is committed without dread of punishment, and the vilest passions of the vilest men rush onward without restraint. For how utterly feeble is the check imposed by human laws when, by denying the Divine existence, they have succeeded in exploding the law of God. But the bad preëminence was reserved for modern France, to teach in a palpable form the awful lesson, that when the Ruler among the nations is openly disowned, the foundations of the earth are out of course, the bonds of society are dissolved, human life is accounted cheap and wantonly sacrificed, and the most horrid deeds are perpetrated under the sacred name of liberty. It was "a grand experiment on human nature." Atheism had never been tried on such an extensive scale before. And it was seen and felt that nations, like individuals, cannot be prosperous and safe, enjoy liberty and be at peace, without acknowledging the living and true God. France was like a troubled sea, a sea of blood, under the reign of atheism. The people at last recoiled from the impious and horrid system. And that same Convention which had publicly disowned the Most High and proclaimed death to be an eternal sleep, was constrained to recognize by enactment the existence of God and the immortality of the soul, and, by an impious festival, professedly to restore the Eternal to the nation's faith and homage. "Vengeance belongeth unto me, I will recompense, saith the Lord." "The republic of these men without a God," remarks Lamartine, "was quickly stranded." Europe has never witnessed the reign of such a bold and undisguised atheism since, and in all probability never will.

Infidel opinions, monstrous and many-shaped enough, are ever and anon thrown up amid the heavings of restless humanity, the natural tendency of which is to lead men to look up to a vacant heaven and down to the dreary gulf, from which, however, they instinctively shrink back, and of such opinions no age was, perhaps, ever more rife than our own. Views of a Supreme Power, of human nature, and of the material world, are emanating from the schools and being diffused throughout the mass of society, which are unquestionably atheistical in their leanings. But there is no broad surface of humanity on which we can look and say, there is atheism absolute and undisguised. Infidelity and atheism are not convertible terms. Atheism is the worst form, the ultimate bound of infidelity; but all infidelity is not atheism. The one is, comparatively, a strange phenomenon; the other is ever floating in innumerable shapes on the surface of society as well as pervading, like leaven, the mass. Men in general will worship. They are naturally led to recognize a Supreme Being, even though he may possess in their imaginings none of the attributes and characteristics of the God of the Bible. We would in nowise be indulgent to the many adverse speculations respecting the Divine Being which are afloat in their subtle and philosophic form, or which are popularized so as to meet the capacities of the multitude, speculations which are dishonoring to God and virtually deny Him. But we would distinguish between the man who believes in the existence of the great First Cause, though holding opinions that rob Him of his glory, and the man who openly avows that there is no God, and denounces the belief in Him as a mere chimera of the understanding. A hypothesis may be atheistical in its bearings, and yet its assertor may be no theoretical atheist. His theism, dissociated from other important beliefs, may be of no moral worth whatever, and in the Scriptural sense of the expression he may be without God in the world, yet so long as positive atheism is not involved in his philosophical creed, and he professes to have faith in God, it were unjust to place him at the bound which he had not yet reached, and write him down atheist. Mr. Hugh Miller justly remarks of the development hypothesis of Maillet and Lamarck, that there is no positive atheism involved in it. "God might as certainly have *originated* the species by a law of development, as he *maintains* it by a law of development; the existence of a first great Cause is as perfectly compatible with the one scheme as with the other."[1] If it were a question of moral influence, and not of dogmatical opinion, we might merge such simple theism in atheism, for, as the author of the "Footprints" observes, "without a belief in the immortality and responsibility of man, and in the scheme of salvation by a Mediator and Redeemer, a belief in the existence of a God is of as little *ethical* value as the belief in the existence of the great sea-serpent." But it is with men's creed, not their practice, that we have at present to do. And men may be living without God in the world, and yet hold that there is a God in the heavens. It is the man who disowns God, who theoretically and practically denies his existence, that bears on his brow the self-inflicted brand, "I am an atheist." Our own age does not lack such daring mortals; they may be found here and there in the schools, and in the workshops, wielding the press, or spouting from the rostrum, or taking up the gauntlet on the platform, but, in general, the mass of society which is not Christian is infidel rather than atheistical. Comparatively few are so foolhardy as to maintain that there is no God, though vast multitudes are foolhardy enough to deprive Him of all his distinguishing glory while professing to acknowledge his existence. Atheism, however, is a fact in human society, and more or less prevalent in every age, and must be numbered as one and the grossest of the forms of infidelity.[2]

[1] Footprints of the Creator, p. 14.

[2] As to the general character of the atheism among the people, we here adduce two competent witnesses. Dr. Krummacher, in his Alliance Paper on Infidelity in Germany, remarks, "that atheism in the lower classes appears as a plant, proceeding more from political interest, than as a proof, proceeding from a clear self-judg-

In atheism the negation of infidelity is complete. Now, before noticing the positive proof for the existence of God, there is an initial consideration, of some importance to the argument, which must be adverted to. We allude to the immense knowledge requisite in certain cases to establish a negative. Evidence may be adduced at once to show that such a thing is or that such a thing has been done, while the negation of this may demand a surprising amount of research and experience. An individual, for example, cast upon what seemed to be a desert island, might affirm that it was, or lately had been, inhabited, and in proof of this he would need only to point to the human footprint on the sand. One such mark would of itself be sufficient to make good the affirmation. But were the companion of his misfortune to contend that the island was uninhabited, and that no traces of a human being having ever been there could be found, it is very obvious that the proof of this negative assertion would be attended with much greater difficulty. In the one case, the single human footmark fresh upon the soil would be proof sufficient. In the other case it would be necessary to explore the whole region, to examine carefully every cavern and locality, before the negative proposition could be substantiated. The one clear print of a man's foot would prove that man was, or had been, in the island; but it would be requisite to see that no human footprint was visible throughout its entire length and breadth, that no vestige of a human inhabitant could be discovered, before an individual would

ment. Religion is looked upon as an invention to press down the people." Mr. Vanderkiste, in his deeply interesting "Notes and Narratives of a Six Years' Mission among the Dens of London," says: "The so-called atheists with whom I have met, have proved, with few exceptions, upon being closely questioned, not *really* to be atheists at all. They have admitted some causation, and when pressed closely upon the subject of intelligent causation, and required to define terms, they have fairly broken down and become angry. Atheism is to be regarded as the desperate shift of an ill-regulated mind, determined to rid itself of responsibility at the expense of all reason and argument."

be entitled to say, that no man was or ever had been there. And the difficulty of making good the negative would increase with the enlargement of the country and the number and size of the localities to be gone over.

The same principle holds with regard to extent of time as to extent of space. Let it be affirmed of the British monarch that, on a certain occasion, she entered, in the most unostentatious manner, into a poor cottage and relieved with her own hands a suffering family. Nothing more would be requisite to substantiate the affirmation than the honest testimony of the favored cottagers, or the truthful word of some competent witnesses. But let the negative statement be made, that the monarch never entered such an humble abode, and never administered relief in such a way, and it is obvious that very much is necessary to make the statement good. No one would be warranted to utter such a negative, but an individual who had closely followed the monarch through every path and winding which she took in private life, or who was, in some way or another, cognizant of all her out-door movements throughout every day of every year since she ascended the throne. Did the individual's experience extend so far as three hundred and sixty-four days of a given year and no farther, for aught he knew, the condescension might have been manifested and the good deed performed on the very day to which his knowledge did not reach. The difficulty of establishing the negative would increase as the time extended to the whole reign, and it would be absolutely insurmountable when made to embrace not only a particular monarch, but all the sovereigns that ever sat on the British throne. Even in the absence of all proof to the contrary, what an amount of presumption would be implied in saying that no English monarch ever entered an humble dwelling and did a benevolent act to its poor inmates; but the arrogance would be complete if the statement was made in defiance of one or more well-authenticated instances of such benignant doings in the annals of English royalty.

These remarks will enable us to see what extraordinary attainments must have been made before an individual would be entitled to say, There is no God. It is a negative proposition which no finite mind can enunciate without being guilty of the most astounding presumption; and the man would only betray his folly who should attempt to demonstrate it. The skeptic may express his doubts of the Divine existence, and give reasons for his doubting, but beyond this, skepticism can achieve nothing. In order to substantiate the affirmative proposition, that there is a God, nothing more might be necessary than to point to some of the footprints of the Creator which are visible in the heavens and the earth. If there be a God, only a very small amount of knowledge and experience would be requisite to prove it. The evidence might lie, as we say that it does lie, in a flower of the field, in a leaf of the forest, in a single hand, or in a single eye. But the negative proposition could be substantiated within no such compass. Even were there no indications of the Creator in that wondrous microcosm the human eye, or in the waving leaf, or in the blooming flower, still it were an illegitimate inference and a manifestation of high presumption to conclude that there is no God. He must needs have traversed not only every part of "this dim spot which men call earth," but he must have wandered from star to star, made himself thoroughly acquainted with all worlds, have searched into the records of all ages, and have found throughout all space and all time no evidence for design, before an individual could be entitled to say that the universe is without a God. This idea is forcibly expressed by

John Foster,[1] and eloquently illustrated by Dr. Chalmers.[2] "The wonder then turns," says the original minded author of the Essays, "on the great process by which a man could grow to the immense intelligence which can know that there is no God. What ages and what lights are requisite for THIS attainment! This intelligence involves the very attributes of Divinity, while a God is denied. For unless this man is omnipresent, unless he is at this moment in every place in the universe, he cannot know but there may be in some place manifestations of a Deity, by which even *he* would be overpowered. If he does not know absolutely every agent in the universe, the one that he does not know may be God. If he is not himself the chief agent in the universe, and does not know what is so, that which is so may be God. If he is not in absolute possession of all the propositions that constitute universal truth, the one which he wants may be, that there is a God. If he cannot with certainty assign the cause of all that he perceives to exist, that cause may be God. If he does not know everything that has been done in the immeasurable ages that are past, some things may have been done by a God. Thus, unless he knows all things, that is, precludes all other divine existence by being Deity himself, he cannot know that the Being whose existence he rejects does not exist. But he must *know* that He does not exist, else he deserves equal contempt and compassion for the temerity with which he firmly avows his rejection and acts accordingly." Atheism is thus shown, at the very outset, to be illogical and to rest on a monstrous assumption, so that we are prepared to welcome whatever evidences offer themselves for the truth of the proposition that there is a God.

But not only is the proof of the non-existence of God an intellectual impossibility; His existence is felt to be an

[1] Essays, 15th ed., p. 35. [2] Institutes of Theology, vol. i, p. 63.

intellectual necessity. The mind of man is so constituted that it cannot be satisfied without it, and hence the monstrous violence done to his intellectual and moral nature when he attempts to banish from him the idea of a First Cause. That there must be a First Cause, is an axiom assumed in all our reasoning upward from the phenomena of nature to nature's God. The snow that is now thickly falling as we write these pages, the stormy wind that is drifting that snow against our windows and doors, are effects the causes of which we investigate and the laws of which we trace; but in our upward track we are seeking after a resting point, we come to the last link in the chain of material causation, and from the very constitution of our minds we repose in a cause essentially different from all others, which is the I AM, the self-existent and independent God. The idea of a great First Cause, is not derived originally from the phenomena of a nature around us, but assumed in our investigations into these phenomena. It is an axiomatic truth which every sound reasoner carries along with him in his ascent from effects to their apparent causes, and to which the mind from a felt necessity fully surrenders itself when it has reached the last link in the phenomena of nature. The Greek logician has said, "all that moves refers us to a mover, and it were only an endless adjournment of causes were there not a primary immovable Mover." Such an endless adjournment of causes can never be resorted to without doing great violence to our mental constitution, and forcibly thwarting its natural tendencies. It is just a perpetual armed attempt to thrust the mind away from the rest to which, from the law of its being, it is ever aspiring. "Our minds cannot be satisfied," remarks Professor Whewell,[1] "with a series of successive, dependent causes and effects, without something first and

[1] Indications of the Creator, 2d ed. p. 198-9.

independent. We pass from effect to cause, and from that to a higher cause, in search of something on which the mind can rest; but if we can do nothing but repeat this process, there is no use in it. We move our limbs, but make no advance. Our question is not answered, but evaded. The mind cannot acquiesce in the destiny thus presented to it, of being referred from event to event, from object to object, along an interminable vista of causation and time. Now, this mode of stating the reply,— to say that the mind *cannot thus be satisfied*, appears to be equivalent to saying that the mind is conscious of a principle in virtue of which such a view as this must be rejected,— the mind takes refuge in the assumption of a First Cause, from an employment inconsistent with its own nature." "That First Cause, indeed, observes Dr. Harris,[1] "must be immensely different, both in rank and *in nature*, from the subordinate physical causes to which it has imparted motion; but still the mind feels the necessity for such a cause with all the force of an intellectual instinct. The mind was constituted to feel this necessity, and thus to supply the last link in the chain of reasoning from itself, as much as it was made and meant to find the preceding links in the phenomena of nature."

Having thus glanced at the intellectual impossibility involved in the negative proposition that there is no God, and at the intellectual necessity for the axiom that there must be a First Cause, we are prepared to consider the real value of the arguments *à priori* and *à posteriori*. And we cannot help remarking, at the outset, that too exclusive an importance has been attached to each of these celebrated forms of proof, as if the one were absolutely independent of the other. The two, in a great measure, go hand in hand, and conduct us to the position that there

[1] Pre-Adamite Earth, p. 151.

is a God, the Great Creator and Parent of the universe. The *à priori* mode of reasoning is the exclusive idol of many of the German logicians, they have an utter contempt for our inductive philosophy and matter-of-fact theology. Experience, the great teacher, is professedly ignored in their argumentation, the world with all its palpable realities is shut out, and from mere mental abstractions they evolve all existencies and all truth. But in their hands this kind of reasoning has completely failed. It conducts the mind to no firm resting-place. It bewilders, instead of elucidating, our notions of God, of man, and the universe. It gives us no divine personal existence, and leaves us floating in a region of mere vague abstractions. Such reasonings are either altogether vain, or are not really what they profess to be.

In our country the name of Dr. Clarke is chiefly associated with the *à priori* argument. He and many others attached to it an immense importance. But however highly extolled in past times, and worthy to be admired as a specimen of intellect, it is now generally set aside as insufficient of itself to demonstrate the Being and Attributes of God. Clarke himself found it necessary to stoop to the argument *à posteriori*, and thereby acknowledged the failure of attempting to reason exclusively *à priori*. In examining his celebrated demonstration, it is found to be really inductive, and not wholly independent of experience as supposed. Our conception of a First Cause is not indeed derived from experience, for it is felt to be an intellectual necessity, but experience is necessary to its development. The very first proposition that something must have existed from eternity, since it assumes that something exists, is *à posteriori*. And in order to prove that this eternal something is not "a blind and *unintelligent* necessity, but in the most proper sense an *understanding* and *really active* being," in which, as he well says, "lies the main question between us and the atheists," he resorts to the world with its orderly arrangements, and, on the ground of fact and experience builds up his argument.[1] The fate of Dr. Clarke's pretended demonstration, and the result, in so far as theology is concerned, of the transcendental reasoning of the continental philosophers, show the futility of attempting to rise up to the height of the great argument for the existence of God on the *à priori* method alone.

The old *à posteriori* argument, while decried by the German logicians on the one hand, has, it must be confessed, been invested with too exclusive an importance by some of our own theologians on the other. It is necessarily limited in its range. It carries us upward from effects to causes, from the evidences of design to a designer; but it cannot of itself carry us to the throne of the Eternal, who is uncaused and the cause of all. We cannot, by a strict process of inductive reasoning, infer from one or more finite effects that the cause of them is absolutely infinite. Design proves a designer, but it does not prove that the designer is God. The argument from external and visible nature leads the way, but, unaided by other proofs or conceptions, would never conduct us to the I AM THAT I AM. The marks of contrivance which are so palpable in everything we see in the fields of creation, give us the logical conclusion that everything has had a contriver. They give us also the idea of great wisdom and goodness and power; but of themselves they do not give us the proof of a Being possessed of infinite and absolute perfections. The argument points, like a finger-post, in that direction; but, strictly speaking, we leave the argument, or it leaves us, and we resign ourselves to the necessary conviction that there is a Great First Designer, and that he is

[1] Clarke's Discourse, Prop. viii.

God. There is nothing elaborate in the process. It is simpler and easier than the simplest step. From effects we ascend naturally to causes, from subordinate laws we rise up to the highest law; but when the inductive philosophy has carried us easily up, and placed us as it were on the highest point in the series of material causation, it has not given us the great First Intelligent Cause. It has, however, conducted us so far that, by our very mental constitution, we repose in the conviction that beyond the series of mere mechanical causes and effects is the Infinite Cause of all. Sir Isaac Newton has truly said, "though every true step made in this philosophy brings us not immediately to the knowledge of the First Cause, yet it brings us nearer to it." Let the chain of material causation be lengthened out ever so far, we only feel however at the topmost link, what is felt throughout all the lower links — the necessity of a cause above all others in nature and rank, a cause uncaused and the cause of all. Induction points to this, but it does not give it. Call it an intuitive sentiment, a primitive judgment, an intellectual necessity, or what you will, the mind is so constituted as in the reasoning process to supply it and rest in it. The starting-point of the *à posteriori* argument, which is the idea of design or causality, is an *à priori* belief, and from the argument itself we pass necessarily to the conviction that there is a First Cause, differing essentially from all others, whose name is God. So that it is vain to assert an exclusive claim for either argument, since they involve and aid each other.[1]

[1] The Atheist, in availing himself of the exclusive importance attached to the *à posteriori* argument, thus reasons: "If design implies a designer, contrivance a contriver, nature's contriver must have been himself contrived." The monstrous assumption, out of which arises this atheistical inference is, that nature's contriver has in himself marks of design. This is the reasoning of a man whose chief distinction is that he is editor of the "Reasoner."

The exclusive claim for either of these arguments being disposed of, we are prepared to notice the indications of the Creator that lie without the field of revealed truth. And here we avail ourselves of the rich contributions in the way of proof which are furnished by the phenomena both of matter and mind; and in doing so we repudiate neither argument, but make use of both. The plain way in which men have reasoned from the beginning, is upward from the evidences of design in the material universe to the existence of the Great Designer; upward from the orderly and beneficial dispositions of matter to the Divine Hand that framed the whole. And this old path is the truest and safest still. It has been adorned by the eloquence of Cicero and Brougham, of Paley, Chalmers and others. It is the argument of the royal psalmist: "The heavens declare the glory of God, and the firmament sheweth his handiwork." Nature in all her departments abounds in such evidences. The discoveries of physical science only enlarge to our view the vast magazine of contrivances, all of which point upward in the direction of the great Infinite Contriver. And our progress in that direction is in nowise arrested by any of the theories which profess to account for the origin of the universe, or to give us the beginning of its existing motions and arrangements. The hypothesis of Laplace, which has been so much vaunted against our Natural Theology, and which would trace backward the earth and the whole solar system to an extremely diffused nebulosity that gradually cooled down and condensed, has been very much discredited by recent discoveries of the telescope. But even supposing that it were verified, it would not destroy the argument for a God derived from the collocations of matter, nor prevent us from going beyond itself to an intelligent First Cause. "Let it be supposed," remarks Professor Whewell,[1] "that the point

[1] Indications of the Creator, p. 63.

to which this hypothesis leads us is the ultimate point of physical science; that the farthest glimpse we can obtain of the material universe by our natural faculties, shows it to us occupied by a boundless abyss of luminous matter; still we ask how space came to be thus occupied — how matter came to be thus luminous. If we establish by physical proofs that the first fact which can be traced in the history of the world is that there was light, we shall still be led, even by our natural reason, to suppose that before this could occur, 'God said, Let there be light.'" It is indeed true, as we before hinted, that the experimental argument of itself does not give us an Infinite cause. But if it carries us to the last link in the chain which is furnished by the phenomena of nature, it leaves us to repose from an intellectual necessity, in the conviction that there is an uncaused Cause which is the cause of all. The old assumption of an eternal succession of finite beings was made to get rid of the idea of One Eternal Being. That the supposition is unphilosophical and absurd has been shown thousands of times. The mind, from its very constitution, disowns it. Men may form as many links in the chain of causes as they choose, but they must, at last, reach an uncaused Cause. It is strictly true that from nothing nothing can proceed. Something must have existed before all finite beings, or whence came these finite beings into existence? *That something* must be self-existent, underived, necessary, and eternal. It is He who is the I AM, and to whom we apply the sublime language of the ancient seer: "Before the mountains were brought forth, or ever thou hadst formed the earth and the world, even from everlasting to everlasting, thou art God." It matters not whether it be in the department of zoology, with its two well-established principles that there is no such thing as spontaneous generation, and that there is no transmutation of the species, or whether it be in the department of a sublime and ever-enlarging astronomy; it matters not whether we extend our survey to the systems of suns that roll throughout the immensity of space, or whether we center it on that wondrous microcosm, the human eye; we meet with teeming evidences of design, which not only carry us to a designer, but hand us over, necessarily, if we may so speak, to the belief that the great First Designer is God. It is no mechanical necessity that we thus reach. It is Jehovah, the living and the life-giving One.

This argument has also received increasingly-rich contributions from a closer study of the constitution of the mind, and a more perfect analysis of its various phenomena. To reason upward from the laws of our mental constitution to the Infinite Mind, who is the Parent Source of the whole, is just as experimental (though in neither case dissociated from *à priori* beliefs) as to reason from material nature up to nature's God. Some of our popular writers on natural theology have either entirely overlooked the evidences of design presented by our mental constitution, or have satisfied themselves with merely adverting to them. Paley, who has written so admirably on material phenomena, never once extends his argument to the intellectual and moral. This omission has been accounted for by the astonishing discoveries of physical science, which, bringing palpably into view a vast assemblage of material evidences, have, for the time, thrown into the shade the proofs of the Divine existence and character derived from the mind. And yet the field of man's inner nature is as legitimate a province of the inductive philosophy as the external world, with its manifold organizations, and furnishes no less numerous and greatly more influential evidences of an intelligent Cause. Lord Brougham, in his "Introductory Discourse of Natural Theology," and Dr. Chalmers, in his

"Institutes," have liberally supplied what, in this department, was lacking in some of our older writers. The mind is a created effect, and, like matter, is a proper subject of observation. It has its own peculiar phenomena and laws, which we can examine, and from them gather proofs of the Infinite Mind, which is the source of all. Between it and matter there is a gulf fixed. The properties of the one are wholly different from the properties of the other. No combination of mechanical forces could ever produce an intelligent and moral being. That mind is a mere modification of matter is no less at variance with the inductive philosophy than is the exploded dogma of the transmutation of the species. Here, then, is an effect, endowed with intelligence, reason, and moral sentiment. This effect must have had a cause. And on the evident principle that no effect can possess any perfection which was not in the cause, we naturally infer that the creator of the human spirit is a moral and intelligent being. This is as much an inductive process of reasoning as the step we take in advancing from material nature up to Him who has designed it. Men have reasoned in this simple way from the beginning. "He that planted the ear, shall he not hear? he that formed the eye, shall he not see? he that teacheth man knowledge, shall he not know?" And since there is an intellectual necessity for a First Cause, himself uncaused, and the cause of all, his seeing must be all-seeing; his knowledge must be omniscience; his moral nature must be absolutely perfect. The most striking phenomenon in our mental constitution is conscience — the man within the breast, as it has been called. It sits enthroned amid the other principles of our nature, and is invested with a rightful authority over them. Its voice — the voice of a sovereign judge — is heard above the tumult of passion and the rebellious uproar of the less noble propensities. And though its high behests are not always obeyed, yet its right to rule is everywhere acknowledged. It is sovereign *de jure* even where it is not sovereign *de facto*. Now, let it be observed that all the authority of this faculty is on the side of righteousness and truth; that it has sanctions for the enforcement of its utterances; that it approves the good, and denounces the evil; and in the righteous supremacy of this part of our nature, we have a strong proof of the existence of a just and holy God. The authority of a law of right and wrong in our moral constitution implies a lawgiver; the setting up of a tribunal within the breast, points to a yet higher tribunal in the heavens; and from the felt presence of a judge within us, denouncing wrong and sanctioning right, we infer the existence of a righteous Judge over us, who is at once its Author and Lord. In the supremacy of this moral principle we have strong evidence, not only of an intelligent Creator, but of one who is just and true in all his ways, and holy in all his works. "And this theology of conscience," as Dr. Chalmers remarks, "has done more to uphold a sense of God in the world than all the theology of academic demonstration." Conscience, however, though the chief, is only a part of our mental phenomena. The mind is replete with other evidences for the being and character of God. These we do not stay to illustrate. Suffice it to say that, in the intellectual powers of man, and their adaptation to external nature — an amazing assemblage of brilliant and magnificent phenomena — in the emotional part of his nature, with the hallowed pleasure inseparable from the indulgence of good affections, and the wretched disquietude attendant on evil ones, speaking loudly, as they do, for a God who loves righteousness, and hates iniquity; — and in the supremacy of conscience, enthroned as it were above the whole, and ever uttering her voice on the side of whatsoever things are true, and lovely, and of good report, and against their opposites; and not only so, but rewarding well-doing, and punishing wrong-doing; — in such mental departments of natural theology as these we gather no less rich contributions to the evidence of a God than from the field of external nature.[1] Indeed, in man himself we have an embodiment of the whole argument. He is fearfully and wonderfully made. The human frame is the noblest structure beneath the heavens. In the exquisite mechanism of his body, and in the primitive judgments and wondrous operations of his mind, we have the clearest indications of the Creator that lie within the range of natural theology. "If you want argument from design," says Mr. Morell,[2] "then you see in the human frame the most perfect of all known organization. If you want the argument from *being*, then man, in his conscious dependence, has the clearest conviction of that independent and absolute *one*, on which his own being reposes. If you want the argument from reason and morals, then the human mind is the only known repository of both. Man is, in fact, a microcosm — a universe in himself; and whatever proof the whole universe affords, is involved, *in principle*, in man himself. With the *image* of God before us, who can doubt of the divine type?"

The argument, then, for the being of a God is neither exclusively *à posteriori*, nor exclusively *à priori*, but partakes of both. Man cannot declare that there is no God, without being guilty of the most tremendous presumption. He is a fool who hazards the assertion, because it involves an amount of intelligence which no creature can possess, the very attribute of omniscience, while He, in whom alone that attribute resides, is denied. And not only so, but there is an intellectual necessity for a Being uncaused and

[1] See Chalmers' Institutes, vol. i, pp. 99–116.

[2] History of Philosophy, vol. ii, pp. 646–7.

the cause of all. The mind cannot be satisfied without it. It refuses to pass along a dependent series of causes and effects, without resting in something that is first and independent. That there must be a first cause, is a primitive belief, a proposition that lies beyond the pale of demonstration,— a principle with which we start in our reasoning upward, and to the full conviction of which we surrender ourselves at the height of the argument. The good old way in which men have reasoned from the beginning, is upward from the evidences of design to a designer, upward from the goodly collocations of matter that meet our view, and the mental phenomena that come under our consciousness, to the great Parent Source of all the orderly relations of matter and mind. And this simple way is the best still. Finite effects, indeed, can never, of themselves, give us an infinite cause. The *à posteriori* argument, strictly speaking, cannot, unaided, carry us up to the throne in the heavens, and prove that beyond the circle of natural causes and effects is the great First Cause of all. But it leads us very far onward in that path. And then, by a soft and imperceptible step, transfers us to the natural conviction that there is an independent existence who is the Alpha and the Omega, the beginning and the ending, the First and the Last. To the height of this great argument we rise from the evidences furnished both by matter and mind. The material universe is full of indications of the natural attributes of the Creator. And our mental constitution is no less full of evidences of his moral nature. We weaken our argument against atheism, if we refuse to avail ourselves of the contributions in the way of proof which are furnished by either department. Both lie within the domain of the inductive philosophy. And with the evidences gathered from both, we logically infer that our Maker possesses transcendent attributes; that he is of great power, and wisdom, and goodness, one who loveth righteousness, and hateth iniquity. From the great we pass, by a different link, to the infinite; from transcendent attributes we pass to absolute perfections. And that link is supplied by the mind itself. The transition, in most cases, is made imperceptibly; but it is done. We have a certain primitive conviction that there is a Being of necessary and unchanging existence, the Maker of all things, and in whom centers, in an infinite degree, every perfection that is found in His works. It is thus that we, apart from the scriptural revelation, rise with a firm step from nature up to nature's God.

The testimony of the Bible now comes and crowns the theistic argument. It authenticates the deductions of enlightened reason, and confirms those primitive judgments, whereby we repose in the belief that God is, and that He is what He is. The very first sublime utterance of Inspiration, *In the beginning God created the heavens and the earth*, sets its seal that our reasoning upward from matter and mind to the Infinite creating Mind, is true. The Bible presupposes the Divine existence, and never formally attempts to prove it. It appeals to that very experimental evidence, which is patent to the eyes of all men, as a witness against irreligion and idolatry, and for the only living and true God, while it throws a luster, peculiar to itself, around his moral character, and his relations to man and the world. In the beneficial collocations of matter, in the orderly relations of this goodly universe, and in the constitution of the mind, with its intellectual powers and moral sentiments, there is a vast amount of clear evidence which points upward to an infinitely perfect Mind. But it is when we reach the Bible itself, "that wondrous monument of past ages, with its firm place in history, and its telling power on men's hearts," that we stand on an elevation, whence, like the angel in the sun, we see in the clearest and most impressive light the glory of Him who created and controls all things. "God never wrought a miracle," says Bacon, "to convince atheism, because his ordinary works convince it." The material phenomena that lie around us, and the mental phenomena that arise within us, give the lie to it. And if men will not believe on the ground of this evidence and the superadded evidence of revealed truth, neither would they believe though the Eternal uttered his voice from the rent heavens, and declared what He has done in His word, "I am God, and besides me there is none else."

Thus far the proof has been dogmatic. But after all, to use the weighty words of Dr. Arnold,[1] "the real proof is the practical one; that is, let a man live on the hypothesis of its falsehood, the practical result will be bad; that is, a man's besetting and constitutional faults will not be checked; and some of his noblest feelings will be unexercised, so that if he be right in his opinions, truth and goodness are at variance with one another, and falsehood is more favorable to our moral perfection than truth! which seems the most monstrous conclusion which the human mind can possibly arrive at."

[1] Life of Arnold, vol. ii, p. 1.

# CHAPTER II.

## THE DENIAL OF THE DIVINE PERSONALITY, OR PANTHEISM.

Pantheism distinguished from atheism—The result of severing two good principles — Pantheism and polytheism a higher and a lower grade — Seduces by its comprehensiveness — Its existence in the past—The doctrine of the Eleatics and of Buddhism — Its prevalence in Germany: Spinoza, Schelling, Hegel, Strauss, Feuerbach — French philosophy accused of it: Cousin — Continental Socialism pantheistic—An exotic in England — Emerson and his school — Intellectual pantheism of Carlyle — Remarks of Professor Garbett — Quotation from Tennyson — Bearings of pantheism: Makes creation an inevitable necessity, destroys responsibility, shuts out prayer, and extinguishes individual immortality —The personality of God argued from our own personality, from consciousness and inward experience, from the language of Scripture—The absolute and the personal reconciled in Christ.

ATHEISM is the ultimate point to which pantheism tends. Both may be said to lie in the same plane. But the one is not to be confounded with the other. The atheist denies the primal truth that God is. The pantheist, on the other hand, admits it. It is, in fact, with him, the sum and substance of all truth, or rather the one great truth in the universe. The atheist sees God nowhere, the pantheist sees Him everywhere. The one looks upon a world wondrously fair and sublime, every department of which is bright with intelligence, and resolves the whole into mere mechanical forces, and thrusts out, by a denial of his being, the all-pervading energy of nature's God. The other sees God really shining in the sun, moon and stars, living in the flowers and the grass of the field; hears Him speaking in the winds and waters, in the songs of the inhabiters of the grove, and in the deep emotions of the human soul. The atheist looks up to the bright heavens and around on the variegated earth, and coolly says, There is nature, but no God. The pantheist points to all the glorious forms of earth and sky, and exclaims with something like enthusiasm, There is God. The Divine Being is with him indeed the only real existence. The universe, with its multitudinous forms of what we call matter and mind, is only phenomenal. Men who have not reached the utmost bound of infidelity — atheism, or who have not come so far within sight of it as pantheism, conceive of the Creator as entirely distinct from his works, though incomprehensibly present with and pervading them. But the pantheist virtually makes of the twain one. Nature is absorbed in Deity; God is extended beneath all that exists, thinks and moves. He is in all and all is in Him. The pantheist, then, has a God, and, strictly speaking, he has nothing else. But his God is merely an infinite substance, a vague immensity — the one essence of Being extended everywhere, of which man and all other existing things are but the modes. The world and all the fullness thereof mirrors to our view the glory of the Infinite, Personal, and Independent One. But the pantheist worships the mirror itself, and sums up his creed by saying that all is God.

Almost every fatal dish contains food as well as poison. Every error in religion lies upon, or side by side with, some truth. Pantheism has within it an element of godliness, but, like the food in the fatal dish, it is overborne and rendered destructive by the element of evil. Or rather, pantheism looks like a good principle severed from another which is necessary to keep it sound and healthy, and in its isolated state transformed into a bad principle. The principle to which we allude is the omnipresence and all-pervading energy of the Creator and Governor of the universe. It is a truth, the vivid recognition of which is essential to piety, that God is everywhere present throughout the vast creation. All nature is full of Him. The luminaries of heaven and the flowers of earth, the perpetual hills, and the wide sea where go the ships, the various animal tribes, and intelligent man, the noblest of all, proclaim the presence of the living God. It might be thought that poetry has carried this principle too far when it represents God as shining in the sun, whispering in the winds, clothing Himself with clouds and storms, and speaking in the rational nature of man. But such poetry is not necessarily pantheistic. It is just an embodiment in living words of sentiments and emotions that burn more or less in the bosom of every man who is susceptible of the influences that come upon him from every department of nature. These influences tend to raise the mind from nature up to nature's God, and such is the tendency of much of the poetry to which we allude. The morning orison which Milton puts into the mouth of Adam and Eve in Paradise, the hymn which Thomson raises to the God of the Seasons, or Coleridge's "Hymn before Sunrise in the Vale of Chamounis," have no tendency whatever to produce or strengthen pantheistic feelings; because however much they clothe with living attributes the grand and lovely forms of nature, they never absorb God in these forms, but rise from the visible to the Invisible, and make "earth with her thousand voices" praise a living, personal and absolutely perfect God. In the last noble hymn which we have mentioned, the whole of Alpine nature is grandly personified, but all its utterances rise, "like a cloud of incense," to Him who in his glorious personality existed before the mountains were brought forth or ever He had formed the earth and the world. It is this latter principle, the principle of personality, that the pantheist sinks or loses sight of. The world, so to speak, is full of vitalities. God is present in them in the immensity of his essence whereby he filleth all things. That is a true devotional principle. God is nevertheless as distinct from them as the soul of man is distinct from his body. That is another true devotional principle. Both must be held fast in order to our having right views of the relation subsisting between the Infinite and the finite, the Divine nature and the divinely-created and divinely-sustained universe. Seize hold of the former principle and let go the latter, recognize a divinity in the vitalities which appear in the world around you, but withhold your recognition of a divinity essentially distinct from these vitalities, and what have you but these collective vitalities for a God. This is pantheism.

Pantheism and polytheism are in fact but a higher and a lower, a more refined and a more vulgar, way which men have taken when they have ceased to walk in a spiritual relationship with God.[1] Their idea of Him —

> "—— who sitteth above these heavens
> To us invisible, or dimly seen
> In these his lowest works,"

has lost its vivid spirituality, and they have fallen from high converse with the Creator down to the creation itself. In such a case, the more learned and philosophic, who were not prepared to take the leap to absolute atheism, would no longer regard the life and thought that appear in the visible world as merely manifestations of the presence and agency of the Great Spirit, but as modes or modifications of the Divine essence. Those, on the other hand, "whose thoughts proud science never taught to stray,"— who had little or nothing of the speculative temperament, and who could not grasp the idea of one great whole,— would see a distinct deity in every different department of nature. The one beheld the same infinite substance under all

[1] See Tholuck on the Nature and Moral Influence of Heathenism, p. 16.

mental and material phenomena. What are called powers of nature, or secondary causes, all of which are controlled by the supreme Intelligent Cause, would be regarded by the speculatist as so many modes of the infinitely-extended One. The collective energies and agencies of the visible world, in his estimation, constituted God. And thus he became a pantheist. The other class, less comprehensive and vigorous in mind, looked at creation in its smaller divisions, and recognizing a distinct energy in every different kind of phenomena, assigned a distinct divinity to the hills and to the valleys, to the woods and to the waters, and thus became polytheists. Pantheism and polytheism, however much they diverge the one from the other, are to be traced up to the tendency in the depraved mind, in its estrangement from the High and Holy One, to confound God with nature, and to lose the pure spiritual world in the phenomenal and visible. The reluctance or incapacity of men to retain God in their knowledge as a Person, self-existent and independent, lies at the bottom of both. The one is the fruit of a speculative philosophy, the other is the grosser manifestation of the same corrupt tendency, unrefined and unarrested by the influence of the schools or the higher influence of Christianity.

It is this very comprehensiveness, this embracing nature of its principles, which distinguishes pantheism from polytheism, that renders it, in Christian lands, the most dangerous foe to Christianity. " Never did a philosophical system take such an attitude toward the Christian faith; it does not make it a superstition, as did atheism; it does not neglect it, as does our popular philosophy; it does not scout its mysteries, as does an irrational common-sense; nor does it attenuate it into a mere ethical system; but it grants it to be the highest possible form of man's religious nature, it strives to transform its grandest truths into philosophical principles; it says that only one thing is higher, and that is pantheism."[1] There is no fear of men becoming polytheists in a country where paganism has been rooted out, and the influences of the Gospel have been deeply and extensively felt. But pantheism flourishes in the very heart of communities called Christian, and coils its pliant form around the very faith whose author and finisher is the Brightness of the Father's glory and the express Image of His Person. The coil indeed is fatal; for, however fair to look upon may be the sinuous folds, it poisons the truth, and destroys everything that is distinctively Christian. "It weaves its subtle dialectics around everything, that thus it may drag all into its terrific vortex. It has a word for almost every man, excepting for the Christian established in his faith. By the very extravagance of its pretensions, it seduces many; by its harmony with the life of sense, it attracts those who love the world; and by its ideal character, it sways such as would fain be lifted above the illusions of sense, and the visions of imagination, and the contradictions of the understanding, into a region of rarer air, where reason sways a universal scepter. Its system includes all things; God is all things; or, rather, all is God. He that knows this system, knows and has God.[2]" It, accordingly, has its attractions for all men who have ceased to walk in communion with the living personal God, and who yet feel the want of something in the shape of religious faith. The philosopher revels in it as in the region of boundless speculation; the poet and the artist find therein a beautiful dwelling-place where they can wander at their own sweet will; and the half-thinking artisan is pleased with a creed which interferes so little with material interests, and summons him so seldom to look at things unseen and eternal. Many such persons in our day are pantheists.

[1] Smith's Relations of Faith and Philosophy, p. 11.

[2] Smith's Relations of Faith and Philosophy, p. 11.

Pantheism is not, however, a thing of yesterday. It has, in its essence, existed in all ages. Some would persuade us that it is the latest result of human experience, a resting-place for the long-tossed mind, reserved for us upon whom the ends of the world have come. But it is not so. Infidelity in our times is throwing up nothing but what has been thrown up before. Its different forms are only old idols in new positions and arrayed in modern garbs. "In every form of it, it has its ancestry, and it must not ask now to be spoken to as if we had not already, and long ago, made acquaintance with it."[1] "Heresies," says Sir Thos. Browne, "are like the river Arethusa, though they lose their currents in one place, they rise up again in another." We meet with pantheism in the speculative philosophy of the ancient world. It has been the faith of millions in India from a remote antiquity down to the present day. Spinoza in the seventeenth century, and Schelling and Hegel in the nineteenth, have only systematized and reduced to a severe logical form what had been floating elsewhere for ages before. This was substantially the doctrine of the Eleatics. They speculated on the great problem of existence, and endeavored to resolve those mysteries which have baffled the human understanding in every age. Zeno, the most distinguished philosopher of his school, maintained that there was but one real existence in the universe, that all other things were merely phenomenal, being only modifications or appearances of the Great One which existed as a substratum beneath the whole. Pantheism, indeed, has appeared in all nations where there have been minds of a speculative cast, ignorant of, or in a great measure uninfluenced by, the revelation of Christ. It seems to be the joint product of an estrangement from God, the eternal and independent I Am, and an effort to comprehend the

[1] The Restoration of Belief, p. 15.

essence of things and the *nexus* which unites the Infinite with the finite, the phenomena of nature with the cause of all that phenomena. The very same doctrine forms substantially the creed of some Hindoo sects in the present day. India has had its philosophies, and has them still. And pantheism is the common form which speculations on the mysteries of existence have there assumed, unrestrained as these speculations have been in the absence of the Gospel. Hindooism and Buddhism are but philosophies of religion. The priests may have been the speculatists, but the system has found a spontaneous welcome with the people, who were too dull of apprehension to rise to the thought of a pure spiritual Intelligence, and too alive to a sense of dependence to say there is no God. The author of the "Recollections of British India," speaking of a philosophical sect called the Gosains, tells us that, "in common with the Buddhists, they believe that the Divine Being is not separate from, but in Himself the universe, so that all its constituent parts are but parts of Himself. The different deities, therefore, are merely portions of the same essential Godhead." This corroborates what has been said of the connection between pantheism and polytheism, and reminds us of the old doctrine of the Stoics, according to which the spirit pervades the whole world as the substratum of its activity, and receives from men various designations according to the different phenomena which it animates. There is, indeed, a striking coincidence between the One substratum of the Eleatics, the Brahma of the Hindoo, and the World-Spirit of the modern German.[1]

Germany, of all the countries of modern Europe, is the most prolific soil of Pantheism. And it is imported from thence into our own among other European states. It is the native fruit of her metaphysics. The mental habitudes

[1] Dr. Vaughan's Age and Christianity, p. 255.

of her people are peculiarly thoughtful and reflective. Philosophy — not the inductive and experimental as with us, but the speculative and idealistic — is natural to the German mind. Her schools have been absorbed in discussing the same great questions which were discussed over and over again in the schools of the ancients. Those mysterious problems which regard the principles of things, the existence and nature of God, the relations between Him and the universe, and the origin of human knowledge,— problems on the solution of which the greatest minds in past ages have been employed with so little profit,— possess a peculiar charm for the philosophers of the Continent. There is this important difference, however, between the pantheism of the old world and that of the new; between that of ancient Greece and India, and that of modern Germany; the one sprung up and flourished in the absence of an authoritative revelation from heaven, while the other has risen and spread in contempt of it. The German has become a pantheist with the Bible in his hand, and his foot in the birth-place of the Reformation. He has refused to follow, humbly and submissively, that light that has come into the world, and which alone has hitherto conducted individuals or communities to rest.

The German philosophy — a philosophy which seeks to reach the one originating principle of all things — has been carried into the region of theology, and there borne its bitter fruit. Spinoza has been justly regarded as the father of modern pantheism. He, by a stern logic, fully developed the system of Descartes. The illustrious Frenchman had endeavored to demonstrate the existence of God from the phenomena of consciousness. The position he assumed was, that whatever consciousness clearly proclaims must be true. Descartes, in short, derived existence from thought. Spinoza identified them, and referred both to the one Infinite Substance of which everything else is a mode or manifestation. According to his logic, God is the only reality in the universe,— the one universal existence that underlies all other existences,— so that everything is in and from God. The distinction between the Creator and his works was thus annihilated, and the system of pantheism became complete. Others had held it as a vague dreamy doctrine, but Spinoza was the first to give it a rigid logical form. It is remarkable that he, too, in a passage in his posthumous works, has anticipated some of the disciples of the Hegelian school in their interpretation of the great doctrines of the Bible. "I tell you," says he, in a letter to Oldenburgh, "that it is not necessary for your salvation, that you should believe in Christ according to the flesh; but of that eternal Son of God, that is, the eternal wisdom of God, which is manifested in all things, but especially in the human mind and most of all in Jesus Christ, we must cherish a very different opinion." [1] It is the philosophy of Spinoza, propounded in the seventeenth century, and diffused over the Continent ever since by his writings, that has given the greatest impulse to the speculative mind of Germany, and produced that wide-spread pantheism so characteristic of German speculations. Schelling and Hegel, whose names are identified with the pantheism of the nineteenth century, are the fruit of his labors. They have refined and carried out the system to which Spinoza gave the form. In both of these philosophic leaders, we see a thorough contempt for what is inductive and experimental, the method by which Newton attained an unprecedented eminence in physical science, and Locke rose to such high distinction in the science of mind. The treasures of knowledge which observation contributes are professedly discarded by them, and those which abstract

[1] Lewes' Biographical History of Philosophy, vol. iii, p. 125.

reason furnishes are exclusively valued. The evidence from design, which has been so fully illustrated by our own writers on natural theology, and which is so patent to the eyes of all men, is set at naught by the heads and disciples of this school. And they pretend to prove all existence by laying down *à priori* axioms, and starting from them in a course of stern logical argumentation. By this process, Fichte, who preceded the two philosophers referred to, brought to a fatal consummation what is called Subjective Idealism. Nature and God in his philosophy vanished. Self became the solitary existence in the universe, and the creator of everything else human and divine. The moral order of the world was all that was left for the world's God, and the philosopher stood on the very brink of absolute atheism. From this the mind of Germany shrunk back; and Schelling reproduced, in an attractive form, the pantheistic system, the tendency toward which is so strong in the great Fatherland. He identified the subject and the object, and made them manifestations of God or the Absolute. Nature with him is but the self-development of Deity. The whole phenomena of the universe have proceeded in one strict chain of necessary evolution. And God has only come to realize Himself, and attain self-consciousness, in man. Everything, according to this system, exists in God, and he is of necessity the All One. The system, in so far as it is intelligible, proclaimed the universe to be God. There was, however, another step to be taken before the climax was reached, and that step was boldly taken by Hegel. He denied the existence of both subject and object, and left only a universe of relation. Everything with him is a process of thought, and God himself is the whole process. The Deity is not a self-existent reality, but a never-ending self-discession, which never realizes itself so fully as in the human consciousness. Creation, according to this, is not a single act, but God is necessarily ever creating. The pantheism of the Hegelian system is obvious amid much of the mysticism that shrouds it. Nature is absorbed in God, and God and the universe, whatever they be, are identified. By this same process of pure philosophic thought, Hegel pretended to deduce the whole of doctrinal Christianity. Schelling before him had made the Gospel revelation one of the modes in which God is manifesting Himself in history. But Hegel, by his philosophy, transformed Christianity into a system of regularly evolved ideas, the value of which is altogether independent of historical testimony.

It is at this point that David Frederick Strauss and his school appear. He has put on the Hegelian armor, taken his stand in the very heart of the Christian theology, scattered into air the grand objective element of the Gospel, and left nothing remaining except a few religious ideas or conceptions of the mind. He is, strictly speaking, neither a rationalist nor a supernaturalist. He disavows all connection with either, and proclaims war against both. He is, however, a pantheist in the extreme. He represents the far left of the Hegelian party, and stands on the very verge of atheism, if he has not fallen into the gulf. God is with him a process of thought. He has no separate individual existence. Apart from the universe, or out of that process which is alleged to be eternally unfolding itself and which attains the highest state of consciousness in the mind of the philosopher himself, there is no God. No room whatever is left in the system for the intervention of a personal God, and in the system a personal God has no existence. Hence his mythical theory. The historical Christ of the Gospels, according to him, was the personified ideas of the church. The Divine Redeemer was a process, a personality gradually formed out of elements contributed by Old Testament history, rabbinical tradition, and the state of the popular mind at the time when the Messiah was expected. In other words, Christ was the creation of the church, not the founder of it. Such a person as Jesus, it is admitted, lived and died, who believed himself to be the Christ. Strauss recognized a small historical element in the person of Jesus, a kind of skeleton which the church gradually clothed with flesh and blood, the distinguishing attributes of which were an investment thrown around it from the mind of the church itself. The fully developed Christ of the Gospel, was thus made the embodied aggregate of the conceptions of the first Christians and the thoughts of the past. This is the latest shape, with the exception perhaps of Feuerbach's, which German infidelity has assumed, the extreme point to which pantheism has been carried, and where it becomes almost, if not altogether, identical with atheism. It leaves no God, but a vague personification of human consciousness. The existence of a divine consciousness separate from the human is ignored. It sweeps the world clean of an historical Christianity. It binds up all the physical and moral movements of the world in one unbroken chain of necessary development. And having left no Supreme and Independent object of worship, it takes away the Bible, and presents us with nothing in its room but mythological ideas embellishing the shadow of a reality. Pantheism in Germany will be found, then, like other forms of infidelity, to have a variety of shades, so that those who stand at the one extreme may hold some opinions that are denied by those who stand at the other. Hegel himself was unquestionably a pantheist, though it may be doubted if he would have gone the length of his bold and admiring disciple Strauss. But Spinoza, the founder of this philosophy, and Schelling,

Hegel, Strauss, and others, who have developed it, agree in this that they sink the personality of God.[1]

Pantheism is not, however, restricted to the schools and literature of Germany. The existing French philosophy is by no means clear of it. While there is reason to apprehend that, in its most unphilosophic form, it constitutes the faith of a large portion of the French people. The system of Cousin, who is regarded as the founder and coryphæus of the modern eclectic school of France, has met with much opposition from various writers on account of its pantheistic leanings. He holds the balance, as Dr. Chalmers has remarked, between the two philosophies of Germany and Scotland, neither being exclusively ontological as the former, nor exclusively psychological as the latter. His idealism, modified though it be, has led him, however, in a pantheistic direction. And though he repels the charge of pantheism, yet what other interpretation can be put on his language, when he speaks of God as "being absolute cause, one and many, eternity and time, essence and life, end and middle, at the summit of existence and at its base, infinite and finite together; in a word, a Trinity, being at the same time God, Nature, and Humanity?" Mr. Morell, an admirer of Cousin's genius, justly remarks, when commenting on his view of the Divinity: "even if we admit that it is *not* a doctrine, like that of Spinoza, which identifies God with the abstract idea of substance; or even like that of Hegel, which regards Deity as synonymous with the absolute law and process of the universe; if we admit, in fact, that the Deity of Cousin possesses a conscious personality, yet still it is one which contains in itself the finite personality and consciousness of every subordinate mind. God is the ocean — we are but the waves; the ocean may be one individuality, and each wave another; but still they

[1] Morell's History of Philosophy, vol. ii, chap. v, sec. 2.

are *essentially* one and the same."[1] Here we have the very notion of Deity which is developed in much of the current literature of the day, and which leads to a system of man-worship. The finite is an emanation or portion of the infinite. The universe is comprehended in God. Men's souls are divine. Every man is an incarnation of Deity. All existences are in God, and God is in all existences.[2]

But the veil of mysticism which shrouds the pantheism of the schools, and often renders its language hard to be understood, is removed from the pantheism of the people. The socialism of the Continent is, in a great measure, pantheistic. The masses, who are incapable of following the philosopher in his metaphysical investigations, readily apprehend their results when popularized, and brought within the sphere of man's interests and duties. This is done by the socialist propaganda. And however much the various sects of socialism war with each other on points of polity, they are generally of one mind in regard to man-worship. Amid the late revolutions which shook continental Europe, it was not difficult to see the divinity to whom the clouds of incense arose. That the highest being is man, was the dogma commonly taught and cordially received. In France, the teaching of Pierre Leroux, who has been counted the metaphysician of socialism, was undisguised pantheism. He knows of no God distinct from the universe of being. And humanity with him is but the incarnation of divinity. The tendency, in

[1] Morell's History of Philosophy, vol. ii, chap. v, sec. 2, pp. 502, 511.

[2] It is but just to admit, what Cousin stoutly contends for, that his system is *not identical* with that of Spinoza and the Eleatics. "I must remind my adversaries," says he, "that the God of Spinoza and the Eleatics is a pure substance, and not a cause. In the system of Spinoza, creation is impossible: in mine it is necessary." But when he tells us that "if God be not everything, He is nothing; — that everywhere present, He returns, as it were to Himself in the consciousness of man," — who can wonder if it be looked upon as pantheism of another phase? See Cousin's Phil. Essays (Clark's edition), pp. 22, 77.

short, of all the socialist sects in France, notwithstanding the religious sentimentalism of the language of some of their leaders, is toward pantheism. Hence their declamations on the perfectibility of the human race, and their exclusion of all motive power but the human will. God, according to them, was in Jesus Christ, and so he is in the French people. And this is the faith which has supplanted the infidelity of Voltaire in the heart of the nation. The diseased patient is perpetually turning himself on the same bed, seeking rest and finding none. The communism of Germany is rampant with the same element. Feuerbach, who is the chief teacher of the more advanced form of socialism, has deified the human race. According to him God is not a being above man, but God is to be found in man. Religion is not a thing that comes to man from without, but the whole contents of religion are derived from human nature itself. Man thus becomes a god to himself. Theology becomes anthropology. And pantheism reaches the point to which it is ever tending, the very verge of atheism. Such has been, and is in a great measure still, the faith of immense multitudes of people on the Continent, in the middle of the nineteenth century. And if there is one lesson more impressively taught than another by the recent commotions, amid which such gross infidelity was thrown up, it is that such a faith can never give rest and happiness to the nations of the world.

Pantheism among ourselves is somewhat of an exotic. The sturdy English mind is not the most congenial soil for it. The philosophy from which it has sprung, is alien to the mental habitudes of our people. But if it does not exist as an intellectual system in our schools, or widely prevail in the communistic form among the masses, it has been imported into our literature in the most alluring guise, and is destined, we think, to prove for a while the great foe of Bible Christianity.

In some of the transatlantic productions which are circulating among us, we meet with the system in its poetic or most attractive form. The Emerson school, which numbers many disciples in our land, is unquestionably pantheistic. Emerson himself, with all his gorgeous mysticism, is a pantheist. Man-worship is the philosophy which pervades his speculations. He comes before the world as a reformer. And whether he addresses a class of divinity students, or the members of a literary society, or a mechanics' association, the one prominent doctrine in his orations is the soul of man. Emerson finds everything in man, and he wages war with all systems that lead man out of himself for an object of faith and worship. His complaint is that "the soul is not preached." The doctrine of the soul, "first, soul; and second, soul; and evermore, soul;" is, according to him, the grand truth that is to regenerate the world, and he seems to consider himself commissioned to promulgate it. He boldly denies the personality of God. It is the "theologic cramp" that bound Swedenborg, one of his favorite Representative Men, that otherwise "colossal soul." After the manner of some of the German Transcendentalists, he holds the totality of being to be God, who comes to self-consciousness only in the individual man. "The universal does not attract us until housed in an individual. Who heeds the waste abyss of possibility? The ocean is everywhere the same, but it has no character until seen with the shore or the ship." Man is at once the worshiper and the object of worship. "Standing on the bare ground, my head bathed by the blithe air, and uplifted into infinite space, all mean egotism vanishes. The currents of the Universal Being circulate through me. I am part or particle of God." Prayer, in perfect consistency with these notions, is shut out. "It is God in us which checks the language of petition by a grander thought." Historical Christianity being a thing from without, is repudiated. Man is a revelation to himself. His soul becomes the fountain of all truth and goodness. And Emerson and his school complain that "men have come to speak of the revelation as somewhat long ago given and done, as if God were dead." The first defect of Historical Christianity with him is, that it "dwells with noxious exaggeration about the *person* of Jesus." For "the soul knows no persons." Mr. Emerson, like many others who would destroy the doctrinal system of the great Teacher, professes much admiration for Jesus Christ. He is no longer denounced as an impostor. He is held up as the true, the model man. "He saw with open eye the mystery of the soul. Alone in all history, he estimated the greatness of man. One man was true to what is in you and me. He saw that God incarnates Himself in man, and evermore goes forth anew to take possession of his world. He said in this jubilee of sublime emotion, 'I am divine. Through me God acts, through me, speaks. Would you see God, see me; or, see thee, when thou also thinkest as I now think.'" But the doctrine of the true prophet was distorted, and Mr. Emerson tells us how. "Because the indwelling Supreme Spirit cannot wholly be got rid of, the doctrine of it suffers this perversion, that the divine nature is attributed to one or two persons, and denied to all the rest, and denied with fury." Man, in short, is thus made the highest being. Every human soul is a wave in the ocean of divine existence. God is the whole sea. And we are divine or a part of God. No wonder, then, that man refuses to receive truth at second-hand, and is taught to believe that all the virtues are comprehended in self-trust. Know yourself, reverence yourself, rely upon yourself, are the law and gospel of this school that claims to regenerate the world.

In this strain does this poetic philosopher discourse to the youth connected with divinity halls, literary societies, and mechanics' institutes.[1]

He is not a logician, but a seer; he announces, not argues; is the language of an admiring editor of his works. This witness is true. Seldom or never does anything in the shape of an argument cross our path in reading the orations and essays of Emerson. He dreams and dogmatizes. All his responses are delivered with oracular authority. "I stand here to say, Let us worship the mighty and transcendent soul." He is unquestionably a man of genius, endowed with exquisite sensibilities and a brilliant fancy. His style, though far from undefiled, is energetic and attractive. It is often, however, far too mystical to be extensively popular. He is, after all that has been said about him, a dreamer—a glorious dreamer if you will—but still a dreamer. Such seers as Mr. Emerson have been in the world before, and have discoursed to young and old, as he has done, about the divinity of the soul, and the duty of self-reliance, and what the better has the world been for such oracles? History attests that it never has been by such dreamers and dreamy systems that society has been quickened and regenerated. Look at the Hebrew prophets who ever and anon appeared, filled with the inspiring Spirit, to rebuke the Israelites for their apostasy, and recall them to the service of the living God. Look at John, the harbinger of the Messiah, the voice of one crying in the wilderness, whose teaching was so influential and impressive for good. Look at Christ Himself, who, "alone in all history, estimated the greatness of man," and for whom Emerson and his disciples profess such veneration, and where in all his discourses do you find him preaching this doctrine of the soul, telling his hearers that

[1] See Emerson's Orations and Essays, *passim*.

there is no atheism but the proposition of depravity, that they are parts or particles of God, and that they ought to rely upon themselves and act a godlike part? The conduct of Judas was honorable compared with such attempts to betray the Son of Man with a kiss. Look at Paul and the noble company of the apostles, men who turned the world upside down when living, and who being dead yet speak, and in vain do you seek for a single point of contact between their doctrines, which alone have been instrumental in the world's regeneration, and this system of man-worship. Look at all the mighty throng, be they poets or philosophers, statesmen or divines, who, by the almost universal consent of mankind, have been counted, in the highest sense of the expression, reformers, and who have left the salutary impress of their genius and labors on their own and succeeding times, and which of *them* ever acted on the belief that in one soul, in any soul, are resources for the world, and that the office of a true teacher is to show God in the soul? "The thing that hath been, it is that which shall be." The world's regeneration will go on as it has begun. And that is not by preaching the pantheistic doctrine of the soul. Go to the heathenism that is abroad, or to the heathenism that surrounds us at home; tell the idolator in the wilderness who drinks out of the skulls of his enemies, or tell the convict in his cell, or the half naked wretch in his hovel, that his soul is divine, and the haggard look and groveling propensities will cry out that the doctrine is a mockery and a lie. But the disciples of this school never venture into such fields as these. Mr. Emerson tells us that in walking abroad, he sees vegetables and trees nodding to him, and he nods to them.[1] But he meets with no salutation from men where, if true, his doctrine would be most welcome. It is only

[1] Emerson's Nature.

among the dreaming men and youth in cities and towns, persons who have a love for the half mystic and half poetic, persons whose religious sentiments are vague and undefined, and who are disposed to be gods unto themselves, that he finds worshipers of this doctrine of the soul. There he may do some mischief. But neither he nor any of his school will ever, by any witchery of language, gain an ascendency over the strong English mind. And of two things they may be assured. Historical Christianity will ever prove too mighty for them. It has overcome vastly more powerful enemies, and traveled on in the greatness of its strength. And this system of man-worship, like every other, will miserably fail to regenerate mankind. The diseased patient must look to the remedy without. And instead of being mocked by the cry, Look to yourself, hearken to the good old invitation, "Behold the Lamb of God that taketh away the sin of the world."[1]

In speaking of Mr. Carlyle in this connection, we are to be understood rather as indicating the religious bearing of much of his writings, than assigning him a definite place in a particular category. There is no great writer in modern times who is ever speaking of men's beliefs or unbeliefs, of whom it is more difficult to say precisely what his own belief or unbelief is. John Foster once said (whether wisely or unwisely we leave the reader to judge), that it would at any time be a great luxury to him to accompany a few athletic men with poleaxes among the

[1] The very able author of "The Restoration of Belief," in putting "in a distinct light what it was which the church of the early age did for mankind in preparation for a new moral era, and under what conditions this necessary function was discharged," and thereby constructing an argument in favor of Christianity, remarks, "the ground of that Christian fortitude (the fortitude of Polycarp and his contemporaries) which, in the end, prevailed over the polytheism of the Roman State, was a BELIEF toward a PERSON; it was not an opinion as to a doctrine,"—"but a belief toward a PERSON whose authority they regarded as paramount to every other." (Pp. 74, 77.) This belief in a personal Savior-God is the grand lever in the world's elevation.

monuments in Westminster Abbey, to be most vigorously wielded, with just here and there an omission, in a process which we might imagine.[1] Mr. Carlyle has a like luxury in vigorously wielding his pole-axe against our churches, as if they were "mere cases of articles;" and against our Bible creeds, as if they were no better than "extinct traditions," "unbelievabilities," "worn-out symbolisms, reminiscences, and simulacra." We might easily conjecture what Foster's excepted instances among the sculptured memorials would have been, but we are without ground on which to conjecture the exceptions, if exceptions there be, in the case of Carlyle. Multitudes of good men read his writings with strong suspicions that, under the cover of assailing the shams, hypocrisies and formalities of which there are unhappily too many in the church as well as in the world, he is assailing the very Bible truth itself; and these suspicions are certainly not weakened by his last interesting work, "The Life of John Sterling." We know that he has said, "Adieu, O Church; thy road is that way, mine is this; in God's name, adieu!" We know that he does worship in "the great Cathedral of Immensity," and acknowledges "the Supreme Silences," "the Destinies and the Immensities," and "the Eternities," and that he is apt to regard our Christian beliefs as a "stealing into Heaven by sticking ostrich-like our head into fallacies on earth."[2] But beyond this we know nothing positively. We are not going, then, to write him down pantheist. But he has given us occasion to say that the tendency of much of what he has written is pantheistical. He does not, indeed, say anything so offensive on the subject of Christianity, as his admirer, Mr. Emerson. He never speaks of it as "an Eastern monarchy, built by indolence and fear," nor charges it with the radical defect of dwelling with noxious

[1] Life of Foster. [2] Life of Sterling.

exaggeration about the person of Jesus.[1] But we are at a loss to gather any better religion from his pages than a kind of man-worship. He sees God-like principles in human nature, especially in great and earnest men, who have made any impression upon the world, and he falls down himself, and calls upon others to fall down and do them homage. Moses and Zoroaster, Jesus Christ and Mahomet, Saul of Tarsus and Paul the Apostle, were, though not in the same degree, alike divinely-inspired men. His hero-worship points to the Emerson doctrine of the soul. He says virtually, what the American says openly, that the doctrine of the divine nature suffers perversion in being attributed to one or two persons, and denied to others. God in man, not exclusively in the man Christ Jesus, but God in every man in whom appear greatness and earnestness, seems to be the religion of this hero-worship. Literature, in short, with him is religion; and "the true sovereign souls" of literature, the Goethes and so on, are the true prophets and gospel preachers. The contents of religion are accordingly regarded by the men of this school as found within the man, not coming to the man from without; the soul is a revelation to itself. Emerson has said, "it is not instruction, but provocation, that I can receive from another soul. What he announces, I must find true in me, or wholly reject; and on his word, or as his second, be he who he may, I can except nothing." And says Mr. Carlyle: "The Maker's Laws, whether they are promulgated in Sinai thunder, to the ear or imagination, or quite otherwise promulgated, are the Laws of God; transcendent, everlasting, imperatively demanding obedience from all men. This, without any thunder, or with never so much thunder, thou, if there be any soul left in thee, canst know of a truth. The Universe, I say, is made by Law;

[1] Emerson's Address to a Senior Class of Divinity.

the great Soul of the world is just and not unjust. . . . Rituals, Liturgies, Credos, Sinai thunder: I know more or less the history of these, the rise, progress, decline, and fall of these. Can thunder from all the thirty-two azimuths, repeated daily for centuries of years, make God's laws more God-like to me? Brother, no. Perhaps I am grown to be a man now; and do not need the thunder and the terror any longer! Perhaps I am above being frightened; perhaps it is not fear, but reverence alone, that shall now lead me! — Revelations, Inspirations? Yes: and thy own God-created soul, dost thou not call that a 'revelation?'" He tells us that religion is "no Morison's Pill from without," but a clearing of the Inner Light or Moral Conscience, a re-awakening of our ownselves from within; the world has looked to the revelation without, but it was "when its beard was not grown as now."[1] And with a sneer at the old churches and the old creeds, he says: "What the light of your mind, which is the direct inspiration of the Almighty, pronounces incredible,—that, in God's name, leave uncredited; at your peril do not try believing that."[2] Where such talk as this is indulged in, the law and the testimony is very little valued. Mr. Carlyle, accordingly, is disposed to make sincerity or earnestness the test of truth and moral greatness. Christianity is thus reduced from its high position as the only true religion, to a level with the other religions of the earth, and what a man honestly believes, and really practices, is counted a good orthodox creed. The revelation is made within the man, and the Outer Light is respected only in so far as it agrees with the Inner Light. All this comes from a dreamy, exaggerated notion about the human soul. Mr. Carlyle does not say, with Proudhon and Emerson, that the highest being is man, and thus make theology anthro-

[1] Carlyle's Past and Present, pp. 307–312. [2] Life of Sterling, p. 78.

pology, but much of what he does say looks in that direction. And his style of expression is frequently such as to lead many of his indiscriminating admirers to that position, or to strengthen those in it who already occupy it. He does not stop with scowling upon the formalism of the age, and calling upon men to be honest, earnest and active, but the scowl seems to be turned toward Christianity and its evidences as a body of fact lying without. He is not satisfied with a natural reverence for what is great and good in any of our race, but the great with him becomes Divine or Godlike In a mighty intellect we recognize the presence and power of the Divinity. And for such he claims something like worship or religious admiration. His hero-worship is just a kind of intellectual pantheism. It is preaching up, though in a somewhat different way from the men of the Emerson school, the doctrine of the divinity of the soul. Much as Mr. Carlyle is to be admired for his original, vigorous thinking, his liberal and independent cast of mind, and his wish to raise up among us an earnest race of men, we cannot but deprecate the religious tendency of a great deal that he has written, as pantheistical.

"The result," says Professor Garbett,[1] "is briefly this. The human mind has awakened into a mighty thrilling consciousness of its *collective capacity;* it has gathered up into one *great unity* and organized humanity, all individual intellects and hearts, all genius and all inspiration; and exulting in this great *corporate* life, and bounding pulse, thus identified with it, it is drunk with pride and worships itself. In its own depth it believes all life and knowledge to lie; the meaning of all outward utterances and phenomena, and the self-evolved solution of all mysteries in heaven and earth. Before the chancery of its own subjective laws and arbitrary requirements, all objective truth is called to

[1] See an admirable sermon on the Personality of God, preached before the University of Oxford.

judgment. It is itself God in fact, and the universe is its product and its mirror." We are reminded of Tennyson's truthful and beautiful description of mere intellectual knowledge:

"What is she, cut from love and faith,
But some wild Pallas from the brain

"Of Demons? fiery hot to burst
All barriers in her onward race
For power. Let her know her place:
She is the second, not the first.

"A higher hand must make her mild,
If all be not in vain; and guide
Her footsteps, moving side by side
With wisdom, like the younger child:

"For she is earthly of the mind,
But Wisdom, heavenly of the soul." [1]

We conclude by taking a bird's-eye view of some of the bearings of this form of infidelity, and with some remarks in disproof of it. The doctrine of an impersonal God, as we have seen, lies at its basis. The universe is the divinity, and men themselves, as "God intoxicated," mingle with it. Out of this fundamental idea rise the following:

1. *Creation*, with the pantheist, *is not a free act, but an inevitable necessity*. It is not a complete effect, but a process that is going on eternally. Hegel says, God did not create the world, he is eternally creating it. Creation is God passing into activity, but neither suspended nor exhausted in the act. Anaximander said substantially the same thing ages before him. And Victor Cousin has repeated it after him. "The distinguishing characteristic of the Deity," says the French philosopher, "being an absolute creative force, which cannot but pass into activity, it

[1] In Memoriam, p. 177.

follows, not that the creation is possible, but that it is necessary." And the men of the Emerson school tell us, that the world is "a projection of God in the unconscious." Pantheism is thus fatalistic. We, according to enlightened reason and Scriptural truth, have been wont to believe that God existed independently, from eternity, in a state of absolute perfection, and that, of his own good pleasure, he called the universe into being. Moses began his historical narrative by declaring, "In the beginning God created the heavens and the earth;" and he sung, "Before the mountains were brought forth, or ever thou hadst formed the earth and the world, even from everlasting to everlasting, thou art God." The pious in all ages, on looking over the creation, have said, "Our God made the heavens." And the heavenly inhabitants cry, "Thou hast created all things, and for thy pleasure they are and were created." But, according to the pantheist, this is all a delusion. The Divine free-will is a nonentity. Creation is but the inevitable development of the one Being that is beneath all and in all. Thus are falsified all these clear marks of design in the universe on which men have looked for ages, the world is robbed of all its moral grandeur, the holy emotions of man's religious nature are repressed, and he has nothing to behold but a creation that has sprung from fate and necessity, and nothing to think of behind the whole, but an absolute creative force ever passing, not from a moral but a physical necessity, into activity. We may theoretically distinguish pantheism from atheism, but assuredly the man who looks upon the universe, and says that it is "a remoter and inferior incarnation of God,"[1] or that it is God necessarily passing into action, is as much without God in the world, as the man who ascribes everything to mechanical forces, and says there is no God.

[1] Emerson's Nature, p. 53.

2. Pantheism *inevitably destroys all moral distinctions*, and makes man irresponsible. "Evil and good are God's right hand and left," is the doctrine of some of our popular literature.[1] And if the whole phenomena of the universe be one chain of necessary development, if man and his actions are strictly inevitable pulsations of the one great source of being, then what is properly called moral evil has no existence. And the Emerson school tells us that it lives only in dogmatic theology. "Evil, according to old philosophers," says the author of the "Representative Men,"[2] "is good in the making. That pure malignity can exist, is the extreme proposition of unbelief. It is not to be entertained by a rational agent; it is atheism; it is the last profanation. . . . The divine effort is never relaxed; the carrion in the sun will convert itself to grass and flowers; and man, though in brothels or jails or on gibbets, is on his way to all that is good and true." This may accord with the generous spirit of the Indian Vishnu; but Christianity and it are wide as the poles asunder. The "Festus" of Mr. Bailey, a poem of great power and of a religious spirit, is pervaded by this bad pantheistic theology. The following is but a specimen:

"The soul is but an organ, and it hath
No power of good and evil in itself,
More than the eye hath power of light or dark.
God fitted it for good; and evil is
Good in another way we are not skilled in."[3]

Hence the notion that all religions are good, but that Christianity is the best. And the conclusion: "All souls shall be in God, and shall be God, and nothing but God be."[4] Dr. Strauss moves in the same plane, though far ahead, when he says: "human kind is impeccable, for

[1] Bailey's Festus, Proem. p. vii.
[2] "Swedenborg; or, the Mystic," p. 68.
[3] Festus, p. 48.
[4] Festus, p. 109.

the progress of its development is irreproachable. Pollution cleaves only to the individual. It does not reach the race and its history. The human race is the Christ, the God-made man, the sinless one, that dies, rises again, and mounts into the heavens."[1] The consciousness of guilt becomes, on this system, a delusion. The sense of responsibility, which is a fact in the natural history of man, is belied. And that voice which comes from the recesses of our moral nature, pointing us from a judge within the breast to a judge without and above, is silenced That God is ever educing good from evil is true, and that the ministry of evil, mysterious though it be, is made under his benign supremacy to subserve most important purposes, agrees at once with experience and Scripture. But that evil has no positive existence, that it is only good in another way, is as repugnant to our moral sentiments as it is opposed to Christianity. We will persist in calling this course of conduct bad, and that opposite course good; and can never act on the belief that both were alike things of fate and necessity, or that each agent is a structure formed by inevitable laws, and part or particle of God. When this creed prevails, the foundations of the earth will be out of course. Only let this doctrine leaven the mass of a community, and the result will be a deluge of sensuality and crime.

3. *This system shuts out prayer.* Man will worship. Here the object of worship is self. And if the soul knows no persons, and is itself "wiser than the whole world,"[2] as the thorough-going pantheist maintains, it were folly to go out of itself for the resources either in the way of a rule of duty or of spiritual influences. Coleridge's "Ancient Mariner" went much too far when he said:

[1] Leben Jesu (last chapter). [2] Emerson.

"He prayeth well who loveth well
Both man and bird and beast.
He prayeth best who loveth best
All things both great and small:
For the dear God, who loveth us,
He made and loveth all."

But Mr. Emerson and his school go much farther. "As soon as the man is at one with God, he will not beg. He will then see prayer in all action. The prayer of the farmer, kneeling in his field to weed it; the prayer of the rower, kneeling with the stroke of his oar, are true prayers, heard throughout nature, though for cheap ends." Mr. Theodore Parker, who, though not a professed pantheist, pretends to have found pantheism in the writings of John the Evangelist, discourses in a similar way. Speaking of what he calls the happy condition of the religious man, he tells us that his "religion demands no particular actions, forms or modes of thought: the man's plowing is holy as his prayer—his daily bread, as the smoke of his sacrifice; his home, sacred as his temple; his work day and his sabbath are alike God's day. His priest is the holy spirit within him."[1] And if Mr. Carlyle does not mean to countenance this pantheistic dogma, why, in "The Modern Worker," does he so frequently talk thus: "Work is of a religious nature. . . . All true work is sacred; in all true work, were it but true hand-labor, there is something of divineness. Labor, wide as the earth, has its summit in heaven. Sweat of the brow, and up from that to sweat of the brain, sweat of the heart; which includes all Kepler calculations, Newton meditations, all sciences, all spoken epics, all acted heroisms, martyrdoms,—up to that 'agony of bloody sweat,' which all men have called divine! O brother, if this is not 'worship,' then I say, the more pity

[1] Parker's Discourses, p. 110.

for worship; for this is the noblest thing yet discovered under God's sky."[1] No doubt this will be hailed by many of the listeners and readers of Emerson, Parker and Carlyle. And there may be here and there, "the poor day-laborer, the weaver of your coat, the sewer of your shoes," who, having no inclination for prayer, may like to be told that "no man has worked, or can work, except religiously," and that he "shall return *home* in honor, to his far distant home in honor."[2] But it will not do for the millions who fail to attain to such a delirium of soul as these poetic philosophers, and whom they will never get to believe that the fountain of all good is in themselves, that they are divine pilgrims in nature, and that everything attends their steps. No. Men's minds, which have not been spoiled by a philosophy falsely so called, will ever, as aforetime, go out in a felt sense of want. They will cry, in spite of all this delirious teaching, "who will shew us any good?" And experience will continue to attest that man will never possess the satisfying good, until as a *beggar* he say, "Lord, lift thou up the light of thy countenance upon us."

4. What becomes of *individual immortality* in such a system as pantheism? It is absorbed and lost. Men in all ages, even in the absence of revelation, have yearned for existence beyond death and the grave. The Gospel, by bringing life and immortality to light, has answered these yearnings. So that with all our moral and religious impressions, is blended the conviction of our individual existence being prolonged on the other side of the tomb. We are conscious of our personal being now, our moral nature points to the continuance of our conscious personality hereafter; and an authoritative revelation has not only set its seal to the truth of the personal immortality of man, but shed an illumination all its own on the grave and

[1] Past and Present, pp. 268, 271. [2] Ibid. pp. 278, 872.

the world beyond. But life with the pantheist is a dream, and death is absorption. It is like the return of a ray of light to the sun whence it emanated, or a drop of water to the great ocean from which it originally came. The disciples of a system do not always go to the full length of the system itself. And so it may happen that some professed pantheists have not discarded the belief of personal immortality. But such is the legitimate issue of the system, and such will actually be its result when, descending from the schools, it becomes the faith of the common people. With the pantheists of the East, the consciousness of separate existence is an illusion, which in a little time will pass away. The souls of men being portions of the divine essence, "parts or particles of God," will ultimately return to their source, so that, apart from the great substance, there will be no conscious existence. Whatever might be Hegel's individual view of the future state of man, Hegelianism, in this respect, is thoroughly pantheistic. "On the doctrine of immortality," remarks Mr. Morell,[1] "Hegel has said but little, and that little by no means satisfactory." But it is a part of his philosophy, that the Divine Being is necessitated to send forth existences and to absorb them again. Reinhard, who is deemed a fair and competent judge of the system, says, that "according to Hegel's speculative decisions, the individual personality of man is perishable in its very nature. In his view, reason demands that the thinking individual should acknowledge the nothingness of his individual essence, and willingly meet self-annihilation in view of his entering into that universal substance which, like Chronos in the old mythology, devours all its own offspring."[2] Strauss, and others of the same school, have gone this length. His words are, "a life

[1] History of Philosophy, vol. ii, p. 190.

[2] Dr. Beard's Voices of the Church, p. 12.

beyond the grave is the last enemy which speculative criticism has to oppose, and, if possible, to conquer."[1] Here, as in some other points, the extremes of sensationalism and idealism meet. The atheist and the pantheist shake hands as believers in the same black creed. Danton, on his trial, said, "My name is Danton, my residence will soon be in annihilation, my name will live in the pantheon of history." And the pantheist says, Let us dream on the day of our existence here, for the night is coming when self must return to the great ocean of being and there be lost for ever. Such are the issues of a system that denies the living Personal God.

---

1. In proof of the personality of God, we might, in the first place, argue from *our own personality*. That we are real, intelligent, and responsible persons, is a matter of consciousness. There is a spirit in man. He has understanding, will, moral sentiment, a power to choose between good and evil, and he knows it. It is this which gives us a decided preëminence over the whole visible creation. It separates at an immeasurable distance from us the flowers of the earth however beautiful, the stars of heaven however bright, and the beasts and birds however wise Were it possible for us to be divested of our complete personality as moral, intelligent individual beings, the crown would fall from our heads, and we would descend in the scale of earthly creatures. Personality — living, moral and intellectual personality — such as man's, is clearly, then, a perfection. And in the very existence of such personal beings we have an argument for a Personal God. Let it be supposed that by intuition, or argumentation, or both, we had come simply to the knowledge of a First Cause; it is evident that the conception of the possession of perfect

[1] Glaubenslehre.

personality by Him would render Him a more glorious Being than the want of it. And this being the case, He must possess it, for our conceptions of the greatest Being in the universe can never surpass, but must always come short of, the reality. "It is clear," says Professor Garbett, "that anything which does not possess personality, or possesses it in a low degree, whether it be like the earth, however exquisitely modeled into beauty and sublimity manifold, or the beasts of the field, however marvelous their living powers, must be inferior to ourselves. And, therefore, Almighty God *must* be a person likewise. For if not, He would be inferior to ourselves, contrary to the supposition on which we go. And the very name imports that, *ὅτι πότ᾽ ἐστι*, He is at all events, the *highest* of beings. You may, indeed, if you please, abandon the intellect to the lawless tyranny of imagination! . . . Drunk with the maddening wine of intellectual licentiousness and creative speculation, you may rave eloquently of a Being of infinite power, who pours forth out of His exhaustless bosom, unfathomable as the abyss of space itself, all glory, all living things, multitudinous and diversified beyond created arithmetic, such as fill the universe. And yet, by the same right of unreason and self-will, you may lay it down that He has not a self-consciousness, nor a choice, nor anything in short of that which makes us, to our fellow-men, objects of love and hope, of dread and hatred, of joy and of misery. And you may then, piling postulate on postulate into the empty air, till you reach, in haze and mist, the limbo of utter unreality, set up this blind and dumb and deaf abomination, with a crown upon its head, on the throne of Him who is, and was, and is to be — the living Jehovah. . . . But this is not a God, according to the supposition; and, of course, is not a living, loving, avenging, awful Deity. Why in such a case, though the spirit within us is clothed in perishable dust and ashes, WE should be far superior, in the order of intelligent being, to such a Deity, with all His immensity."[1]

2. Men in general feel, in the *most solemn and affecting moments of their lives, that God is a real Person.* Demonstration is not necessary. Consciousness and inward experience, more powerfully than any argumentation, attest it. This truthful evidence is given forth at times from the bosoms of the worst and the best of men. How true to nature are such parables as those of the Prodigal Son, and the Pharisee and the Publican. And the most life-like feature in each picture is, when the Prodigal coming to himself exclaimed, "Father, I have sinned;" and the Publican, conscious of his burden of guilt, cried, "God be merciful to me a sinner." The very cry for help which, under an irresistible impulse, ascends from the human soul when in imminent danger or stricken under a sense of sin, is a testimony of conscience to the personality of God. It is the witness of unsophisticated nature to the truth that He is a Being who can save from danger, who has displeasure to be dreaded and mercy to be sought after. The mind, *then*, unrestrained by philosophical theories or other artificial hindrances, recognizes Him in the personality of the judge, the sovereign, or the savior. The consciousness of the most excellent ones of the earth, gives a yet clearer evidence for the Divine personal existence and attributes. Men who have been renewed in the spirit of their mind, and who long for closer union with the best and greatest Being in the universe, never think of Him as a substance "stretched uncouthly through infinite space," which has only arrived at self-consciousness in their own souls. But they thirst for God — for the living God. They, clothed with humility, bend the knee and, with hearts uplifted to heaven, say, in filial confidence, "Abba Father." They

[1] The Personality of God, pp. 26–29.

gather up, as it were, into one, all the glorious attributes by which he is distinguished, and contemplate Him as Creator and Lord, Father and Friend, Judge and Savior. This we regard as real evidence, uttered from amid the indestructible elements of man's moral nature, for the perfect personality of God.

3. The *Sacred Scriptures throughout are full of the Divine Personality.* Every page breathes or burns with it. From the opening sentence of Genesis to the closing chapter of Revelation, in its unadorned histories as well as in its magnificent poetry, in the language alike of its threatenings and its promises, the Bible moves with the living Personal God. This places an impassable gulf between the religion of the pantheist and that of the Christian. And the Bible owes much of its telling power over men's hearts, as a divine instrument, to this pervading element of personality. Be it remembered that this is the book which has done vastly more than all others to regenerate and elevate our race, and that, under the agency of the Divine Spirit, it exerts this influence by bringing the mind into contact with God, not as a vague immensity, but as a glorious, awful, benignant person with whom we have to do. The sinner has been arrested in his wickedness, his spirit has quailed within him, and he has become a new creature, by hearing the living God of Holy Scripture speak to him in solemn warning and melting invitation. The saint has been refreshed and armed anew by the thought that the same Divine Being who clothes the grass of the field, and cares for the fowls of the air, loves, as a father, his own redeemed children, and surrounds them with his favor as with a shield. Yes; the Spirit, by whose inspiration the Word was given, beareth witness with our spirit to the perfect personality of God. And could this be separated from the Bible, and a pantheistic creed substituted in its stead, it

would be as if the sun had been shorn of its beams, and the ocean had lost his voice. "Ye shall know," said Joshua to the Israelites, "that the living God is among you." "It is a fearful thing," says Paul, "to fall into the hands of the living God." And in such winning words as these, of which the sacred volume is full, how near does the personality of Him whose name and nature are love, come to the heart: "Incline your ear, and come unto me; hear, and your soul shall live." "Look unto me, and be ye saved, all the ends of the earth: for I am God, and there is none else." The relational conception of the Most High, as our Maker, King, Father, Savior, Judge, guards us as effectually against a pantheistic view on the one hand; as the absolute conception of Him does against an anthropomorphic view on the other. Both conceptions blend with each other in the Bible. No book gives us such exalted ideas of the Infinite Intelligence, and none is less in harmony with the system of pantheism. "It is all in the same spirit; burning, powerful words; real above everything in this world; piercing, as living words must needs do, to the dividing of the very hearts and reins. They have the impression, they are stamped with the seal of the living God. The tetragrammaton is on them."[1]

4. *In Jesus Christ we see the absolute and the personal reconciled.* Pantheism and anthropomorphism, though traceable to the same source, are two extremes, toward one of which the mind, in the absence of revelation or in the want of faith in it, has ever shown a strong tendency. Men have been apt either to limit the Infinite, and think of Him as being such an one as themselves, or to conceive of Him as an infinite substance of which all things are but the modes and manifestations. How to reconcile the personality with the infinitude of the Divine nature, seems to be one of those sublime mysteries pertaining to the Divine existence

[1] Professor Garbett's Discourse, p. 45.

which unaided reason cannot solve. Such knowledge is too wonderful for us; it is high, we cannot attain unto it. As principles of abstract theology they may be clearly made out, but really to grasp them in our religious belief as attributes of the Almighty, is a great achievement of faith. The two are, however, reconciled before our view in Him who is the Word made flesh, at once the Son of God and the Son of man. The creation of the world was the work of an infinite Being. The everlasting God, the Lord, is the Creator of the ends of the earth. And by Jesus Christ were all things created, that are in heaven and that are in earth. The redemption of the world demanded the interposition of Him who made it. It was Jehovah's prerogative to say, "Behold I create new heavens and a new earth." And in Emmanuel, God in our nature, God with us, we see the Redeemer of man. The judgment of the world is an act of the Absolute. None else is judge but God. And the Son of man, coming in his glory, occupies the judgment throne. The Divine Being, without any limitation of his absolute perfections, is thus revealed in the person of Christ. Great, indeed, is the mystery of godliness. The incarnation is a stupendous fact that surpasses reason; for whatever pertains to the Divine nature must be incomprehensible by the human mind. But it contains in itself the solution of the mysterious problem how the absolute and the personal agree in One. And with all its mysteriousness, it becomes a resting truth to the minds of men and angels, when attempting to grasp the idea of an infinite and yet a personal God. The Lion of the tribe of Judah, the Root of David, has opened the book and loosed the seals thereof. And happy the mind that returns from its wanderings, that leaves off raving about a vague immensity which it can neither love nor fear, and rests in Jehovah-Jesus, God manifest in the flesh.

# CHAPTER III.

## THE DENIAL OF THE DIVINE PROVIDENTIAL GOVERNMENT; OR, NATURALISM.

Distinctive characteristic of Naturalism — Denounces every idea of Divine interposition — Not peculiar to any age or country — Broadly manifested in some works on Physical and Moral Science — System of Auguste Comte — "Vestiges of the Natural History of Creation" — Humboldt's "Cosmos" — Combe's "Constitution of Man" — The Owen School — Naturalism in the department of Bible Theology: Anti-miracle School of Germany — Spinoza — Paulus — Strauss — Miracles considered — Hume and Strauss alike guilty of a *petitio principii* — Denial of Special Inspiration of the Scriptures — Theodore Parker — Inspiration viewed as a fact — Mr. Morell's position — General remarks upon Naturalism as a whole — The idea of a self-sustaining universe based upon false analogy — Chargeable with anthropomorphism — Opposed to palpable evidence of Geology — Assigns no adequate cause for Christianity and its effects — Diametrically opposed to the religion of the Bible — Naturalism unnatural.

NATURALISM, or, as it is sometimes called, Rationalism, is distinguishable enough from atheism and pantheism. The rationalist is distinguished from the atheist by his theoretical belief of a Supreme Power, and he is distinguished from the pantheist by his denial of an ever-present and all-pervading Divine energy. The pantheist says, Cod is at hand; the rationalist says, God is afar off. Pantheism sees the Divine Being in all things, and confounds the Creator with the creation. Whereas naturalism, though distinguishing Him from His works, banishes Him into a distant solitude. It is not essential to this system that the evidences of design in proof of a creative intelligence be denied, however much it may tend in that direction, and though many of its abettors may have gone that length. But its distinctive characteristic, as a form of infidelity, is, that while admitting the world to have been originally created by God, it as it were extrudes Him from that world, by reducing it to a self-sustained mechanism, and by resolving what are generally understood by the works of Providence into a regularly successive series of necessary developments. The seed, having the vegetative power in itself, is cast by the husbandman into the soil, and there, aided merely by natural agencies, it is left to develop itself into the full-grown plant or tree. The watch, complete in its wheels and mainspring, is wound up, and continues to move, though ever so far distant from the maker. The ship-builder having finished and launched the ship, leaves it entirely to the care of the sailors.[1] Such are specimens of some of the analogies by which men would exclude God from his own world, and make the universe, if not independent of his creative power, altogether independent of his presence and control. The falsity of the analogy is obvious, and will be noticed by us hereafter. At present we wish to get as full-sized a view as possible of the system itself.

Men, whose piety is both rational and scriptural, have been accustomed to consider God as continually present in the world with the same power by which He made it. They reckon up no less numerous indications of a designing providential agency than of an original creating intelligence, and feel that they would be as much warranted to deny the presence and power of God in creating, as to deny his presence and power in sustaining and controlling. The heavens and the earth, in their estimation, furnish as clear and impressive tokens of the agency of the Divine Preserver as of the Divine Creator. The seasons roll on in beautiful harmony, but God is there present as the source of that harmony. We may speak of the universe as a huge machine moved by natural powers or mechanical laws, but it is the finger of God that touches the subordi-

[1] "Ut faber discedit à navi exstructâ et relinquit eam nautis."—*Melancthon.*

nate agencies which move the whole. He acts in every place, upon all things, and throughout all time. And but for his pervading influence, the world would become an inactive mass without form and void, and darkness would again cover the face of the deep. The language of Thomson, according to the creed of Christian piety, is as philosophically true as it is poetically beautiful:

> "But wandering oft, with brute unconscious gaze,
> Man marks not Thee, marks not the mighty hand
> That, ever-busy, wheels the silent spheres;
> Works in the secret deep; shoots, steaming, thence
> The fair profusion that o'erspreads the spring:
> Flings from the sun direct the flaming day;
> Feeds every creature; hurls the tempest forth;
> And, as on earth this grateful change revolves,
> With transport touches all the springs of life."

This is neither pantheism nor naturalism. It distinguishes the great Intelligent Spirit from the material world which He pervades, while it acknowledges his presence and energy acting upon all secondary causes as the primary action of the whole. Hence the ample room which such a system opens for the outgoings of a grateful and lofty devotion. Hence its firm faith in the well-attested Divine interpositions of the past, and its expectation that, if need be, similar interpositions will take place in the future.

Naturalism denies all this. It denounces it as the progeny of ignorance and fanaticism. It demolishes it at once, just as a man on awakening demolishes the airy castles which he built during sleep. If naturalism admits of a special and supernatural interference at all, it restricts such an interference to the original act of creation. The Almighty is allowed to come forth, create, give life, set in motion, and look on the scene, but afterwards He retires, and leaves the whole to nature and nature's laws. All the phenomena of matter and mind however rich and magnificent, all the events of history however influential and unprecedented, all the changes that have taken place in nations and individuals however thorough and beneficent, have, according to this system, occurred in a merely natural way, just as the engine speeds along the line of rail by the natural force of steam. The poet spake with a poetic license, or under the hallucination of genius, when addressing the god of the seasons, he said, "The rolling year is full of Thee." King David, in a dark age, sang very beautifully but not truly, when he said to Jehovah, "Thou visitest the earth, and waterest it: Thou greatly enrichest it with the river of God, which is full of water: Thou preparest them corn when Thou hast so provided for it: Thou makest it soft with showers: Thou blessest the springing thereof. Thou crownest the year with Thy goodness; and Thy paths drop fatness." Jesus Christ merely accommodated Himself to the views and circumstances of his followers, when He said to them, "Behold the fowls of the air: for they sow not, neither do they reap, nor gather into barns; yet your heavenly Father feedeth them." Miracles are impossible, just because they are unnatural. And what in theology is called the doctrine of Divine influence, is a mystery, a thing supernatural, and, therefore, not to be believed. The rationalist traverses the wide fields of space and makes himself familiar with the laws that regulate the movements of suns and stars; or he penetrates into the bowels of the earth, and reads, amid its rocky beds and their wreck of animal existence, the history of a past world; but neither in the heavens above nor in the earth beneath does he recognize the presence or interposition of God. He may admit that the Creator has left the impress of his finger there from a past eternity, but he sees no such finger amid the continued harmony of the spheres on high, or amid the convulsions and up-heavings that have taken place in the depths below. He virtually, if not openly, says, the Almighty was once here present, but He has withdrawn ages ago; nature reigns, and all physical phenomena are the necessary result of mechanical laws. The rationalist reads history too, but he sees not God in history. Its marvelous events, however unforeseen by men, however much they startled and baffled the calculations of the wise who were contemporaneous with them, and however mighty and protracted have been their influence in succeeding times, are drawn by him into that iron chain of necessary development in which he binds up all things. He looks too upon vast masses of men sunk in ignorance and vice, so sunk notwithstanding the play of many influences upon them which rationalists deem beneficial, and he will admit any or every agency into the work of their regeneration but the special agency of the Former of men's bodies and the Father of men's spirits. "Is it not strange," remarks John Foster,[1] "to observe, how carefully some philosophers, who deplore the condition of the world, and profess to expect its melioration, keep their speculations clear of every idea of Divine interposition? No builders of houses or cities were ever more attentive to guard against the access of flood or fire. If *He* should but touch their prospective theories of improvement, they would renounce them, as defiled and fit only for vulgar fanaticism. Their system of Providence would be profaned by the intrusion of the Almighty. Man is to effect an apotheosis for himself, by the hopeful process of exhausting his corruption. And should it take a long series of ages, vices, and woes, to reach this glorious attainment, patience may sustain itself the while by the thought that when it is realized, it will be burdened with no duty of religious gratitude. No

[1] Foster's Essays, p. 177, 15th ed.

time is too long to wait, no cost too deep to incur, for the triumph of proving that we have no need of a Divinity, regarded as possessing that one attribute which makes it delightful to acknowledge such a Being, the benevolence that would make us happy. But even if this noble self-sufficiency cannot be realized, the independence of spirit which has labored for it must not sink at last into piety. This afflicted world, 'this poor terrestrial citadel of man,' is to lock its gates, and keep its miseries, rather than admit the degradation of receiving help from God."

This form of infidelity is no novelty. It is not peculiar to any age or country. And while it may be said of other forms, that they slay their thousands, it must be said of this that it slays its ten thousands. This was the doctrine of the ancient atomists and Epicureans. They were not, theoretically considered, atheists. They believed in the existence of the gods, but denied that they interfered with either the physical or moral concerns of the universe. Plato held the doctrine in abhorrence, and made it one of the three kinds of blasphemy punishable in his republic with death. Justin Martyr, speaking of the philosophers in his time, tells us they taught it to be "useless to pray to God, since all things recur according to the unchangeable laws of an endless progression." Some of the English deistical writers of the last century, held substantially the same infidel opinion. Lord Herbert, "the first and purest of our English free-thinkers," who lived in the century preceding, includes the doctrine of Divine providence and the duty of worshiping God, in his five articles of religion. But others of the free-thinking school advanced ahead of him, and either denied that the Supreme Being interposed in the affairs of men, or held such a vague idea of a general providence as virtually excluded him from the government of the world. Chubb seems to have maintained that

God kept aloof from human affairs, and that whatever happened to men depended entirely upon secondary causes. Bolingbroke's idea of a providence that regarded things collectively but not individually, was such as left no room for the special interposition of God either in the physical or moral world. Hume, in his essays on Miracles and Providence, sapped the very foundations of natural and revealed religion, and would preclude us from believing that the same power which created the world, can continue to sustain it. The French Encyclopædists, who flourished during the latter half of the same century, built the whole of their metaphysical philosophy upon the basis of materialism, a system that began by removing God to a distance from the world, and explaining everything by secondary causes, and that ended in excluding Him altogether from their conceptions, and elevating nature to his throne. Men of science and literature were then resolutely bent on disregarding everything that seemed to admit the interference or idea of God, and on shutting themselves up in a system of blind fatalism and stern materialism. The bold skepticism and gross impiety of such schools have, in a great measure, passed away, yet much of the spirit that animated them is manifested in our own times. From the elaborate work on science down to the cheap journal that circulates among the masses of the people, there is not a little, both in our own country and on the Continent, that is avowedly opposed to the idea of Providence, crying out upon it as a bugbear in men's paths, or seeking to explode the doctrine by maintaining a studied silence respecting it, when it might most naturally have been introduced.

Such, in an undisguised form, is the philosophical system of M. Auguste Comte, who has been styled the Bacon of the nineteenth century.[1] He has given to the world a

[1] Lewes' Biographical History of Philosophy, vol. iv, p. 255.

large work of profound science,[1] built entirely on palpable facts, which are said to have occurred in a chain of necessary development, and to need no dogma of a Divine Providence to account for them. It interdicts every investigation beyond phenomena and the laws of phenomena, as without the reach of the human mind. And not only so, but every philosophical theory admitting the intervention of the First Cause is denounced as bearing a drag that obstructs the march of science and human improvement. This is very broadly laid down in the law of mental evolution or human progress, which he applies to every department of knowledge. According to him, the intelligence of mankind passes successively through three distinct stages: the supernatural, the metaphysical, and the positive. The first is the lowest or infant state of human society. The last is the period of progressive development, in which the mind advances onward to perfection. It belongs to the former, to attribute all the operations of nature to a Divine cause, and to admit the intervention of supernatural power to account for every unusual phenomenon. It belongs to the metaphysical stage, to ignore all such supernatural interpositions, to bring in the idea of abstract forces, and to personify them under the one agency of Nature. While it belongs to the last, the age of advanced science, to exclude all search into causes, and to apply itself to palpable phenomena, their relations and laws, so as to classify and generalize them. David, in a distant age, looked upward, and said, "The heavens declare the glory of God, and the firmament sheweth his handiwork. O Lord, our Lord, how excellent is thy name in all the earth! who has set thy glory above the heavens." Newton declared that "every true step made in inductive philosophy, is to be highly valued, because it brings us nearer to the First

[1] Cours de Philosophie Positive, 6 vols.

Cause." "A God without dominion, providence, and final causes," said the author of the "Principia," "is nothing but fate and nature." And again, remarks that greatest name in science, "it no doubt belongs to natural philosophy to inquire concerning God from the observation of phenomena." But according to the great French philosopher, David lived in an infantile state of society, when men sought the supernatural in everything; and Newton was fettered in his glorious career of discovery by the theological chimera of a Providence and a God. These heavens and this earth, the bare contemplation of which has filled with holy rapture many of the greatest minds of our race, and the investigation into the phenomena of which has drawn a Newton and others nearer to God, are, in the view of Auguste Comte, and his disciples, but a magnificent piece of mechanism, in the harmonious movements of which nothing higher is to be recognized than mechanical laws. It is said of the ancient Epicureans that they believed in the existence of the gods, but neither believed them to have created nor to govern the universe. And if the brilliant French philosopher admits a God at all, he excludes Him from creation and dominion, by resolving this goodly universe, both in its formation and government, into the spontaneous operation of purely physical principles. The system which is impressed by his great name, if not absolutely atheistical, looks certainly in that direction, and is, to say the least, as massive a structure of naturalism as ever scientific genius exhibited to the world.

It might have been expected that such a work of profound science, characterized as it is by high intellectual powers, would be greatly prized by the scientific men of our own country. But assuredly it is to be regretted that the author of so useful a book as "A Biographical History of Philosophy," should be found identifying himself with so much of its most objectionable principles. Speaking of Comte's system as the key to decipher past history, Mr. Lewes says,[1] "when we see so great a writer as Niebuhr unable to give any other explanation of the stability and progress of the Roman people than that of destiny—unable to read any signs but those of the 'finger of God'—it is high time to bestir ourselves to rid the world of this *supernatural* method of explaining facts." It is striking and gratifying that about the same time that this little work, in a cheap form, is endeavoring to propagate such principles among us, one of the most graphic historical works[2] that was ever given to the world, and embracing one of the most remarkable portions of the world's history, should follow as its guiding star the sentiment "God in history." And, to say the least, it is surely more philosophical to believe that the Supreme Being operates through the medium of natural laws, than that these laws are independent of the Law-maker, — that the world with all its grand and beautiful phenomena, and that history with all its marvels, bear traces of the directing finger of God, than that all should be wrapped up in an iron chain of necessary development. "The finger of Providence was on me," said the Duke of Wellington, in one of the brief notes that he dispatched from the field of Waterloo; and this sentiment, expressed at the close of the dreadful fight that decided the fate of nations, and under a solemnizing impression of the many brave that had fallen, belongs, we are told, to the lowest stage of human intelligence! "I had rather," said Bacon — and the remark is as applicable to the denial of Divine Providence as to the denial of the Divine Existence — "I had rather believe all the fables

[1] Biographical History of Philosophy, vol. iv, p. 258.

[2] D'Aubigné's History of the Reformation.

in the Legend, and the Talmud, and the Alcoran, than that this universal frame is without a mind."[1]

A work producing considerable excitement, calling forth a storm of opposition from the man of science and the divine, and which excludes God as effectually from the concerns of the universe, as that to which we have just adverted, has, but a few years ago, proceeded from the press of our own country. We allude to the "Vestiges of the Natural History of Creation." The naturalism of this anonymous publication, notwithstanding the term Providence is occasionally on the author's lips, appears without disguise. The theory is one of those extreme systems of development, according to which the world, with all its varied phenomena, moves on in its stern necessary course, guided only by physical laws, to the exclusion of the Divine agency. It assumes the nebular hypothesis — an hypothesis which, resting originally on insufficient data, is falling more and more into discredit as science steadily advances — and from the nebulous matter of space, which "must have been a universal fire-mist," it evolves, on the principle of pure physical law, the whole system of worlds. This universal fire-mist being granted, we have, as it were, the original germ of the material universe. The germ may have been created by God, and have received from Him its first impulse, but out of itself, and solely through the operation of physical laws, have been gradually unfolded

[1] M. Comte is not inactive in carrying out his principles. He knows that man will worship. But he is determined, as much as in him lies, to lead France and the other European nations from the worship of the supernatural to an idolatry of science or a systematic worship of humanity. With a view of utterly exploding the theological element, he has recently constructed a "Positive Calendar" of Infidel Worship, on the model of the festivals and saints' days of the Romish Church. It is nothing more than a public periodic commemoration of great men; and while Moses and Paul have a place in it, with such heroes as Confucius and Mahomet and Voltaire, the divine man, the model man, Jesus Christ, is ignored. These be thy gods, O France, and this worship of "Positive Philosophy" is first to regenerate thee and then the world!! — See *North British Review*. May, 1851.

those forms of magnificence and beauty which we see in the heavens and the earth. The theory may admit of a Divine interposition in calling the original constituents of the universe into existence, but it dispenses with or extrudes all Divine interposition in giving to matter its wondrous and richly-varied collocations. It may allow God in the beginning to utter his fiat, summon matter forth in its shapeless form from the void, and impress on it certain laws, but it allows not the Creator henceforth to interfere with his creation, or even to touch any of its springs of motion, so that, after the first creating act, He might as well have ceased to be. The universe, according to this theory of naturalism, has moved on in its glorious path of evolution, from the hour of the creation of the nebulæ, without the interposition of God; his existence and agency being deemed necessary to give it beginning, but not necessary to fashion, dispose, continue and control it. To the questions, whence this universal fire-mist, this nebulous matter, diffused throughout space, and the natural laws with which it has been endowed? you may get the answer, "from God." But you get no such answer when you ask who fashioned matter into such grand and beautiful forms, and disposed them so orderly and beneficially. The Most High seems now to have abdicated, and to have enthroned the physical laws, and left them to mould and govern the worlds. The Bible, in its sublime simplicity, tells us that "God made two great lights; the greater light to rule the day, and the lesser light to rule the night; he made the stars also." But the author of the "Vestiges" declares, the "masses of space are formed by law; law makes them in due time theaters of existence for plants and animals."[1] "It is impossible," he says,[2] "to suppose a distinct exertion or fiat of Almighty Power for the formation of the earth,

[1] Vestiges, p. 372, 5th ed. [2] Ibid. p. 204.

wrought up as it is in a complex dynamical connection, first with Venus on the one hand and Mars on the other, and secondly with all the other members of the system." And not only so, but he endeavors to interpret the first chapter of Genesis so as to discountenance "special efforts of the Deity." The sublime expression, "Let light be," indicates no special interposition of the great Creator, but merely a process of law. And such statements as — God made the firmament, God made the beasts of the earth, etc., are said "to occur subordinately . . . . not necessarily to convey a different idea of the mode of creation, and indeed only appear as alternative phrases in the usual duplicative style of the East."[1] This is naturalism without a cloak.

We dwell not here on the strong presumptive proof which advancing science is bringing against the nebular hypothesis. The fact that so many of the supposed nebulæ have been resolved into starry systems, makes it highly probable that all are resolvable. Lord Rosse's powerful telescope has revealed suns and systems where nothing but dim nebulæ were supposed to exist. And could another instrument of considerably greater magnifying power be constructed, the hypothesis, already so much damaged, might be completely destroyed. "As thrown out by Laplace," remarks Professor Whewell,[2] "it was a mere conjecture. It is a mere conjecture still. Hitherto it has lost ground in the progress of astronomical researches." But let us suppose it to be true, "that the primary condition of matter was that of a diffused mass, in which the component molecules were probably kept apart through the efficacy of heat; that portions of this agglomerated into suns, which threw off planets; that these planets were at first very much diffused, but gradually contracted by cooling to their present dimensions:[3] still, on this suppo-

[1] Vestiges, p. 167, 5th ed. [2] Indications of the Creator, p. 27, 2d ed.
[3] Vestiges, p. 43, 5th ed.

sition, we demand the presence and agency of God. The orderly and varied dispositions of matter bespeak a Divine interposition, as well as the origination of matter itself. In view of the collocations and motions of the material system, we no less naturally infer a Divine Providence than in thinking of the existence of matter we infer the agency of the creating God. The *à posteriori* argument has as firm a footing amid these collocations, as it has on the existence of matter, and its laws. Yea, more; it is in these collocations that we see the most legible evidences of design, and it is not so much from the bare existence of matter as from its dispositions and motions that we rise up to the Great Designer. The nebulous mass diffused throughout space, supposing such to have existed, came not there without the fiat of the Almighty; and suns and planets were not formed out of that mass without the intervention of Infinite Wisdom. The Book of Creation, beautifully written and well arranged, points up to the Divine hand that garnished and disposed it, no less than it proclaims the Divine Power that called from nothingness the materials of which it is composed. The author of the "Vestiges" tells us that law formed the masses of space into goodly theaters of existence for plants and animals. But what are natural laws without a Divine intelligence working in them and by them? Not realities, but merely abstractions. The existence of law not more truly presupposes the Lawgiver, than does the harmonious and uniform operation of law indicate the presence and control of the Governor. It is quite an illusion to speak of the laws of nature as if they were things distinct from the natural phenomena, and to invest them, like independent deities, with fashioning and regulating powers. "It is a perversion of language," says Dr. Paley,[1] "to assign any law,

[1] Natural Theology, vol. ii, pp. 9, 10. (Knight's edition.)

as the efficient operative cause of anything. A law presupposes an agent; for it is only the mode according to which an agent proceeds: it implies a power, for it is the order according to which that power acts. Without this agent, without this power, which are both distinct from itself, the *law* does nothing; is nothing." "Opus," remarks Lord Bacon, "quod operatur Deus a primordio usque ad finem."

But this theory of progressive development explains how the world was peopled, as well as how it was formed. It includes within its sweep both the animate and inanimate phenomena of the universe. It would not only evolve from a universal fire-mist, and by the exclusive operation of physical law, all the forms which matter has assumed, but it would trace the whole organized system, in a regularly advancing series, up from an infusorial point, to the noblest being, man. "No organism is, nor ever has one been, created," is the language of a chief philosopher of this school,[1] "which is not microscopic. Whatever is larger has not been created, but developed. Man has not been created, but developed." "We call in question," says the author of the "Vestiges,"[2] "not merely the simple idea of the unenlightened mind, that God fashioned all in the manner of an artificer seeking by special means to produce special effects, but even the doctrine in vogue amongst men of science, that 'creative fiats' were required for each new class, order, family, and species of organic beings, as they successively took their places upon the globe, or as the globe became gradually fitted for their reception." According to the Bible, "God said, Let us make man in our image, after our likeness. So God created man in his own image, in the image of God created He him." But, according to this theory, God created only microscopic monads or em-

[1] Professor Oken. [2] Vestiges, p. 161, 5th ed.

bryotic points, and from these, by a process of natural development, extending through cycles of ages, arose all the animated tribes. Creatures of "the simplest and most primitive type gave birth to a type superior to it in compositeness of organization and endowment of faculties; this again produced the next higher, and so on to the highest; the advance being, in all cases, small, but not of any determinate extent."[1] Man was not, then, the special workmanship of the living God. Moses is to be understood as speaking of ordinary law when he says, "The Lord God formed man of the dust of the ground, and breathed into his nostrils the breath of life." David's devotion is to be set down as enthusiasm, when, addressing God, he exclaimed, "Thou madest man a little lower than the angels." We must go back to the infusorial point, "whose seed was in itself," for the germ of human existence, and then, in retracing our steps, notice how, throughout the whole marvelous process, there is no mixture of the supernatural. The Creator is thus bidden to retire to the utmost bound of creation. No room is left for Him to interpose and create new species. He gave the first impulse at a dateless period in the past, and all subsequent formations and dispositions, however wondrous and varied, are the necessary results of fixed laws. This is the order of God's universe. Yea: "the system ought to be described as *a System of Order in which life grows out of dead matter, the higher out of the lower animals, and man out of brutes.*"[2]

The theory is no less opposed to the well-ascertained facts of science than it is to the scriptural record. The most illustrious names in the scientific world have condemned it. Geology, as it unfolds leaf after leaf of the "great stone book," gives the lie to it. The maxim is indeed true: *Natura non operatur per saltum*, understand-

[1] Vestiges, p. 232, 5th ed. [2] Whewell's Indications, p. 12, 2d ed.

ing that "Nature is but a name for an effect, whose cause is God."[1] But it is a wild fancy, a reckless mode of philosophizing, to conclude that since there are no gaps in nature, there have been no interpositions of the Creator from the period when He formed the first and smallest organism. The stars in their harmonious courses have been called to fight against God, and now the orderly gradations of the vegetable and animal kingdoms are summoned to give evidence against his agency and dominion. But the earth beneath and the heavens above refuse to be perjured. And, as Dr. Chalmers has remarked, "these two doctrines, the all but universal faith of naturalists, that there is no spontaneous generation and no transmutation of the species, are two denials, in fact, of nature's sufficiency for the origination of our races, and shut us up into the faith of nature's God." Had the development theory been founded in truth, it is obvious that the earlier fossils would have been very small in size and very low in organization. But such is not the case. We meet with giants where we should have found dwarfs, and creatures of a high organization instead of creatures of a low one. In the last, and one of the ablest replies to this fanciful hypothesis, Mr. Hugh Miller shows that the oldest ganoids yet known are, both as to size and organization, in direct opposition to it. "Up to a certain point in the geologic scale we find that the ganoids *are not;* and when they at length make their appearance upon the stage, they enter large in their stature and high in their organization."[2] The Fossil Flora also contradicts it. At the base of the Old Red Sandstone where, according to the development theory, "nothing higher than a lichen or a moss could have been expected, the ship-carpenter might have hopefully taken axe in hand to explore the woods for some such stately pine as the one

[1] Cowper. [2] Footprints, p. 105.

described by Milton."[1] The stubborn facts of science thus conflict with this baseless theory, a theory adopted before ever geology had a place among the inductive sciences, and which no eminent geologist is found to advocate. We are warranted, then, with the author of the "Footprints," to say: "Had an intelligent being, ignorant of what was going on upon earth during the week of creation, visited Eden on the morning of the sixth day, he would have found in it many of the inferior animals, but no trace of man. Had he returned again in the evening, he would have seen, installed in the office of keepers of the garden, and ruling with no tyrant sway as the humble monarchs of its brute inhabitants, two mature human creatures, perfect in their organization, and arrived at the full stature of their race. The entire evidence regarding them, in the absence of all such information as that imparted to Adam by Milton's angel, would amount simply to this, that in the morning man *was not*, and that in the evening he *was*. There, of course, could not exist, in the circumstances, a single appearance to sanction the belief that the two human creatures whom he saw walking together among the trees at sunset, had been 'developed from infusorial points,' not created mature. The evidence would, on the contrary, lie all the other way."[2] Such is at once the evidence of Scripture and geology. The "vestiges of the natural history of the creation" become the "footprints of the Creator," and vain becomes the attempt to explain the world's genealogies so as to banish from it the Omnipotent Father and Sovereign Lord.

In the domain of physical research, the "Cosmos" of Humboldt, a work of considerable value and popularity, bears on it the stamp of naturalism. Unlike the book on which we have been animadverting, it propounds no theory

[1] Footprints, p. 120. [2] Ibid. p. 104.

to account for the formation and peopling of the world, though the author favors the nebular hypothesis, but gives, what it professes to do, a physical description of the universe. It is more guilty by its omissions than by its assertions, though in some of these the naturalism is obvious enough. It is the most striking illustration with which we are acquainted of a work setting aside the doctrine of Divine Providence by maintaining a studied silence respecting it, when the author, if a believer in the doctrine, would have been naturally led by his subject to advert to it. It is just as if one were to give a glowing description of the pictures of Raphael without alluding to the genius of the artist; just as if Addison and Macaulay, in their dissertations on the grand poem of "Paradise Lost," had never mentioned Milton, "that mighty orb of song;" or, as has been remarked,[1] just as if a critic were to give a correct and eloquent account of the contents of "Cosmos" itself, without referring to its illustrious author, and the mental manifestation which he has made of himself in its pages. Baron Humboldt, in this work, makes no reference to a living omnipresent God. He sinks the spiritual in the material. He can, with much picturesque animation of style, exhibit the phenomenal harmony of the heavens, and describe his path from the remotest nebula to the minutest organism, and ignore Him who is the source of all that life and order. We perused a considerable portion of this interesting book while wandering on a lovely day of June over a beautiful tract of country, and were struck with the contrast between its repeated references to the active forces of nature and no reference to nature's God, and the glorious volume of creation that lay open before us, every page and line of which were radiant with the Creator's glory, and spoke of his power, wisdom and goodness. We lifted

[1] Dr. Harris' Man Primeval, p. 313.

the eye from the page of the philosophic traveler to the grand scenery above and around us, and involuntarily asked, Is there, then, amid this magnificent spectacle of earth and sky, no other power pervading and animating the whole but physical forces? We wondered to what specific cause it was to be attributed, that so keen and enthusiastic an observer of natural phenomena could, "in the late evening of an active life," present a sketch of a Physical Description of the Universe, "whose undefined image had floated before his mind for almost half a century," in which no reference is made to the Eternal One, but in the outset of which, as if to prevent disappointment, he uses such language as the following: "In reflecting upon physical phenomena and events, and tracing their causes by the process of reason, we become more and more convinced of the truth of the ancient doctrine, that the forces inherent in matter, and those which govern the moral world, exercise their action under the control of primordial necessity, and in accordance with movements occurring periodically after longer or shorter intervals."[1] The illustrious German, after having traveled over a considerable portion of the earth's surface, and made himself acquainted with all that is at present known of the physical phenomena of the universe, thus acknowledges, in the midst of his fourscore years, no higher agency than inherent material forces acting under the government of a primordial necessity. Divine Providence is thus interdicted, and this goodly universe moves onward, unfolding its forms of life and grandeur, without the hand of Him that made it. This may consist with Hegelianism, or with some other form of the transcendental philosophy, but it does not consist with the deeper philosophy of man's inward nature. It *might* do if we had heads and no hearts. The intellect may rest in it for a

[1] Cosmos, vol. i, p. 30.

while, but the soul, with its capacities and cravings, cannot repose there for a moment. Our very heart-strings must be torn out, the emotional part of our nature must be overborne, and all our upward aspirations repressed, before we can be satisfied with this thing of fate, this primordial necessity, in the room of the living and ever-ruling God. Even in an æsthetic view this method of philosophizing stands condemned. Robert Hall has truly said: "The exclusion of a Supreme Being and of a superintending Providence, tends directly to the destruction of moral taste. It robs the universe of all finished and consummate excellence, even in idea."

Combe's "Constitution of Man," a work of vastly wider circulation, and more adapted to the masses of the people than any to which we have referred, is, notwithstanding much that is valuable in the book, notorious for its naturalism. Mr. Combe and his school are not satisfied with discarding ignorant and superstitious notions about Providence, but their philosophy explodes the very idea of a Providence who controls and orders all things, and without whose permission not even a sparrow can fall to the ground. We meet, in such writers, with much that is worthy of attention respecting the influence of natural laws both on physical health and mental and moral training, and the evil consequences of disregarding or violating these laws. And we are quite willing to admit with the author of the "Vestiges," that to Mr. Combe's Essay, among other publications, "may be ascribed no small share of that public movement toward improved sanitary regulations which is one of the most cheering features of our age."[1] But the good in this respect is more than counter-balanced by the evil of erecting the natural laws into a sort of independent control, and holding out this principle as the true key to

[1] Vestiges, p. 397, 5th ed.

the government of the world.[1] It is a good service to rescue natural laws from the hands of ignorance and superstition, and to set forth their operations in a clear light. Mr. Combe has, in some measure, done this. But evil is done when these laws are taken, as it were out of the hand of the superintending Lawgiver, when either a studied silence about God as working in and by them is preserved, or intimations given that they are all in all, and that God does not interfere with their operations. And Mr. Combe and his school have done this.

It is the extreme of superstition or fanaticism, to repose implicit faith in Divine Providence while neglecting or going counter to the clearly defined laws of the human constitution, or those which regulate the physical and moral worlds. The type of such fanaticism is to be seen in the man who expects, as it were, bread to drop from the clouds into his mouth, or treasures to fall into his pockets from the same source, while doggedly refusing to work. But it is rushing to a godless extreme, the extreme of naturalism, to rest in mere secondary agencies without rising upward to Him who touches all the springs of action, or to ignore his presence in and superintendence over the world. It is confessedly mysterious how human instrumentality and Divine agency blend in bringing about events. But the mystery of things is not a whit lessened in cutting the link that connects the two together, in virtually saying, Let us loose our hold of the heavens above, and attach ourselves exclusively to the earth and things therein. Is the world's history, or is individual history, less mysterious, by shutting out from the sphere of human things the Divine Providence, and leaving room for nothing but the operation of natural laws? Or rather is not all history, by such an exclusion, made much more mysterious than ever? In the

[1] Constitution of Man, p. 6, People's Edition (6th).

one case, we have the human agency moving freely under the moral control of the Divine, we have in full play the elements of human action and piety, and yet mysterious relations. In the other case, we have only the human agent and the physical and moral laws, we have excluded the hand of God and taken away the elements of piety, and still the relations are mysterious. The choice then lies between a mysterious world in which God is ever present and ever felt, and a mysterious world that moves onward in its glorious evolutions without his continued agency. He is the better philosopher and the happier man who prefers the former, and holds a key to things inscrutable which can never be solved by the man who chooses the latter.

Mr. Combe sets up for a reformer, the advocate of a philosophy which would turn the pulpits of our churches and the chairs of our schools upside down.[1] Spiritual religion must be supplanted "by teaching mankind the philosophy of their own nature and of the world in which they live. Human depravity is a doctrine which he cannot away with, and it is set down to "an age when there was no sound philosophy, and almost no knowledge of physical science."[2] That Christianity is "a system of spiritual influences, of internal operations on the soul," is the representation "of men who knew extremely little of the science of either external nature or the human mind."[3] Prayer has no power with God, but is merely reflex in its influence, affecting only the mind of the petitioner.[4] And death is not,[5] as Moses and Paul have written, and Milton sung, the penal effect of man's first disobedience. Hence the necessity, as he asserts, of the religious instructors of mankind being taught over again, and of "a new direction"

[1] Constitution of Man, pp. 99, 100. [2] Ibid. p. 4. [3] Ibid. p. 92. [4] Ibid. p. 95. [5] Ibid. p. 58.

being given to their pursuits. He means modestly to insinuate, that were it possible to summon such men as Butler and Edwards, Howe and Charnock, Hall and Chalmers, "men who knew extremely little of the science of either external nature or the human mind," back again to this world, they would have to learn in his own school, the philosophy of human nature and material things, in order to prove, in this age, effective instructors of mankind! Not to dwell, however, on the inconsistency of such statements with facts, we readily grant that there is much in them consistent with naturalism or the denial of Divine providence. It is with such a denial that we have now to do. If, as Mr. Combe asserts,[1] "supernatural agency has long since ceased to interfere with human affairs," then it were time that spiritual Christianity should give place to a philosophy of nature, and that the worshipers of God were asking what profit should we have if we pray to Him.[2] But if, as seems to be admitted, such an agency once interposed in the concerns of the world, why may not that agency be there still, operating through the medium of those natural laws which the school of Combe would exalt into a sort of independent dominion?

There is a double illusion into which writers of this class fall when speaking of natural phenomena. In the first place, they represent the laws of nature, not, as they really are, modes of the Divine procedure, but as if they were real and independent existences. And then they suppose that because things happen according to fixed laws, the Divine agency cannot be in them. This, viewed merely as a philosophy, not to speak of its utter repugnance to Scripture, is extremely superficial. Men, by

[1] Constitution of Man, p. 99.

[2] Cicero, speaking of the philosophers of this school — not the "magni atque nobiles" — asks: "Quorum si vera sententia est, quæ potest esse pietas? quæ sanctitas? quæ religio?" — *De Nat. Deorum*, lib. i.

knowing, and adapting themselves to, fixed laws can often work out their own will. But this does not warrant the conclusion that the Divine Lawgiver cannot or does not, in such cases, make them subservient to the accomplishment of his higher will. An army, at the will of a monarch bent on enlarged dominion, is marched into a foreign state; or a voyage of discovery is made for mere commercial ends. The designs of men in both instances are served. But the accomplishment of a much higher design, to which these inferior ones are rendered tributary, follows. The gospel of peace enters into the respective territories, civilization comes in its train, and by the truth multitudes are made free. God's will was thus paramount; and under his moral control, the human will, acting by the fixed laws, was made the pliant minister of the Divine. Take one of Combe's own examples. In the reign of Charles the Second, London was, in a great measure, depopulated by the plague. "Most people of that age," says he,[1] "attributed the scourge to the inscrutable decrees of Providence, and some to the magnitude of the nation's moral iniquities." But, according to his views, "there was nothing inscrutable in its causes or objects. These appear to have had no direct reference to the moral condition of the people;" and the calamity "must have arisen from infringement of the *organic laws*, and have been intended to enforce stricter obedience to them in future. Now we ask, can disease or suffering not be an infringement of organic laws, and also a dispensation of Providence? Mr. Combe assumes that it cannot; and because an individual or a community, neglectful of sanitary conditions, falls a victim to plague, we are to believe that the natural violation leaves no room for the Divine operation. This, however, is nothing less than an assumption — an assumption, too.

[1] Combe's Constitution of Man, p. 36.

which fails to account for much of the afflictive, both in the history of individuals and communities. The human or secondary agencies do not exclude the Divine or first agency, the natural laws by no means supersede the presence and interposition of the Lawgiver. Mr. Morell, speaking of these secondary agencies, justly remarks: "They are all under the *moral control* of Deity from first to last, so that the penalty, which seems at first to be simply the result of breaking a natural law, is really an effect of that providential power which governs the world." And what he says of the world's history, may be said of the history of many a community and individual: "To the man who looks unbelievingly upon Divine Providence, the world's history is a problem that can never be solved."[1]

Combe's view of prayer,—bolstered up though it be by such names as Lord Kames, Dr. Hugh Blair, and Professor Leechman,[2] men of no high authority, verily, in such matters,—stands condemned also as most unnatural, not to say most unscriptural. It is, indeed, quite of a piece with his philosophy, but it consists not with the deeper philosophy of the heart and the Bible. Men have never prayed under the persuasion that the sole efficacy of prayer is reflex, that it has an influence only upon the mind of the worshiper. The wisest and best of the Greeks and Romans, the unsophisticated children of the desert, as well as the most enlightened and devout Christians, have resorted to prayer under the conviction that it is effectual to secure blessings directly from above. The reflex influence of prayer is valuable, but the value is realized just in proportion as the heart goes out after the direct influence. A rational theory it truly is, which would thus make the value of men's devotions to arise from men's illusions! The

[1] Morell's History of Philosophy, vol. ii, p. 571.

[2] Combe's Constitution of Man, pp. 95, 96.

reflex influence supposes the direct influence, and for men to enjoy the former without faith in the latter, resembles, as Isaac Taylor remarks,[1] "the supposition that we might continue to enjoy the accommodation of moonlight, even if the sun were blotted from the planetary system." As to the stale objection, which is ever and anon brought forth,[2] that the direct influence of prayer supposes that we can alter the Divine determinations, it is sufficient to reply, that it is according to these determinations that men must ask in order to receive, and knock in order to the door being opened. God discloses unto us the treasures of his grace, and says, "I will yet for these be inquired of."

What is insidiously taught by such a writer as Combe, has been advocated more boldly, and with less fear of giving offense, by the Owen school. Rationalism is here defined to be the science of material circumstances. And the philosophy of Owenism ignores everything else. It denounces other systems for having spiritualized man, and it professes to look upon him, to all practical purposes, as a material being. Humanity, in its estimation, contains within itself the germs of indefinite moral improvement, and needs only to be brought under the genial influences of earth to ripen into perfection. Supernatural aid is interdicted at the threshold, lest it should beget an indifference to self-exertion, and foster a habit of dependence. The first and last lesson given to its disciples is, that men's opinions and actions result exclusively from their original susceptibilities, and the influences of the world around them, over which they have no control. Hence its oft-

[1] Spiritual Christianity, p. 51.

[2] Mr. R. W. Mackay, who, after the manner of Combe, confines "the circle of our real knowledge to phenomenal succession and its laws," with all the coolness of the sensational school, serves up this oft-refuted objection. He falsely assumes that prayer presupposes changeableness in God, and then settles the matter by telling us that the Creator is not "to be diverted from his purposes by entreaty."—*The Progress of the Intellect*, vol. i, pp. 25, 109.

repeated injunction, Study yourself and mind external circumstances. This is the sum and substance of its commandments. It admits the existence of error and vice in humanity, for these are too palpable to be denied, but it charitably calls them misfortunes, and as a remedy for all moral ills, insists on a rational education. The favorite analogy of this system is derived from the influence which the sun exerts upon the earth. This is at once the grand image in its poetry, and the grand illustration of its philosophy. Human nature is compared to the earth, and external influences to the sun which vivifies and adorns it. Rationalism says, Bring a man of good susceptibilities into a favorable position as regards external circumstances, and hence results a good character. This is the system ushered forth with big pretensions, and propounded in innumerable little books and pamphlets, which is "to renovate the social state, recast and elevate humanity!"

The crude elements of the system have been found floating on the surface of society in every age. Its modern form may be said to have been cut by Rousseau and French philosophy, and to have assumed a still more palpable shape in the hands of Owen and his followers. It is gross naturalism, naked and not ashamed, and as such, though now fast in the wane, it has been greeted by masses of the people who were disposed to throw off every species of religion as an intolerable yoke. Such writers as the author of the "Vestiges," do not more effectually exclude Providence from the government of the spheres, and from the whole domain of natural history, than do the disciples of the "new moral world" shut out the idea of supernatural interference in educating man. Rationalism in this form, and what is called communism, are often associated, though they are by no means to be identified or confounded. Its politics rise out of its philosophy. The great lesson of its philosophy is, External circumstances are the agents of fate, look well to them. Its politics may be summed up in ascribing demoralization and crime to the factitious arrangements of society. It cries out, Alter these, place society in a favorable position, educate man aright, and then will be realized the new heavens and the new earth, wherein dwelleth righteousness.

Viewed merely as a system of philosophy, it is the shallowest that rationalism ever offered to the world. No one denies the vast influence of external circumstances upon the human character, and the importance of attending to them. It will also be admitted that improved systems of education, and altered arrangements in civil society, would tend greatly to lessen crime, and ameliorate the condition of man. But to rest the world's regeneration on these alone, exposes the system to the charge of being one-sided and empirical, as unphilosophical as it is ungodly. It takes up one idea, an important and a true one, but, to the neglect of other ideas no less true and important, this is exalted, carried everywhere forth, and all men and things are called to fall down and worship it. Material circumstances are something, but the school of Owen makes them everything. The human will is no doubt influenced by them, but our rationalists maintain, in opposition to consciousness, that it is controlled by them. Man is made a passive creature. This is plainly implied in the fond analogy of the sun acting upon the earth. Emerson has said,[1] "Man is here, not to work, but to be worked upon." And the men of this school tell us that our characters are the necessary result of our organization at birth, and subsequent external influences over which we have no control. "The germs of intelligence and virtue are expanded or blasted by them," and thus the whole human character is

[1] Representative Men, p. 92, Bohn's edition.

formed. It is not so. Our subjective constitution is not such an inert, helpless thing. We are conscious of possessing a faculty which gives us control over external circumstances; so that, taking this into account, it is true that character is the result of our subjective nature, and of the objective influences acting upon it. But, in this system of naturalism, the great facts of man's moral nature are ignored. One portion of the field of phenomena is dwelt upon as if it were the whole, and the other portion, which to a reflective mind is no less obvious, is overlooked. The eye is turned outward and lost in material things. It does not direct its glance down into the depths of human consciousness, and fails to perceive the more wondrous things of the spirit. A sense of responsibility and moral sentiment are great truths in the natural history of man. They are phenomena just as palpable to the eye that looks inward, as any of the material circumstances are to the eye that looks outward. But the Owen school either loses sight of these phenomena in human nature, or would assign them to a blind necessity, a source from which the unsophisticated mind refuses to receive them. Then there is the stubborn, though mysterious fact of human depravity, which it either winks at or entirely overlooks, and for counteracting which it accordingly makes no provision. The wonder is how the abettors of such a system can read history, or look upon the world around them, without perceiving, on the one hand, how individuals and communities, placed amid the most favorable external circumstances, have continued corrupt and corrupters; and how, on the other hand, persons more unfavorably situated have, notwithstanding, become exemplars of virtue. A theory that ascribes so much to the mere outward relations, and leaves no room for an influence counteractive of bad ones or efficacious to good ones, is condemned by experience as well as by religion. But perhaps its advocates would remove it from such a tribunal by affirming that no community has ever yet been placed in such a paradisiacal state as rationalism would place it. In such a case, it must bear the double stigma of being godless and utopian.

Hitherto we have viewed naturalism as broadly manifested in some works on physical and moral science, and now we have to notice its appearance in the department of Bible theology. Germany, in this respect, though not exclusively its seat, has attained a bad preëminence. Thousands of men, professing to be Christ's ministers and expounders of his Word, have, during the last half-century or more, propounded from the halls and pulpits of Germany a creed which no more admits of supernatural influence than any of the philosophical systems to which we have adverted. In their teaching, God is as effectually excluded from the province of the Bible, as in the "Vestiges" and similar works He is excluded from the solar system. The brilliant and beneficent miracles which ushered in the Gospel dispensation are exploded, or explained away on purely natural principles. And what is properly meant by Divine influence is denied a place either in the mode of inspiring the sacred writers, or in the mode of enlightening and renewing the minds of the readers. Spinoza, whose philosophy has exerted such a mighty influence on the thinking of Germany, had said, "All that is recorded in the books of revelation took place in conformity with the established laws of the universe." On this principle, interpretation after interpretation has been given, until the sacred record has been swept as clear of its mighty signs and wonders, as some would sweep the starry firmament of the evidences of an ever-present and all-controlling God. In Germany, speculative philosophy and theological doctrine are more closely linked together than in any other country in Europe. The pervading principle of its speculative philosophy, that God never intervenes specially, but that all things move on in a chain of necessary development, has been carried into the region of its theology. Hence the axiom, laid down at the threshold, "miracles are an impossibility." The very first principle which Strauss brings to the study of the evangelists is, that when the events narrated are incompatible with known and universal laws, it must be maintained that they did not happen in the manner recorded. Divine Providence is thus interdicted at the onset.

We have been accustomed to consider Christianity as a second creation, and to conceive that as the first creation took place by a special intervention of Divine Power, so did the second. The philosophy of the rationalist will not admit this, and therefore his theology must be shaped so as to exclude it. The first miracle in Christianity is the birth and manifestation of the Savior. This cannot be a true literal history, says the rationalist, for it is incompatible with the laws that regulate the succession of events. The miraculous texture of the gospel narrative may be admitted, but the wonders recorded must be accounted for in accordance with the assumed principle that there is no supernatural intervention in the world's history. Hence the theory, formerly adverted to,[1] that Christ did not make the church, but the church made Him. He is represented as a pious Israelite, educated in the bosom of a pious family in Nazareth, who endeavored to realize in Himself the Messianic conceptions that prevailed among the people. He believed Himself to be the Messiah of promise; the Jews, in process of time, transferred their conceptions to Him, and recognized Him as the expected deliverer.

[1] Chapter II, p. 55.

Thus, out of the existing Messianic notions, and the impression which Jesus made by his personal qualities and actions, does rationalism derive the first miracle of Christianity—the birth, incarnation, and appearing of the Son of God. The great mystery of godliness having been thus stripped of its grandeur, and made to assume the shape of a natural event, the whole train of mighty works wrought by Christ and his apostles must undergo a similar denuding process. Rationalism admits that, according to the conceptions then prevalent among the Jews, the Messiah was to be a worker of miracles; and it infers that, in consequence of these conceptions, they ascribed to Him the power of performing them. "The chain of endless causation," says Strauss, "can never be broken, and a miracle is an impossibility." They must be resolved, therefore, into purely natural principles.[1]

The earlier school of rationalists, which took hold of Spinoza's principle, endeavored to show that the gospels were not miraculous in their texture, that the writers never intended to assert miracle, and that the events recorded were simple facts magnified by the impression which they made on the senses, or exaggerated by the false coloring of copyists and others. This school of rationalism has well-nigh become obsolete. It was too materialistic for the ideal tendencies of Germany. Strauss assailed it. He declares in that misnomer, the "Leben Jesu," "that it was time to substitute a new method of considering the history of Jesus for the worn-out idea of a supernatural intervention and a naturalist explanation." He is, however, but a naturalist in another shape. He admits the gospels to be miraculous narratives. And in this admission there is

[1] It may be here noticed that the "Progress of the Intellect" goes on the pantheistic assumption that a miracle is God at variance with Himself; and then, taking a leaf out of Strauss, accounts for the development of a supernatural Messiah. See vol. i, p. 20. and vol ii, chap. 8.

assuredly no more virtue than in the recognition, on a clear frosty night, of the stars that shine out of the depths of the blue sky. Miracles, as Dr. Newman has well said,[1] "form the substance and groundwork of the narrative, and, like the figure of Phidias on Minerva's shield, cannot be erased without spoiling the entire composition." But, while admitting the gospels to be supernatural in their texture, or to have miracles interwoven with them, he aims to show that they nevertheless originated without an historical foundation; as if the stars of night were mere mental illusions, and the form of Phidias on the shield a fiction, not a reality. His fundamental position is a naturalist one: "miracles are not, and never were." Every narrative that surpasses the ordinary course of events proves itself not to be historically true. The allegory, the legend, the myth, must explain all the bright and beneficent miracles that astonished the Jews before whom they were wrought, and that have drawn forth the homage of the church in every age. The naturalism of Strauss and his followers may differ in some features from that of Paulus and the older rationalists, but it is sheer naturalism still.[2]

Is the feeding of five thousand men with five loaves and two small fishes to be accounted for? This has generally been regarded as one of the most striking manifestations of the divine power of Christ, and so great was the impression produced on the multitude, who witnessed it, that they cried, "This is of a truth that Prophet that should come into the world." But, according to our rationalist, this great miracle dwindles down to the event of Christ having had such an influence over the minds of men, as that the more wealthy in the crowd, who were well

[1] Newman's Dissertation on Miracles, Encyclop. Metrop.

[2] See Dr. Beard's Voices of the Church, p. 35.

supplied with provisions, were constrained to distribute of their abundance to the destitute multitudes; or it may be regarded as a copy of the story of the manna in the desert. The calming of the storm on the sea of Galilee is another of those mighty works that have strikingly displayed the supernatural power of the Savior. It led the observers in wonder and awe to exclaim, "What manner of man is this, that even the winds and the sea obey him!" Rationalism, however, has the explanation at hand. Jesus, by his calm and dignified demeanor, tranquilized the troubled minds of his disciples. By a happy coincidence, the raging elements of nature at the same time became still. And the event was thus magnified into the miraculous. In short, is it the most magnificent of all miracles, the resurrection of Christ, that is to be accounted for? The rationalist acknowledges that the surprising revolution in the minds of the disciples, from the deep despair into which they had sunk at the death of Jesus, to the fearless energy with which they shortly afterwards pleaded his cause, shows that during the interval something extraordinary had happened. What that something was, the gospel narratives tell us — the miraculous resurrection of Christ, which powerfully declared Him to be the Son of God. But naturalism admits no miracle. Strauss says, the return of a dead person to life is impossible. And the change which took place in the minds of the disciples is resolved into visions, and these visions are resolved into their own excited feelings. The most stupendous events in the world's history are thus made to vanish before a naturalist explanation.[1] And Strauss coolly and remorselessly looks on, as the bright train of beneficent and mighty deeds, which have drawn forth men's faith and reverence, disappear. No wonder that the German mind, on reflecting, drew back

[1] See Tholuck, in Dr. Beard, p. 151.

from, or refused assent to, such critical principles as these, inasmuch as they were seen to uproot all our hold upon the past, and to involve all history in a mythical illusion.

Pantheism and naturalism may be said to meet in this theory, which we denounce as one of the most unphilosophical that was ever attempted to be imposed upon the world. Its dogged adherence, in spite of all evidence, to the position that miracles are impossible, is consistent only with absolute atheism or pantheism. Men who adopt, as a fundamental principle, the impossibility of supernatural intervention, must either deny that God is, or deprive Him of his personality. Strauss, as we have already noticed, is a pantheist in the extreme. He stands at that point where atheism and pantheism face each other, and shake hands. And just as one impiety naturally follows another, does his theory of Christianity arise out of his other infidel views. But admit the existence of a first Intelligent Cause, the Creator of heaven and earth, the living God,— a necessary truth granted by all sound reasoners — and where is the rationality in denying that He either does or can interpose in the system of things which He has established? Reasoning *à priori*, and in accordance with a pure theism, we would have been led to conclude that He who made the worlds would continue to govern them, and that, for great and special ends, He would interpose in a special and extraordinary manner. Whether He has done so or not must be decided on the broad ground of evidence. The axiom of Strauss contravenes the very foundation principles of the inductive philosophy. A miracle is neither impossible nor incredible, on the supposition of a God.

Miracles are supernatural facts, things which bespeak the intervention of a cause superior to and having a supreme control over all natural causes. It matters not, in our present argument, whether we strictly define them as lying beyond the sphere of natural laws, or as involving the idea of suspension of or opposition to these laws. In either case we demand the interposition of God. To raise a dead man to life, or to walk upon the sea, may be viewed either as above the range of the established laws of nature, or as directly contrary to them; but, on either supposition, the operation is divine. The latter point of view is commonly, though not universally, taken by evangelical men in our country; the former is the stand-point of distinguished Christian divines on the Continent. Strauss and his school lay down the position that nature is but a development of God. He says the chain of endless causation cannot be broken; and taking the common idea of miracles, as violations or suspensions of natural laws, he declares a miracle to be impossible. Neander, Müller, D'Aubigné, and other Continental divines, without conceding anything to the rationalists, oppose them, by maintaining that miraculous phenomena lie beyond the sphere of those laws, and are not violations of them. And in this theory they are joined by some of our own eminent evangelical writers, such as Trench, Vaughan, Westcott, and the author of "The Restoration of Belief."[1] The idea of supernatural intervention is prominent, however, in either view, and that is not to be tolerated by naturalism. Miracles may be perfectly natural, viewed in reference to a higher world, but they are supernatural viewed in reference to this. "At the establishment of Christianity," says D'Aubigné, "the superior world acted upon the inferior world, conformably to the laws which are peculiar to it, a miracle is nothing more than this."[2] Be the miracle contrary to, or lying beyond, the subordinate laws of physical nature, it is doubtless in conformity with the moral and supreme law of the universe.

[1] See Tholuck, in Dr. Beard, p. 232. [2] The Miracles; or, Two Errors.

"God, therefore," says Gioberti, "far from disturbing universal harmony, maintains it, by interrupting the course of physical forces in certain determinate cases, and for a most wise end."[1]

Hume and the older deists said a miracle is incredible. Strauss and the modern rationalists affirm a miracle to be impossible. Hume's fallacy, as has often been shown, lay in confounding two distinct experiences, the uniform experience of the individual and the uniform experience of mankind viewed as a whole. He reasoned as if his own experience embraced a knowledge of all causes, and as if his knowledge of the power of all causes was so complete that he was warranted to say, There is not a cause able or willing to work miracles. His own uniform experience, as an individual, bore testimony to the constancy of the laws of nature. And the fallacy consisted in exalting that experience into the experience of the human race. In short, the argument is based upon a gross assumption. By it he arrogates to himself a knowledge which no finite intelligence can possess. The argument fails also in the principle on which it would set aside the testimony of witnesses adduced to prove a miracle. Hume reasons thus: there

[1] Dr. Wardlaw, in his recent able work "On Miracles," advocates what may be called the old view, and offers some strictures on Drs. Vaughan and Beard and Mr. Trench, who contend that miracles are not "*contra* naturam, but *præter* naturam, and *supra* naturam." And yet he says of the miraculous event, "it does not to me seem very material whether we speak of it as beyond nature, or above nature, or beside nature, or against nature, or contrary to nature,—whether as a suspension, an interruption, a contravention, or a violation of nature's laws; provided we are understanding 'nature and nature's laws' as having reference to the physical economy of our own system."—(P. 31.) This, we presume, is just *their* understanding when, according to Mr. Westcott, they say, "that there is nothing in miracles contrary to nature, while all is above nature; that the laws of existences around us are not broken, but resolved into higher laws."—*Gospel Harmony*, p. 17. We are disposed to regard this discussion as not "much more than a logomachy," for the great idea of supernatural intervention is unaffected by it. At the same time, the "above and beyond nature" view seems the more advantageous one in cutting away the ground from beneath the German anti-miracle school.

are two testimonies in the case — the testimony of uniform experience in affirming the constancy of the laws of nature, and the testimony of witnesses in favor of a miracle or deviation from these ordinary laws. No number of witnesses for the miracle can equal the evidence for the constancy of nature. It is more probable that the witnesses should have been deceived, however apparently strong their testimony, than that the laws of nature should have been departed from. Thus all miracles are denied, without any regard to the kind or quality of proof by which they are supported. The rationalist intrenches himself behind the position of the incredibility or impossibility of miracles, and levels to the ground the whole structure of Christianity. Now, it is sufficient to say to this, that, in the ordinary concerns of life, we value testimony rather for its quality than for its quantity. If a few witnesses of known veracity attest an extraordinary occurrence, we confide in their testimony as naturally as we do in the testimony of thousands of persons who had previously deposed to the ordinary course of events. On the very same principle, then, we should, as has been satisfactorily argued, credit testimony unexceptionable in its quality when it is adduced not only in proof of the extraordinary, but when it carries us a step higher — to the supernatural or miraculous. Well-attested miracles can consistently be denied only on atheistical, or, what in this case amounts to the same thing, pantheistical principles. Once admit the existence of a Personal God, Himself uncaused and the cause of all, and you cannot rationally deny that He may interpose in the concerns of the universe. Grant that the Almighty intervened in calling into existence the first creation, and you cannot reasonably withhold your assent, that, if evidence in support of it exist, He may have intervened in originating Christianity, the second creation. The rationalist who, in the face of all evidence, takes up the position that miracles are impossible, must be driven back to another position — viz., the non-existence of a Being who can perform supernatural works. Strauss in maintaining the impossibility of miracles, as well as Hume in asserting their incredibility, has been flagrantly guilty of a *petitio principii* — a begging of the question. It is nothing more than his *ipse dixit.* The world has had more than enough of this philosophy, falsely so called, which would supersede all investigation into the testimony for miracles by proclaiming it as an axiom that miracles are impossible, or that no evidence can substantiate them. It is alike opposed to the cautious philosophy of Bacon, and to the facts and principles of Holy Scripture. It is the taking of a one-sided, and consequently a very erroneous view of God's universe. The moral system is ignored, a system as real and palpable as the physical, though immeasurably superior to it. And the remark is as applicable to the men of the Strauss school as to the men of the Hume school: their antecedent objections against miracles "will be found nearly all to arise from forgetfulness of the existence of moral laws. In their zeal to perfect the laws of matter, they most unphilosophically overlook a more sublime system, which contains disclosures not only of the *Being* but of the *Will* of God."[1]

But Scripture itself, under the system of naturalism, is, as a whole, disrobed of its glory. The special interposition of God in inspiring the sacred writers, is as much excluded as his interposition in working the Bible miracles. And, if the mighty deeds recorded sink down to the level of common events, why should not the Holy Book itself descend to the level of a common treatise? John Foster has said: "Surely, it is fair to believe that those who received from heaven superhuman power, received likewise

[1] Newman's Dissertation, Encyclop. Metrop.

superhuman wisdom. Having rung the great bell of the universe, the sermon to follow must be extraordinary." Naturalism, having denied the superhuman power, consistently with its own principles, denies the superhuman wisdom. The bell, according to it, was nothing uncommon, and the sermon that followed was nothing transcendent. The denial of the miracles has, in fact, led to the denial of the inspiration. It must be admitted that the Bible records miracles. It must be admitted also that the Bible claims special inspiration. Naturalism cannot admit the miracles, and consequently it cannot concede that the prophets and apostles, holy men of God, spake as they were moved by the Holy Ghost. De Wette and others attacked the Old Testament, and Strauss has made a similar onslaught on the New, from the same naturalist position. The books must be treated as spurious, because they narrate predictions and miracles, things which naturalism cannot away with. We find, accordingly, in the writings of the old English deists, in the Wolfenbüttel Fragments, and in a succession of such like productions, down to that paragon of honest book-writing—"Phases of Faith"—a heap of apparent contradictions raked together from all quarters, the fruit of a shallow criticism and an irreligious spirit, in order to falsify the Book which claims to have been given by inspiration of God. Hatred of the supernatural, which is interwoven with every page of Scripture, has led to the various disingenuous attempts to depreciate the testimony of the inspired writers. It is related that a Swedish traveler, in looking through the library of Voltaire, found Calmet's Commentary with slips of paper inserted, on which were written the difficulties noticed by Calmet, without the slightest reference to the solutions given by the commentator. The Swede, who, in other respects, admired the brilliant Frenchman, denounced this conduct as dishonorable. And yet, as Hengstenberg remarks,[1] our modern rationalist critics have acted in a similar manner. Theodore Parker, Francis William Newman, and Robert William Mackay,[2] who make no secret of the Gamaliels at whose feet they have been sitting, serve up the often-refuted objections against the infallibility of the sacred writers, as if they were a fresh course, and then, on the assumption of their gross mistakes and contradictions, conclude against their miraculous inspiration.

The age in which we live is universal in its tendencies. It must have all things in common. The mind has become intolerant of monopolies. And not a few writers in our own and other lands are laboring to bring the Bible down from its proud pre-eminence, stripping it of its solitary grandeur, and allowing it no other inspiration than that which is common to men. The controversy may be said to have shifted its ground, or to present a new phasis, in consequence of a new philosophic influence. Formerly, our Christian apologists had to contend for the very element of inspiration in the sacred books, as they had to contend for the miraculous texture of the gospel narratives; now, we have to strive for their special claim to the Divine inbreathing, against those who would merge them in an influence common as the light or air of heaven. Thus Mr. Parker,[3] speaking after the Emerson fashion, tells us, "inspiration, like God's omnipresence, is not limited to the few writers claimed by the Jews, Christians, or Mahometans, but it is co-extensive with the race." Minos and Moses, David and Pindar, Leibnitz and Paul, Newton and Simon Peter, "receive into their various forms the one spirit from God most high." Yea, "this inspiration is lim-

[1] Hengstenberg on the Pentateuch, vol. i, p. 47.

[2] See Parker's Discourses, Newman's Phases of Faith, and Mackay's Progress of the Intellect, *passim*.

[3] Parker's Discourse, pp. 161–171.

ited to no sect, age or nation. It is wide as the world, and common as God." The Bible thus ceases to be the law and the testimony, the only infallible directory of faith and morals, and men may turn it into myths and legends, receive or reject it, as they please. But this attempt to confound inspiration and omnipresence goes on the assumption that as God is present everywhere, He cannot be specially present anywhere; that as he may be said to exert a common influence on the minds of all men, He cannot be said to exert a supernatural influence on the minds of a chosen number of men. An assumption of the same nature and philosophic value as that of Strauss — miracles are impossible.

The Bible comes to us claiming to have been given by miraculous inspiration of God — an inspiration separated by an impassable gulf from that of mere genius — and, in support of its claims, presents a large amount of clear and strong evidence. There is an impregnable external testimony encircling it "as the mountains are round about Jerusalem," and, on its pages, the finger of God is not less clearly manifested than on the starry heavens. This Book stands above and apart from the sublimest effusions of human genius, revealing truths bearing on man's highest interests and lying beyond the sphere where science and genius make their discoveries — having a history quite unparalleled and miraculous — and producing on individuals and communities such radical and beneficent changes of heart and life, as no other book in the world has effected. It professes to have received its grand revelations directly from above, and to have transmitted them under such infallible guidance as entitles it to be regarded as the oracle of God. We meddle not with the question of degrees of inspiration. We advocate no theory of mechanical dictation. It is enough, but not more than enough, that we hold a special influence ranging from the highest point, or direct revelation, down to the lowest limit, or superintendence as a guard against error. We take the fact as it stands — all Scripture is given by inspiration of God. The mode does not trouble us. Scripture, in its rich diversity of style, evinces free mental action on the part of the sacred writers, while it asserts that action to have been under the infallible guidance of the Divine Spirit. The plenary inspiration we hold in perfect consistency with the human peculiarities. Our position "presupposes that the same providential power which gave the message selected the messenger, and implies that the traits of individual character and the peculiarities of manner and purpose which are displayed in the composition and language of the sacred writings, are essential to the perfect exhibition of their meaning. . . . It preserves absolute truthfulness with perfect humanity, so that the nature of man is not neutralized, if we may thus speak, by the Divine agency, and the truth of God is not modified, but exactly expressed in one of its several aspects, by the individual mind. Each element performs its perfect work, and in religion, as well as in philosophy, we find a glorious reality based upon a true antithesis."[1] This is the Bible claim. And if this be not conceded on the ground of the internal and external evidence, then the Bible, in its structure, in its characteristic truths, in the simplicity and majesty of its style, in its matchless character of Christ, in its influence on and present position in the world — is a greater miracle than the miraculous inspiration which naturalism would set aside. Discrepancies we admit, such discrepancies as might have been expected to result from the transmission of a book through so many hands, languages and ages, unless shielded so miraculously at every point that the finger of no copyist could inadvertently have

[1] Westcott's Elements of the Gospel Harmony, pp. 9, 10.

introduced a wrong date or omitted a letter. But what is the chaff to the wheat? A large number of discrepancies, on which infidel objections were grounded, have vanished before the application of a true and searching criticism, and we anticipate that the residue will be still further diminished till it shall be accounted as nothing. There is no discrepancy in regard to the substantial contents of Christianity, and to found an argument against the miraculous inspiration of Scripture on a few unresolved variances, is no less irrational than to argue against the perfections of God because of some conflicting natural phenomena.[1] The Bible, in its disclosures, history and position, is as unaccountable without the admission of special inspiration, as the world and the fullness thereof without the creating and upholding hand of God.[2]

The position taken up by Mr. Morell on this question, however stoutly he, in other respects, denounces rationalism, is little better than a rationalist one. He indeed admits supernatural agency, but it is a mere vivifying operation, a heightening or clearing of the power of intuition, not generically different from the inspirations of genius or the spiritual elevation common to Christians. "Inspiration," according to him, "depends upon the clearness, force and accuracy of a man's religious intuitions.[3] . . . It does not involve any form of intelligence essentially different from what we already possess.[4] . . . It is a higher

[1] Butler's Analogy, p. 8. (Dublin, 1849.)

[2] We make no use of the *petitio principii* in the above remarks. We do not say to our opponents, The Scriptures are inspired, and therefore their statements must be true. But we ground an argument for their inspiration on their internal structure and external position. The author of "The Restoration of Belief" observes, "We are often told that we timidly hold up this 'Inspiration' as a screen, lest the documents of our faith should come to be dealt with severely, in the mode that is proper to historic criticism." With him we say, "Only let this Historic Severity take its free course, and Disbelief will be driven from its last standing-place. . . . It would wither like the grass of the tropics."—P. 127.

[3] Morell's Philosophy of Religion, p. 176.

[4] Ibid. p. 151.

potency of a certain form of consciousness, which every man to some degree possesses.[1] Indeed, if his theory be true, inspiration is not only a much less extraordinary thing than the church has imagined, but there is nothing to hinder it taking place again, and a supplement being made to the volume of revelation. Let the religious consciousness be elevated, the moral nature purified, and the power of spiritual vision increased, and, as he asks, what do we require more in inspiration? He denies that any special Divine commission to write was given to the sacred penmen, "that each book came forth with a specific impress of Deity upon it,"[2]—or that the providence of God watched over the composition and construction of the Bible in any other sense than Providence superintends every event bearing upon the welfare of man.[3] The inspired Word, with him, is just a transcript of the religious consciousness of the writers, a representation of "the bright impressions of apostolic men,"—the result of "the Divine light which was granted to the age, and to the mind of the author—a gift which he was left to make use of as necessity or propriety might suggest."[4] He thus cuts up infallibility by the root, that error which, he and Mr. Newman hold, has been introduced into the idea of inspiration. And then he thinks that, without irreverence,[5] he can speak of misstatements made by the evangelists, and of false reasoning in Paul, the most logical of the apostles.

It is the strangest part of this unsatisfactory theory, that inspiration cannot apply to processes of reasoning, that "it can neither give any certitude, nor guard against any errors which an accurate thinker could not detect for himself."[6] He confounds logic as an instrument with the understanding that employs it, when he speaks of inspired

[1] Morell's Philosophy of Religion, p. 166. [2] Ibid. p. 160. [3] Ibid. p. 183. [4] Ibid. p. 161. [5] Ibid. p. 173. [6] Ibid. p. 174.

logic as an absurdity. Let us suppose a reasoner so accurate that he errs only once in a hundred times. That one error, however, may have been very important. What impossibility is there in the supposition of a supernatural influence carrying up the mind from general to universal accuracy — as effectually excluding error from the hundredth process as it had been excluded up to the ninety-ninth? God, assuredly, can suggest a train of reasoning to the mind of an individual, and control that mind so as to lead it to a right conclusion, and extend that control over the writer so as to enable him to convey to others both the process and the result in terms free from error. This, we maintain, has been done in the case of Paul. In this there is no absurdity. Without this we have no security that Scripture is inspired of God.

All the inspiration which Mr. Morell allows is restricted to brightening and elevating the intuitional faculty so as to render it receptive of truth. He leaves the whole after-process, involved in giving a formal expression to the intuitions, to the natural working of the human faculties; and denounces the idea of Scripture being written under the special direction of the Spirit as a pernicious and indefensible dogma. This we regard as nothing less than an attempt to strip Scripture of its supernatural character. Inspiration is denied to the written word, contrary to its own claims, and it is attributed exclusively to a certain form of man's own consciousness. The Bible, in this case, is not God's word, but man's. The writers may have seen visions, and had the truth revealed in their minds, but we have no security that they have been kept from error in recording what they received, or that they have conveyed the truth purely to us. The idea that they had no special commission to write and no special guidance in writing, does not harmonize with the solemn announcement with which they often begin their oracles, "Thus saith the Lord," or with the statements, "Holy men of God spake as they were moved by the Holy Ghost," and "All Scripture is given by inspiration of God." The elevation of the religious consciousness, by special and extraordinary agencies, may account for the divine conceptions of the sacred penmen. But, without a continued supernatural agency, under which the minds of the writers were allowed to develop their characteristic peculiarities, it is difficult to account for the structure of the books, the "halo of Divine glory" in which these conceptions are expressed. The internal evidence shows, that in the work of composition, the hand of the Lord was with them.

Mr. Morell fails to substantiate the old charges adduced to weaken that evidence. He urges[1] the imperfect morality of the Old Testament, as if the word of God necessarily implied approval of all that it records. He urges[2] discrepancies between some of the Scriptural statements and scientific truth, as if the Book of Genesis pretended to give a scientific account of the creation, or as if it were in open conflict with the result of geological research. He charges Paul with errors in reasoning, without specifying a single instance; and Peter with arguing perversely about the circumcision, whereas everybody knows that Peter only acted against his own conviction.[3] In this way he backs his assertions that it would not be very reverent to suppose the Spirit of God had anything to do with such statements, and that the writers of them were left to the influence of the imperfect religious, moral and scientific ideas of their times. These are things much more easily said than proven. The only discrepancies on which objections against plenary inspiration can be raised are but as the small dust in the balance, compared with the weight of proof that the book

[1] Morell's Philosophy of Religion, p. 167. [2] Ibid. p. 170. [3] Ibid. p. 176.

is, what it claims to be, the word of God. Even that small dust, we are warranted from the past to believe, will become yet smaller, and may ultimately vanish away. Mr. Morell's theory of inspiration may naturally result from his own philosophical principles, but it explains nothing, is at variance with palpable evidence, at open conflict with Scriptural claim, makes room for the most latitudinarian interpretations, and, if brought to bear upon the progress of the church, would be long in ushering in the brighter day of which he speaks, when the Gospel would come to us, not in word only, but in demonstration of the spirit and in power.

Our investigation into naturalism has led us from the point where Divine Providence is ignored in sustaining and garnishing the material universe, to the point where his presence is excluded from the Bible — his holy temple. We might have passed on to notice the denial of Divine influence in regenerating the souls of men. But this will find a place in the next chapter, when speaking of the denial of the Divine redemption. We have tracked the rationalistic spirit up to the very shrine of the holy oracle, and found it there lurking under the Christian name and professing adherence to the Christian faith. Between the two points there is doubtless a gulf, but it is not an impassable one. The man who excludes miraculous inspiration from the Bible, may admit supernatural agency in the heavens and the earth, and even in giving birth to Christianity; but in that exclusion he occupies a naturalist position. On reviewing our track, then, we see that, in physical science, naturalism has given rise to the mechanical theory of the universe; in moral philosophy it has led men to attach an exclusive importance to external circumstances as influencing human conduct; and in theology, it has banished the supernatural from the sphere of Christianity, so as to account for its origin and influence on ordinary principles, or has left but partial room for its operation. With a few summary remarks upon the theory as a whole, we shall close our notice of it.

1. *The idea of an entirely self-sustaining universe is based upon a false analogy.* The regularity of nature's operations may have given rise in some minds to the opinion. And not a few of its abettors may maintain, that it is a more exalted conception of God to represent the multiplicity of effects which take place in nature as the result of a single original act of his power, than to conceive of Him as ever interposing in the affairs of the world. Order is the law of heaven. The very regularity which is adduced to favor the mechanical theory, is adduced more justly in proof of the Divine presiding agency. And it is surely more exalting to God to view the universe as directly dependent on his arm, and ever pervaded by his presence, than to compliment him out of it by attributing to it a self-sustained action. The falseness of the analogy, however, is obvious. The movements in a piece of mechanism do not, properly speaking, originate with the mechanist. He only employs pre-existing forces, such as gravity, elasticity, cohesion and repulsion. Now, these powers are the very things to be accounted for in the theory which likens the universe to a machine.[1] In a piece of human mechanism, we can account for these properties irrespective altogether of the workman. They were there before he existed, and they continue after he is gone. But that the universe, after having been constructed and set in motion by the Almighty, has continued to revolve and develop itself ever since, without his providential agency, is a theory that is unsupported by any analogy whatever. And, in the absence of all true analogy, it is more rational to view the creation as always directly dependent on the Creator,

[1] Dugald Stewart.

than to view it as self-sustained. In fact, it is as easy to conceive of a self-originated world as of a self-subsisting world. The thing is an impossibility. Dr. Harris says,[1] "The reasoning which compliments God out of the material universe not unfrequently ends in excluding Him from the Throne of his moral government." May it not be said that the one is done for the sake of the other?

2. This theory, as it is often advocated, *is chargeable with anthropomorphism*. While professing to exalt God, it virtually degrades Him. It thinks of Him as if He were such an one as ourselves. The piece of human mechanism saves the labor of the artist. He can set it in motion and go his way. And the machine is considered to be more ingenious and complete, the more that it dispenses with the interposition of the constructor. But to reason in a similar manner regarding the Almighty and his works, is to ascribe unto Him the limitations and imperfections of the human faculties. His presence in one part of his dominions does not imply his absence elsewhere. An infidel philosophy has often, by the anthropomorphism of its reasoning, endeavored, with a feigned homage, to exclude the Eternal from the management of the universe. This was involved in the astronomical objection against Christianity, which has been so eloquently repelled by Dr. Chalmers in his "Astronomical Discourses." The modern astronomy has wonderfully enlarged our conceptions of the magnitude and extent of the material universe, and shown that this earth occupies but a small place in the vast creation. Philosophical infidels urged that our world, being comparatively so insignificant, could not have had centered upon it such special regards of the Almighty as the Christian scheme represents. At the very root of this objection lay the principle of conceiving of the Most High as acting

[1] Pre-Adamite Earth, p. 128.

after the manner of men. It is just clothing the Divine Being with the impotency of the human. "It is our imperfection that we cannot give our attention to more than one object at one and the same instant of time; but surely it would elevate our every idea of the perfections of God, did we know that while his comprehensive mind could grasp the whole amplitude of nature to the very outermost of its boundaries, He had an attentive eye fastened on the very humblest of its objects, and pondered every thought of my heart, and noticed every footstep of my goings, and treasured up in his remembrance every turn and every movement of my history."[1] And as this would be the most glorious conception of God, it must be the true one; for, as John Foster remarks,[2] "to say that we can, in the abstract, conceive of a magnitude of intelligence and power which would constitute the Deity, *if He possessed it*, a more glorious and adorable Being than He actually is, could be nothing less than flagrant impiety." The anthropomorphising view of the Almighty is brought out very palpably in some of our modern books of science which advocate the natural development hypothesis. The author of the "Vestiges" speaks of it as "nothing less than a mean view of the Great Author, to suppose Him obliged to come in on frequent occasions with new feats or special interferences." And the question is asked, "Is it conceivable, as a fitting mode of exercise for creative intelligence, that it should be constantly paying especial attention to the creation of species?"[3] Here, the Divine Being is assimilated to the human. He is stripped of the attributes of omnipresence and omniscience which enter into the glories of his incomprehensible character. This is a damning evidence against this theory of naturalism. It makes God

[1] Chalmers' Astronomical Discourses.
[2] Foster's Contributions to the Eclectic,—"Review of Chalmers."
[3] Vestiges, pp. 165, 169, 5th ed.

like to corruptible man. Whereas, on the supernatural theory, while his name is excellent in all the earth, his glory is set above the heavens.

3. The theory which excludes the Divine agency from the universe, and abandons it to natural laws, *is opposed to the palpable evidence of geology.* This science has established, beyond a doubt, not only that our globe has repeatedly undergone great changes previous to its becoming the habitation of man, but that during these changes several successive creations of animal and vegetable life have taken place. The organic remains imbedded in strata, that had been formed ages anterior to the existence of the human race (these strata being separated from each other by considerable periods of duration), furnish evidence of whole groups having been swept away by some violent agencies, and of entirely new races having been called into being to supply their place. Geology tells us that the temperature of the globe in a remote antiquity was such, that our present races of animals and vegetables could not then have existed, and that the creatures then existing could not have lived now. This being the case, the inference is obvious, that new creations of animal and vegetable life must have occurred, between whose natures and the changed earth there subsisted a nice adaptation. Now it is for the production of these new races that we demand the interposition of God. There is no power in the laws of nature to produce them. "The growth of new systems out of old ones," says the great Newton, "without the mediation of Divine Power, is absurd." Man, compared with the ages that elapsed before his creation, is but a very recent being on the earth. For the production of a creature so distinct in his intellectual and moral qualities from the whole animal creation, a new exertion of the creative power of God was necessary. Theories of

spontaneous generation and of transmutation of the species have not been wanting. But these theories have never risen any higher than vague fancies. The records of geology furnish no indication of such phenomena. And, as Cuvier asks, why, if such transmutations have occurred, do not the bowels of the earth preserve the records of such a curious genealogy? In the domain of fossil geology, we discover abundant remains of distinct species, but not a single specimen of any species being in a state of transmutation has been met with. The faith of the most distinguished geologists and anatomists is very unanimous on this point. The first proposition which Cuvier establishes is, that the species now living are not mere varieties of the species which are lost. "For myself," says Agassiz, "I have the conviction that species have been created successively at distinct intervals, and that the changes which they have undergone during a geological epoch are very secondary, relating only to their fecundity, and to migrations dependent on epochal influences."[1] Lyell gives it as the result of a careful inquiry, "that species have a real existence in nature, and that each was endowed at the time of its creation with the attributes and organs by which it is now distinguished."[2] "Everything," says Sir Charles Bell, in his "Bridgewater Treatise," "declares the species to have its origin in a distinct creation, not in a gradual variation from some original type; and any other hypothesis than that of a new creation of animals suited to the successive chang.s in the inorganic matter of the globe — the condition of the water, atmosphere and temperature — brings with it only an accumulation of difficulties." On the strength of all this high testimony, we may say with Dr. Chalmers, that it places our argument for the

[1] Dr. Harris' Pre-Adamite Earth, p. 287.

[2] Lyell's Principles of Geology, vol. ii, p. 65, 1st ed.

interposal of God on firm vantage ground, to assert that, were all the arrangements of our existing natural history destroyed, all the known forces of our existing natural philosophy could not replace them. The records of geology are thus shown to be the records of a special Providence. And, as Conybeare justly remarks, the geological evidence strikes at once at the root of every skeptical argument against miracles. If God has specially interposed in the ages preceding the present state of the globe, is there not a strong presumption that He has done so at the most wondrous epoch of our earth's history—the introduction of Christianity; and that, at some future period, He will again interpose for the accomplishment of his high purposes. Geology convicts naturalism of falsehood, while it warrants us to credit the miracles and revelations of the Bible, if authenticated on the broad ground of evidence. The Almighty had not withdrawn from the world in the remote past, but presided over it as sovereign Lord, and, on befitting occasions, made bare his arm in new exertions of creative energy. And why should it be questioned that He is there still, touching all the springs of life and motion, and upholding all things by the word of his power?

4. *Christianity and its effects are phenomena for which naturalism assigns no adequate cause.* The theory of Strauss, that the church *made* its founder in the natural progress of events, and out of the Messianic conceptions existing at the birth of Jesus,—that the grand miracles which signalized his history were merely a kind of mythological clothing gradually thrown around Him by his followers in order to exalt their hero,—is a more idle fancy than any of the hypotheses of spontaneous generation and transmutation of the species, which have been formed to account for the origin of our races. Geology gives not a more

decided negative to the one theory than historical facts do to the other. It is a foolhardy attempt to account for a creation without the intervention of the Great Creator. Christianity is a new creation, and naturalism ascribes it to a cause which did not at the time exist, and which, if it had existed, would have been altogether inadequate to the effect. The conceptions of the Hebrew nation respecting the mission, character and kingdom of the Messiah, were far from being realized in Him who claimed to be the Son of the Highest and the Christ of promise. Indeed, the notions of his immediate disciples, up to the time of his leaving the world, were ever coming into conflict with his sayings and doings; and their attachment to his cause, notwithstanding, can only be accounted for on the belief of an evidence and agency that lay beyond the influence of these conceptions. The character of Christ, it has generally been admitted, even by infidels, is altogether unique; and some of them have granted that the invention of such a noble character by the first disciples would have been a greater miracle than any that is recorded. It is magnifying the effect much above the cause; it is investing the creation with a glory that did not belong to the creator, to assert, that a character so absolutely complete in all the elements of moral grandeur, and standing alone in its majesty on the pages of history, originated in Jewish conceptions thrown around the skeleton of an historic reality. "The author of a new creation," remarks D'Aubigné,[1] "must not himself come of the old creation which he is to change. The regenerator of the human race must not himself be a polluted member of the corrupt body which he is going to purify. He who comes to bring a divine life into the world must himself emanate from that life and possess it in its fullness; for how otherwise

[1] D'Aubigné's Discourses and Essays, p. 336.

can he communicate it? The first man of the new creation must issue from the hand of God, as did the first man of the old creation." There are two stubborn things which the theory of Strauss cannot solve. The first is, Why, if Christ answered to the conceptions of the Jews, was He persecuted by them, and the more in proportion as He manifested Himself? The second is, Why, after his death, the death, according to them, of an impostor and blasphemer, was He received by so many thousands of the people who had formerly rejected Him? To ascribe all this to the mere natural course of things, exclusive of a Divine interposal, is, if possible, more absurd than to account for the creation of the universe without the agency of the Great First Cause. Whether we consider the age — an age of unbelief and derision — in which Christianity as a "myth" is said to have arisen, or the men with their strongly-rooted adverse prejudices to whom the origin of the myths is assigned, we see the wild, unphilosophical character of the Straussian theory. It accounts still less for the success of such a myth as Christianity among the Gentiles, opposed as it was at all points to their systems of superstition and philosophy. "In truth," as Mr. Henry Rogers remarks,[1] "nothing less than a universal lunacy of the nations will account, under such circumstances, for its reception by them."[2]

[1] Appendix to Rogers' Reason and Faith.

[2] "German theories, though they have broken down in quick succession at home, have been imported as if still good, and have been done into English without scruple." To this remark of the author of "The Restoration of Belief," the theory of Strauss is no exception. Germany is getting ashamed of it. Yet this is substantially the theory, though Gfrörer is the great authority referred to, that Mr. Mackay has reproduced, in his "Progress of the Intellect." chap. 8, vol. ii. He fathers the idea of a superhuman Messiah on "a visionary suggestion" that rose in the Hebrew mind when suffering under Persian oppression — this suggestion or wish "filled up the blank of political disappointment"— this wish, in due time, assumed "the fixity of dogmatical theory"— and this wish threw around "the Messianic champion" miraculous glories and God-like qualities. In other words, the church created its

And as the origin of Christianity cannot be accounted for, except on the belief of a supernatural interposition, so it is impossible to account for the mighty effects of Christianity, except on the belief of an accompanying supernatural influence. It has been soundly argued that the marked contrast between the writings of the apostles and those of the most ancient fathers, can only be explained on the supposition that the sacred penmen wrote under the inspiration of the Spirit of God.[1] And the radical and beneficent change which the progress of Christianity has wrought on individuals and communities, argues that it has come in demonstration of the Spirit and in power. Human depravity is a stubborn fact which no theory of naturalism can get rid of. Individuals and nations have been placed in the most favorable external circumstances, and yet their depravity has grown with their growth, and strengthened with their strength. The power of mere natural influences has failed to reach the depths of that depravity, and elevate man to a high and holy character. The Christian revelation, accompanied by that Divine energy which originated it, has been

founder. Mr. Mackay has no doubt of it. He describes the process as coolly and deliberately as if it were a piece of art, the fashioning of which he had witnessed in the artist's studio. Like some of his German prototypes, however, he overshoots the mark when he tells us, in the face of historical evidence to the contrary, that the record of Christ's life, having "a supernatural coloring," was given to the world "when the generation of his contemporaries was extinct." He makes Christ to have been an ingenious impostor, the evangelists to have been very clever knaves, and the skeptical age in which Christianity was received to have been an age of great simpletons. All this has been said over and over again long ago. There is *here* no "Progress of the Intellect."

1 "The interval between the Scriptures and the very best of the Fathers is so immense, that not a few have testified that it forms to them the most convincing proof of the inspired origin of the former; it being, in their judgment, absurd to suppose that any man — much less a number of men — could have composed such a volume as the Bible, in an age in which their immediate successors, many of them possessing undoubted genius and erudition, and having the advantage of such a model, could fall into puerilities so gross, and errors so monstrous. For ourselves we could sooner believe that Jacob Böhmen could have composed the 'Novum Organum,' or Thomas Sternhold the 'Paradise Lost.'"—*Rogers' Essays from the Edinburgh Review*, vol. ii, pp. 123, 124.

brought to bear on human nature, and that nature, in thousands of instances, it has thoroughly renewed and maintained in its moral dignity in a world where so many natural influences tend to debase it. This fact, taken along with another — viz., that the best men in every age have been firm believers in the doctrine of Divine influence — goes to prove that Christianity and its benignant deeds are effects which point to the agency of the Great Spirit that at first moved upon the face of the waters and garnished the world.

5. It need scarcely be remarked, that naturalism, whether viewed as excluding Divine Providence from the government of the spheres, or from interposing in the concerns of men, *is diametrically opposed to the religion of the Bible.* The constant concurrence of the Divine will with the operation of secondary causes, is alike the doctrine of sound reason and scriptural truth. "My Father worketh hitherto, and I work," said the Great Teacher — an expression which seems to refer to the conjunct agency of the Father and Son in producing the Chistian miracles, and the works of Providence in general. It is said of Him who is God manifest in the flesh, that "by him all things consist, and that he upholdeth all things by the word of his power." Passages like these, with which the Book of God is thickly strewed, show that any attempt to remove God to a distance from the creation, or to explode the idea of Providence, wars with the record of revealed truth. The Scriptures, as we have seen, assert their own inspiration. And their testimony is clear in regard to the necessity of Divine influence to regenerate men. This is a great mystery, who then can believe it? Its mysteriousness is admitted in the very passage that asserts its necessity.[1] Strip Christianity of its mysteries, and you strip it of its glory. "A religion

[1] John iii, 7, 8.

without its mysteries," says Robert Hall, "is like a temple without its God.

But you cannot get rid of the mysterious. Naturalism banishes the Creator to a distance from the creation, resolves everything into the unaided operation of established laws, and thinks that the mystery is greatly lessened. But, in truth, it is greatly increased. The stupendous systems of worlds on worlds moving in harmony throughout the fields of space, without the ever-present agency of Him who made them, is a mystery more baffling and less sublime than the same system viewed as directly dependent on the presidency and power of God. It is confessedly mysterious how the Divine Spirit works on the human mind, so as in the case of inspiration to allow free intellectual action, and in the case of regeneration not to infringe on moral liberty. But so it is. Scripture attests it, and the subjects of Divine influence in either case have been conscious of it. Naturalism guards the human mind and human concerns from such an interposal, and thinks that it has cleared the moral world of a mystery. But it is not so. The Bible, in its grand disclosures and robe of solitary majesty, is much more inexplicable without inspiration than with it. And how moral evil — that most insoluble of all mysteries — should be counteracted, and men rescued from its power, by the mere play of natural influences, is assuredly more mysterious and unaccountable than that it should be accomplished by the Spirit of God.

In fine, naturalism, viewed in all its bearings, is most unnatural. It has a universe independent of Him who created it. It has a Christ, a Gospel, and a Church, for the existence of which no higher cause is assigned than Jewish conceptions and traditions. It has a world in which moral evil abounds, and depraved human hearts exist, for overcoming and regenerating which, it ignores all but natural influences. In attempting to get rid of mysteries the most sublime and ennobling, it falls into mysteries far more perplexing, but less elevating. Were the two systems to be tested by the attribute of mysteriousness, we would prefer supernaturalism, with its mysteries, to rationalism, with its mysteries.

# CHAPTER IV.

## THE DENIAL OF THE BIBLE REDEMPTION, OR SPIRITUALISM.

Change in the enemy's tactics — Rationalism confessedly beaten on the field of Biblical criticism — Coleridge's remark — The doctrines of redemption granted by rationalistic theologians and philosophers to be in the sacred text — The warfare shifted from the ground of critical interpretation to that of speculative philosophy — Change that has come over Unitarianism: its pretensions philosophical rather than exegetical — The "School of Progress" — Parker's "Discourse on Religion" — Newman's "Phases of Faith" — Mackay's "Progress of the Intellect" — Tendency of Mr. Morell's speculations — Examination of the moral argument against the evangelical doctrines — The argument stated — Refutation of it: unsupported by analogy — View given by it of the Divine character is one-sided and partial — Scripture doctrine of depravity accords with actual condition of man — Pardon on the ground of an atonement consistent with the paternity of God — Reasonableness of the Scripture doctrine of spiritual regeneration — Sustained by an appeal to three undeniable facts — Charge of gloominess against the doctrines of redemption shown to be unfounded — Quotations from Jonathan Edwards and Cowper.

MORE than half a century ago, the battle raged keenly between the defendants and assailants of the New Testament doctrines on the field of Biblical criticism. Neology and rationalism in Germany brought a large though unhallowed amount of scholarship to the attempt to expel from the sacred volume those doctrines which have been generally regarded as its distinguishing truths. And the same warfare was prosecuted with much vigor in our own country. The cool daring of the French atheistical philosophy infected men's minds; and individuals who professed to interpret the Divine Book, set about demolishing one text after another that favored the obnoxious articles of atonement and spiritual regeneration, as men set about destroying the underwood of a forest in order to build them houses on the clear ground. Christendom for a while looked on appalled. But the work of destruction was soon seen not to be the work of interpretation. And, after the alarm and heat of the first onset were past, the attempt to expunge the doctrines of the incarnation, atonement, and regenerating influences of the Spirit from the sacred record, was pronounced a more complete failure than the attempt in France wholly to explode the idea of God from the heart of society. On the ground of criticism, then, the dispute, as is generally admitted, has been decided in favor of the great doctrines of redemption. It is only such a man as Mr. Foxton, late of Oxford, that ventures now to say that "in the teaching of Christ Himself there is not the *slightest allusion* to the modern evangelical notion of an atonement."[1] It is only such a kindred spirit as Mr. Newman, formerly fellow of Balliol, whose faith, having passed through so many phases, has at last got into the eclipse that "can testify that the atonement may be dropt out of Pauline religion without affecting its quality."[2] Such a style of writing as this is only to be rivaled by asserting that Hamlet would still be Hamlet though the part of Hamlet were omitted. Nothing but a system of monstrously forced interpretation — so forced that, if applied to extract a meaning from any human composition, it would raise the shout of dishonesty— could expel these doctrines from Holy Writ, strip the text of all that is peculiar to the Gospel, reduce its theology to a mere theism, and the teaching of Jesus to a morality somewhat elevated above the best of the heathen. The mode of attack, accordingly, has been changed, the ground of warfare has been shifted. But there is the sacred text, speaking as loudly and clearly for the atonement, and the doctrines inseparably connected with it, as the stars in their courses and the earth with its teeming productions speak for the existence and providential agency of God. Coleridge

[1] Foxton's Popular Christianity, p. 67. [2] Newman's Phases of Faith, p. 103.

spoke strongly, but not more strongly than truly, when he said that "Socinians would lose all character for honesty, if they were to explain their neighbor's will with the same latitude of interpretation which they do the Scriptures," "I told them,"— at a time when he was far ahead of them, as he himself informs us —" I told them plainly and openly, that it was clear enough John and Paul were not unitarians."[1]

Such has become the opinion of many of the rationalistic theologians and philosophers of Germany. Christianity with them may be either true or false, but they are constrained to admit that what are usually regarded as its peculiar doctrines are contained in the sacred volume. Schelling and Hegel[2] assume the existence of the doctrines of the Trinity, incarnation, atonement, the lapsed condition of man, and the regeneration of the soul by the Holy Spirit; and attempt, in the true rationalistic mode, to deduce the whole from philosophical principles. Their Christology, in so far as doctrinal articles are concerned, differs but little from the evangelical creed. The Trinity and incarnation may be explained according to a theory of development which denudes them of their surpassing glory. but that they are in the Bible is not denied. The idea of the doctrine of the fall and of redemption by Christ, as enunciated in their philosophy, agrees in the main with evangelical principles, however contrary to these may be the attempt to deduce them on principles of pure science. The doctrine of the fall is explained as being the disunit-

[1] Mr. Theodore Parker thus speaks of the "Old School" of unitarians, which he has outgrown, though in a very different way from Coleridge: "If the Athanasian Creed. the thirty-nine articles of the English Church, and the Pope's bull 'Unigenitus,' could be found in a Greek manuscript, and be proved to be the work of an 'inspired' apostle, no doubt unitarianism would in good faith explain all three, and deny that they taught the doctrine of the Trinity or the fall of man."—*Discourse on Religion*, p. 357.

[2] Morell's History of Philosophy, vol. ii, pp. 152, 190.

ing of the human will from the Divine will. And redemption is regarded as the reunion of man's will to God. The rationalism of the system is broad and palpable. But it is something in advance of former speculations, that the Christian doctrines are admitted to be in the text of the Bible. Such intrepid thinkers, the very spirit of whose philosophy is destructive of the influence of the Gospel, virtually declare that the attempt to extrude the evangelical doctrines from the sacred record is vain, and that, be they true or false, they must be recognized as occupying a prominent place in that book which claims to be from heaven.

Strauss, who is a true Hegelian, and who, as we have seen, has exploded an historical gospel for the sake of a philosophical creed, has adopted and more fully developed the same view of the leading Christian doctrines. He denounces as strongly the old rationalistic method of interpretation as he does the idea of a supernatural intervention. He denies the historical truth of the New Testament, but he admits the gospels to be miraculous in their texture, and that the orthodox tenets are contained in them. His principle is, not that there are no miracles in the sacred record, but that the miracles there related cannot be literally true, for miracles are an impossibility. His principle is, not that the dogmas of the Trinity, incarnation, atonement, the fall of man, and his regeneration by the Spirit, have no place in the Scripture text, but that they are a series of myths or philosophical figments, which can be explained on the principles of Hegelianism. Thus, in Germany, the attempt to interpret the New Testament so as to expunge from it the peculiar doctrines of the Gospel, and reduce it to little more than a mere theism,— the attempt to make John and Paul Socinians,— has been for the most part abandoned. The hostility to these doctrines, as principles of evangelism, may not a whit be abated, but it is granted that they are in the sacred canon. And the warfare against them is, to a considerable degree, shifted from the ground of critical interpretation to that of speculative philosophy.

It has been said that unitarianism gravitates toward rationalism. And, accordingly, the change that has come over German rationalism, has, in some measure, influenced English and American [1] unitarianism. It is assuming something like the shape of a religious philosophy. We seldom meet it in the field of critical exegesis, and, generally, wherever we do meet it, the weapons of the new philosophy are found in its hands. It was from the sensational philosophy that the unitarianism of the last century took its character. In the time of Priestley, and subsequently, it was deeply stamped with his own fatalism and materialism. And everybody knows how D'Alembert and Voltaire exulted in its progress, and hailed it as an ally in the war in which they themselves were engaged. A writer in the *Encyclopédie* remarks: "The unitarians have always been regarded as Christian divines, who had only broken and torn off a few branches of the tree, but still held to the trunk; whereas they ought to have been looked upon as a set of philosophers, who, that they might not give too rude a shock to the religion and opinions, true or false, which were then received, did not choose openly to avow pure deism, and reject formally and unequivocally every sort of revelation; but who were continually doing, with respect to the Old and New Testaments, what Epicurus did with respect to the gods,— admitting them verbally, but

1 "It is probable," says Dr. Baird, "that unitarianism in the United States will disappear in process of time very much as it arose — *gradually*. The more serious will return, if proper measures be pursued, to the evangelical churches — many have done so within the last twenty years. Those who have embraced the transcendental and pantheistic views will go farther astray, until they end in downright infidelity and deism. Indeed, that is their present position, so far as concerns their opinions of the inspiration of the Scriptures and the Divine nature." — *The Religious Condition of Christendom*, p. 605, 1852.

destroying them really. In fact the unitarians received only so much of the Scriptures as they found conformable to the natural dictates of reason, and what might serve the purpose of propping up and confirming the systems which they had embraced. . . . From Socinianism to deism there is but a very slight shade, and a single step to take; and the Socinian takes it."[1] And not only the French encyclopædists, but the German rationalists looked favorably upon the progress of Socinianism, both in our own country and on the other side of the Atlantic, as helping them in their attempt to extrude from the Gospels the miraculous and supernatural element. But the reign of the sensational philosophy having passed, and the idealistic philosophy having gained the ascendant, unitarianism, at least among many of its adherents, has, without losing any of its virulence toward evangelical truth, undergone a somewhat corresponding change in its character. It has, in a great measure, laid aside the old rationalistic method of attempting by forced interpretations to thrust out from the Bible text the doctrines of redemption. Its pretensions are philosophical rather than exegetical. It exhibits Christianity as a system of spiritual philosophy founded in the nature of things, rather than a body of truth derived from the New Testament fairly and literally interpreted. It does not so much deny that the evangelical doctrines are there, as assume that if they were they could not be literally true. Accordingly, the more modern unitarianism pays less deference to the Bible, viewed as a revelation from heaven, than even did the old. It heeds far less what saith the Scripture, than what says human reason, or this and that oracle of the speculative schools. The chiefs of this system of religious philosophy consequently rid themselves of many of the embarrassments which their predecessors had to encounter. Holding an increasingly

[1] Dr. Smith's Scripture Testimony, vol. i, pp. 135, 136.

lax theory of inspiration, or tossing aside the idea of inspiration altogether, the doctrines of the Trinity, incarnation, atonement, and Spirit's influences, become not so much a question of scriptural truth as of philosophical possibility. The stubborn texts have been abandoned, and the weapons of transcendentalism have been resorted to. Reason is to be the umpire in every dispute. There are laws of the mind, say the disciples of this school, which are exact and uniform. These are absolute tests to man, and by means of them the pretensions of every doctrine must be decided. "What is of use to man lies in the plane of his own consciousness, neither above it nor below it."[1] This is the motto of the class of writers referred to. Strauss takes up the position, "miracles are impossible;" and, being pinned there as firmly as a man in the stocks, proceeds to examine the miraculous gospel history. In like manner, the more liberal unitarians fix themselves on the assumption that the Trinity and atonement cannot rest on evidence; and then, either deny that they are to be found in the Bible, or finding them there, discard them as false because not according with their own sense of fitness.

Socinianism, then, properly so called, is not the goal in which such speculations terminate. Emerson, Parker, Blanco, White, F. W. Newman and others, have touched at this point, but they have passed beyond it. There is no great gulf, indeed, fixed between them and their former associates. It is only the difference between men who seeing clearly whither the road leads have shot along it, and men halting dubiously at an intermediate post yet looking onward to the advanced station. The "School of Progress," conscious of a common linking principle between itself and unitarianism in all its shades, is calling upon it to come on. "It must do this, or *cease to represent the*

[1] Parker's Discourse on Religion, p. 33.

*progress of man in theology.* Then some other will take its office; stand God-parent to the fair child it has brought into the world, but dares not own."[1] Mr. Parker, in America, has taken the office; and Mr. F. W. Newman aspires to it in England. Our amazement is that such persons should still profess a vague reverence for Christianity, clothe themselves so frequently in the language of its cast-off Bible, and claim the privilege of being accounted Christians. "A certain man," we read, "went down from Jerusalem to Jericho, and fell among thieves, which stripped him of his raiment, and wounded him, and departed, leaving him half dead." Had such depredators turned again upon their victim and professed friendship, it would have been somewhat parallel to the conduct of many in our day, who, while stabbing Christianity in the heart, speak of it as something divine.

Mr. Parker, as a member of the Unitarian body, grew too fast for the body itself, and has been detached from it. His writings are highly appreciated by the men of the new school, and they seem not unwilling to acknowledge him as a leader. He is a strenuous advocate of what he calls "absolute religion," or those simplest elements of moral and religious truth which are supposed to underlie all theologies, Pagan, Jewish and Christian. His talk on this point is not unlike the rhapsodies of Emerson. "There is but one religion," he tells us, "as one ocean."[2] And again, "There can be but one kind of religion, as there can be but one kind of time and space." Of course, the different names given to it indicate "our partial conceptions," or distinctions belonging "to the thinker's mind, not to religion itself."[3] Just as in looking over the world, we see only one race of men, taking the name of Britons or Esquimaux, etc., according to artificial or local distinctions;

[1] Parker's Discourse. p. 357. [2] Ibid. p. 6. [3] Ibid. pp. 33, 34.

or just as it is one and the same element of water though parts of it be named the Pacific, the Atlantic, or the German Ocean. Two things follow from this view which occupy a prominent place in Mr. Parker's writings. The one is, that "there is no difference but of words between *revealed* religion and *natural* religion,[1]— all religions being more or less true, and the essence of Christianity being made independent of all circumstances, "all those extraneous matters relating to the person, character and authority of him who first taught it."[2] The other is, that each man possesses in his own mind the power of discerning the absolute truth, so that everything supposed to be included in religion is to be tested by this intuitive susceptibility or power. "Christianity is dependent on no outside authority . . . we verify its eternal truth in our soul."[3] He, in common with some of our own men of progress, resolves, after the example of Schleiermacher, the religious element in man into a sense of dependence. This religious sentiment or sense of dependence, supposed to exist at the root of all religions, is made everything; while the character, nature and essence of the object on which it depends are made of little or no importance. The objects of worship are "accidental circumstances peculiar to the age, nation, sect, or individual." This religious sentiment is the "eternal element," all else is "mutable and fleeting." The problem of our times which he deems himself commissioned to solve, is: "To separate religion from whatever is finite — church, book, person — and let it rest on its absolute truth."[4] Mr. Parker is a sort of Luther in his own way: "Protestantism delivers us from the tyranny of the church, and carries us back to the Bible."[5] Philosophical spiritualism is to effect the next Reformation. "Our

[1] Parker's Discourse, p. 33. [2] Ibid. p. 183. [3] Ibid. p. 209. [4] Ibid. p. 37. [5] Ibid. p. 364.

theology," he says,[1] "has two great idols — the BIBLE and CHRIST." And Mr. Parker is the iconoclast who would break them in pieces. It is, after all, however, but the exchange of one infallibility for another — an infallible Bible for an infallible Self — the outward for the inward oracle. *There* is an idol still.

We meet with strange reasoning and a confounding of things, in "A Discourse of matters pertaining to Religion." Thus, in order to cut away the external evidences, he argues, that if it could be shown that Christianity rested on miracles it would prove nothing in its favor, because other religions appeal to the same authority: which is something like saying that because there is a great deal of counterfeit coin in the world there can be no genuine, or because there are multitudes of knaves there can be no true men. It is overlooked that Christ has "done the works that none other man did," that his miracles, in their simplicity and sublimity, in their power and benevolence, stand apart from and in contrast to all the pretended miracles alleged in support of false religions.

The character of Jesus is a link in the chain of proof, and, in order to rend it asunder, it is sophistically argued,[2] that as the truth of a demonstration in Euclid is independent of Euclid's character, so what is true in Christianity is independent of the character of Christ "If it depends on Jesus, it is not eternally true . . . if not eternally true, it is no truth at all. . . . Personal authority adds nothing to a mathematical demonstration." Now, in the first place, we protest against the infidel assumption that Christianity rests exclusively on this or that thing which forms only a part of the whole ground of evidence.[3]

[1] Parker's Discourse, p. 369.

[2] Ibid. pp. 181, 198.

[3] Our opponents, with great unfairness, charge us with resorting to a sophism when we hold that the external and internal evidences, the miracles and the doctrines corroborate each other. This is well met by trying it in a single case. "You

And, then, secondly, we can conceive nothing more unphilosophical than this attempt to place mathematical and moral truth, in point of evidence, on the same plane. Mathematical truth has no influence on moral character; and the bad or good life of a mathematical teacher does not affect the truth of his demonstrations. But the character of one who claims to be a teacher sent from God enters into that amount of evidence by which his message is substantiated. Common sense never thinks of a connection between a man's life and the truth of his theorem, but it does think of such a connection between moral truth and the character of him who reveals it. The Jews felt the force of this, and, in order to resist his doctrine, they endeavored to fasten upon the Great Teacher the charges of being a blasphemer and in league with Beelzebub Besides, religious doctrines may be true without being eternal — such is the doctrine of the incarnation And a doctrine may be eternal and yet historical — such is the doctrine of the Trinity. Mr. Parker should know that eternally true and eternally known are quite different things. It is a similar fallacy, and adduced for the same end — ridding the world of a fixed doctrinal standard — which is involved in the assertion that "the phenomena of religion — like those of science and art — must vary from land to land, and age to age, with the varying civilization

have to do with one who offers to your eye his credentials — his diploma duly signed and sealed — and which declare him to be a Personage of the highest rank. All seems genuine in these evidences. At the same time the style and tone, the air and behavior of this Personage, and all that he says, and what he informs you of, and the instructions he gives you, are in every respect consistent with his pretensions, as set forth in the Instrument he brings with him. It is not, then, that you alternately believe his credentials to be genuine, *because* his deportment and his language are becoming to his alleged rank; and then that you yield to the impression which has been made upon your feelings by his deportment, because you have admitted the credentials to be true. Your belief is the product of a simultaneous accordance of the two species of proof: it is a combined force that carries conviction, not a succession of proofs in line."—*The Restoration of Belief*, p. 103.

of mankind."[1] The progress of physical truth no more indicates a similar progress in religious truth, than a man's bodily growth indicates the enlargement of his soul. And to conclude that, as we have outgrown the geology of a past age, we ought to outgrow its religious belief, is as good as saying that a people who have railways and huge reflecting telescopes, must be sounder in the faith than those who ride upon asses and never have resolved the nebulæ in Orion's belt. "It may be shown," remarks an able reviewer,[2] "that, while what is merely historical in physics may be of small value, the historical in morals and in religious faith may embrace all the truth of that nature the world will ever need, and greatly more than the world would ever have discovered had it been left to itself."

But the great fallacy in this theory of spiritualism — that which lies at the very core of the system — consists in making the religious principle in man find its proper object, in the same way that the senses — the eye or the ear — find theirs. Two things are here confounded; the capacity for receiving religious truth and the capacity of unaided reason to discover it. "This theory," says Mr. Parker,[3] "teaches that there is a natural supply for spiritual as well as for corporeal wants; that there is a connection between God and the soul, as between light and the eye, sound and the ear, food and the palate, truth and the intellect, beauty and the imagination." He thus cuts off the miraculous provision. And then, "as we have bodily senses to lay hold on matter, and supply bodily wants, through which we obtain, naturally, all needed material things; so we have spiritual faculties to lay hold on God, and supply spiritual wants; through them we obtain all needed spiritual things." He thus excludes the supernatural influence

[1] Parker's Discourse, p. 37. [2] British Quarterly, No. XXI.
[3] Parker's Discourse, p. 160.

which opens the heart to receive the miraculous supply. Here is a point of fact. Do men obtain peace of conscience and rest for the soul, as naturally as their eyes obtain light or their palate obtains food. Do the spiritual faculties and the spiritual objects come together in the merely natural way here represented? We trow not. Universal history and individual history disclaim the analogy. "Each animal, in its natural state, attains its legitimate end, reaches perfection after its kind."[1] Yes. But man is the anomaly here. He fails of reaching the perfection that is proper to him. It is easy to descant, as our author does, on the relation of supply to demand in the animal kingdom, and on the sufficiency of instinct in the ox and the sparrow. But to conclude that because the natural circumstances attending them are perfect, it must be so in the case of man; that because they obtain rest and satisfaction in a natural and not miraculous supply, by a natural and not supernatural guide, therefore the human race needs no miraculous provision and no other than natural guidance; is as consistent with fact as to infer that since the fowls of the air fly, man must have wings. It *is* true that we find a race of men, though "we never find a race of animals, destitute of what is most needed for them, wandering up and down seeking rest and finding none."[2] That capacity implies the object, and that there are supplies to meet the spiritual wants of man are truths. But the fact, however mysterious, in reference to man, is, that the capacity and the object do not, as in the irrational animals, come naturally together. There is no discrepancy between the proper destiny and the actual condition of the sparrow, but there is much between the proper destiny and the actual condition of man. A sense of guilt is a real and powerful element in man's religious consciousness, which this theory of

[1] Parker's Discourse, p. 136. [2] Ibid.

spiritualism ignores, and for which, consequently, it makes no provision. That sense of guilt is a fact in the natural history of man, which remains in spite of all such teaching, and to talk, amid this felt discordance between actual condition and proper destiny, of throwing man upon himself or upon the religious sentiment at the bottom of his heart, is something like bidding a man brood over his disease when he feels the need of going out after a remedy. Mr. Parker tells us that "for the religious consciousness of man, a knowledge of two great truths is indispensable; namely, a knowledge of the existence of the Infinite God, and of the duty we owe to Him."[1] These, of course, may be known, independently of all revelation and supernatural influence, by intuition and reflection. Now supposing that man needed no more than this knowledge, it is asked, does his own unaided intuition furnish it, or is he found in this state of nature discharging his duty? Let the world's history, actual observation and personal experience answer. Our question *is* answered when we think of "many a swarthy Indian, who bowed down to wood and stone — many a grim-faced Calmuck, who worshiped the great God of Storms — many a Grecian peasant, who did homage to Phœbus-Apollo when the sun rose or went down — many a savage, his hands smeared all over with human sacrifice," although Mr. Parker assures us, in his catholicity, that "they shall sit down with Moses and Jesus in the kingdom of God."[2] But much more than this knowledge is wanting. Men who have it are wandering up and down seeking rest and finding none; they know that the Infinite God exists, but they want to know how he can pardon guilt and justify the ungodly; they know their duty, but there is the want of inclination or moral power to act up to it. And — amid all this fine talk about the light of nature, world-wide

[1] Parker's Discourse, p. 158. [2] Ibid. p. 83.

inspiration, and the power of intuitive sentiment,— the actual condition of the race, without the external teaching of Christianity, rises up in dark contrast, and forces from us the exclamation, Has this intuitive power given to the soul its proper object, as instinct has given to the beast and bird theirs?

It will be seen, then, what is the attitude taken by this system of spiritualism toward the Christian revelation. "It bows to no idols, neither the church, nor the Bible, nor yet Jesus, but God only. . . . Its redeemer is within — its salvation within; its heaven and its oracle of God."[1] The intuitive susceptibility or power of the mind is placed on the judgment-seat, and made the sovereign determinator of what is truth or the "absolute religion." The Bible, irrespective altogether of its evidences, is stripped of its authority as the law and the testimony, and is received as a help only in the degree that its utterances accord with the sentiment of the mind. The claims of Christianity are settled, not on the ground of its grand divine peculiarities, but in proportion as its statements are found to contain the simple, unchanging principles of the religion called absolute. It "sponges out nine-tenths of the whole: or, after reducing the mass of it to a *caput mortuum* of lies, fiction and superstitions, retains only a few drops of fact and doctrine,— so few as certainly not to pay for the expenses of the critical distillation."[2] Christianity, or what is generally understood to be its distinguishing principles, is, of course, well blackened and grossly misrepresented, in order to insure its condemnation. Spiritualism, we are told, "calls God father, not king;" whereas popular Christianity "makes God dark and awful; a judge, not a protector; a king, not a father; jealous, selfish, vindictive. He is the Draco

[1] Parker's Discourse, p. 361.

[2] Rogers' Essays from the Edinburgh Review, vol. ii, p. 330.

of the universe; the author of sin, but its unforgiving avenger."[1] This we can characterize only as a great untruth, and we cannot help thinking that Mr. Parker knew it. The design is to array man's moral nature against the external divine revelation, and to represent the doctrines of atonement as conflicting with the imperishable religious sentiments common to the race. But, as we shall afterwards show, spiritualism is as much at variance with analogy in calling God father and refusing to call Him also king, as it is dishonest in making evangelism call Him king only and not father also.

Mr. Parker, like many others, would shift the contest from the field of the external evidences (by affecting to despise them as, even if true, of no value), to the matter of Christianity itself; the intuitive susceptibility or power of the mind being supreme arbiter. We, without abating a jot of our regard for these evidences — being more and more disposed to tell these towers and mark these bulwarks — are willing to abide by a fair trial of the contents of the revelation itself. It is part of the disingenuousness of infidelity to represent us as fixed on the one ground, and reluctant to do battle on the other. The nature of the doctrine must be taken into account, as well as the external evidence which attests it. But we demur to making any inward power of depraved man, be it called intuition or religious sentiment, a sufficient guide or test in such a question as this. It is enough that our moral nature, in its clear imperishable utterances, be not overborne or brought into collision. But it is not entitled to demand that it should be made the revealer of truth, or that an external revelation should disclose nothing but what lies within the range of our natural faculties, for that were to deny the possibility of a revelation properly so called. This, how-

[1] Parker's Discourse, pp. 342, 359.

ever, is the high claim of modern spiritualism. Common sense refuses to yield to any such intolerable dogmatism. It is inconsistent with our dependent condition in this world, and with the felt wants of the human spirit. We are led to look for a revelation from without, and if attested by sufficient evidence, if its documents be proved genuine, and if its contents, though above the power of our moral nature to discover, be in harmony with its broad principles and with what we otherwise know of the Divine government, nothing on our part should hinder its reception. It is the alleged discordancy between the two that runs throughout the whole of Mr. Parker's illogical and intolerant book, and which is the sharp sword in the hands of philosophical spiritualism. But let us hear another chief of the same school, before we turn the weapon.

"Modern spiritualism has reason to be deeply grateful to Mr. Newman" So says a London journal[1] that numbers among its contributors men of like stamp. He seems to have done great things for them whereof they are glad. His recent work, "Phases of Faith; or, Passages from the History of my Creed," is looked upon as having thrown up a highway on which the "new reformation" may safely advance. People, in certain regions, are thankful for what in other places would be counted but very bad roads. And surely the pathways of spiritualism must have been loose and insecure that it needed Mr. Newman's work to tread on, and for which it is so grateful. We willingly accord to this book the praise of a simple and good English style; but we deny it the merit of cleverly sustaining the part of honesty which it assumes. There is reason to suspect that a man has not overmuch of this virtue, when at the end of every paragraph in his speech, he is making loud professions of it. Mr. Newman becomes an unbeliever,

[1] The Leader.

and then he writes a book to tell us that he could not help it. He would have us to look upon him, in passing through these "phases," as a man whose sympathies were mainly in favor of the old doctrines, but who, under a strong sense of duty, had to sacrifice them and suffer loss. And these professions, be it observed, are not unfrequently made after grossly perverting Scripture, or misrepresenting the evangelical creed. He "struggled to the last, to rest on the practical soundness of Paul's eminently sober understanding. . . . But Paul also proved a broken reed."[1] And why? Because, in his treatment of the gift of tongues, he speaks, according to Mr. Newman, like an Irvingite; and because the Christ of Paul's epistles is a different being from the Christ of the evangelists! Again, he tells us that the 53d chapter of Isaiah and some of the other Messianic prophesies "were the very last link of his chain that snapt." After severe tugging, "it still remained strange that there should be *coincidences* so close with the sufferings of Jesus: but he reflected that he had no proof that the narrative had not been strained by credulity. . . . And herewith (he adds) my last argument in favor of views for which I once would have laid down my life, seemed to be spent."[2] We are thus to judge of the way in which he has made such mighty sacrifices. And our conclusion is, that Mr. Newman's statements must be taken with some qualification, when he assures us of being forced, against all his prepossessions, to yield to the authority of Strauss; or, of being thrown every now and then into great disquietude, because his "moral sentiment and the Scripture were no longer in full harmony."[3]

The impression made on most minds in reading the "Phases," we are persuaded, will be that its author never was, in the proper sense of the expression, a Christian.

[1] Phases of Faith. p. 177. [2] Ibid. p. 197. [3] Ibid. p. 81.

Indeed, his ignorance or perversion of Christian doctrines and evidences is manifested in almost every page. He divides the progress of his creed into a number of periods. In the first period, or what he calls his "youthful creed," we have the picture of a young man sent to Oxford without armor, and wounded by all the little fighters that surround him. We may sympathize with his detestation of formalism and of priestly assumptions. But he lacks judgment to discern the things that differ. In the second period, or "strivings after a more Primitive Christianity," he occupies the position of a man in open conflict with other men's opinions, and yet chagrined that they do not hug and embrace him. He is caught and tossed about by every wind. He throws aside the leading Christian doctrines as intellectual propositions or dogmas, while pretending much reverence for Scripture. In the third period, his religion has assumed the shape of moral sentiment, ("if shape it might be called that shape had none,") which is independent of our belief in the Bible. The inward power of judging is here made everything. He touches at unitarianism, but it cannot afford him "half an hour's resting place."[1] And before this inward power, "whether called common sense, conscience, or the Spirit of God,"[2] he brings, after having in a great measure perverted them, the doctrines of depravity and the fall, election and future punishment, the atonement and divinity of Christ, and having surrendered them, indorses them "Calvinism abandoned." And yet he would have us believe that in all the workings of his mind about these doctrines, they had little to do with the inward exercises of his soul toward God. "He was still the same, immutably glorious; not one feature of his countenance had altered to my gaze, or could alter."[3] Surely, then, a dishonest man might say, after his

[1] Phases of Faith, p. 101. [2] Ibid. p. 82. [3] Ibid. p. 104.

work of plunder, What has this to do with my integrity? The fourth period, or "the religion of the letter renounced," represents him afloat far from land. He lays hold of all the old objections to the Bible, grounded for the most part on such things as wrong dates and names, most of which have been refuted a thousand times. He would have us infer, that as John and Paul did not understand astronomy so well as Sir W. Herschel, that as their science as men might be at fault, so might their teaching as inspired apostles.[1] It is in vain to tell Mr. Newman it is not in their character as men, but in their peculiar character as apostles, that we claim for them inspiration and infallibility; that as they were not commissioned to teach human science, they might have been wrong in astronomy, but that as they were commissioned and inspired to teach Christian truth, they could not have been wrong in theology. He has here reduced the Bible to almost nothing, being greatly aided, he confesses,[2] by some German divines, especially by De Wette, and yet he professes to hold by Christianity. He would have us to imagine him "resting under an Indian fig-tree, which is supported by certain grand stems, but also lets down to the earth many small branches, which seem to the eye to prop the tree, but in fact are supported by it. If they were cut away, the tree would not be less strong. So neither was the tree of Christianity weakened by the loss of its apparent props. I might still enjoy its shade, and eat of its fruits, and bless the hand that planted it."[3] This may seem beautiful, but it is not true. The tree, in so far as Mr. Newman is concerned, has disappeared with all its props and stems. And that under which he is sitting is as like the tree of Christianity as the bramble bush is like the oak. In renouncing the letter he has renounced the spirit. And the flagrancy

[1] Phases of Faith, p. 121. [2] Ibid. p. 138. [3] Ibid. p. 143.

is, after having openly done the deed, to vaunt of his innocence. In the fifth period, or "faith at second-hand found to be vain," he has reached the position that miracles cannot be admitted as evidence of moral truth. He does not attempt so much to deny the miracles as to depreciate them. The assertion on which he lays stress is, "that miraculous phenomena will never prove the goodness and veracity of God, if we do not know these qualities in Him without miracle."[1] Granted: but this does not preclude miracle attesting a special manifestation of the Divine goodness. That God is good, is indeed a truth "discernible by the heart without the aid of miracle;" but that He would manifest his goodness in the way implied in the Christian redemption is not so discernible. And though such a manifestation, after it has been made, may answer the yearnings of the heart, yet the want of special evidence to attest the special and extraordinary interposition is felt. Mr. Newman and his school can never make good the proposition that moral truth cannot be substantiated by miracles of sense. Men are so constituted as to associate (unless willfully blinded by prejudice) the truthfulness of the moral teaching with the undoubted manifestations of miraculous power on the part of the teacher. And what he does to weaken or nullify them, is to represent Jesus as "solely anxious to have people believe in Him, without caring on what grounds they believed;"[2] to represent the logical notions of the apostles as at variance with ours, and to speak of our moral judgments as at conflict with the Gospel and its evidences.[3] Did he never read the Scripture, how that Christ, resting his claims on his miracles, said, "The works that I do in my Father's name, they bear witness of me. If I do not the works of my Father, believe me not. But if I do, though ye believe not me, believe the

[1] Phases of Faith, p. 157. [2] Ibid. p. 146. [3] Ibid. p. 147.

works; that ye may know and believe that the Father is in me and I in him?" And when he assumes that, because the astronomy of Paul's day was defective, so was the logic; or asserts [1] that, because we cannot cross-examine the apostles, we have no means of assuring ourselves that they held correct principles of evidence — we tell him that, though men may have different data in different ages, it by no means follows that they must have different principles of reasoning; and we ask if he is prepared to set aside all but contemporaneous history, to place no confidence in Thucydides or Josephus, because he cannot interrogate them. And then he assumes, what never has happened, and never can happen, the existence of a miracle that would authorize him to violate his moral perceptions. It is, we repeat, a disingenuous resort of infidelity, to separate two things which God hath joined together — the character of the doctrine and the character of the external evidence attesting it — and to represent us as resting on the latter, exclusive of the former, whereas the faith of the Christian has regard to both. In the sixth phase of Mr. Newman's faith, he attempts to cut up historical religion by the roots, and represents religion as a state of sentiment toward God that is independent of any outward creed whatever. He assumes that because we contend for an historical foundation to Christianity, we make it a mere problem of literature; and then argues,[2] that as he cannot solve literary problems concerning distant history, and as they lie beyond "the religious faculties of the poor and half-educated," they can form no part of religion. Here is obviously a confounding of two different things: the mind's susceptibility of religious sentiment, and the outward law and testimony which appeals authoritatively to that susceptibility. And, to use the words of Dr. Vaughan,[3] we ask,

[1] Phases of Faith, p. 148. [2] Ibid. p. 199.
[3] Dr. Vaughan's Letter and Spirit, p. 64.

"What means this constant insinuation, that historical evidence must be wholly without value to men not learned in history? Is it not manifestly the sentiment of our nature — a sentiment so common and rooted as to seem to be instinctive, that there is a credibility in historical testimony, even as relating to the mass of mankind, sufficient to bring the remote past into a certain and living connection with the present? Not only is it a fact, that the least learned are influenced by historical testimony as truly, if not as immediately, as the most learned, but it is manifestly a law of Providence that it should be so; and it remains to be shown why the law which embraces testimony to this effect concerning Cromwell or Alfred, should not embrace testimony to the same effect concerning Paul and Esaias." Mr. Newman, referring we presume to some of the difficulties connected with this subject, says,[1] "If I have been seven years laboring in vain to solve this vast literary problem, it is an extreme absurdity to imagine that the solving of it is imposed by God on the whole human race." Now, let him spend seven times seven years in laboring to solve some of the problems that lie before him in the domain of natural religion,— for example, the problem of moral evil — and what will he make out? Nevertheless, God certainly has not imposed the solution upon him or upon any of the race.

But Mr. Newman's drift is to get rid of an historical Christ. He insinuates that Jesus was far from perfect — that his portrait as drawn by the evangelists is in a great measure imaginary — and, if asked to specify the faults in that matchless character, he maintains that he is not bound to do so, because this were presuming Him to be perfect until we find Him to be imperfect.[2] Yes. If a man is generally reported to be honest, and claims to be accounted so,

[1] Phases of Faith, p. 199. [2] Ibid. pp. 210, 212.

you, if you deny it, are obliged to establish the charge of dishonesty. It is generally acknowledged that every mere man is imperfect — every sane mind admits it. The *onus probandi*, therefore, lies on him who denies it. So with the man who denies the sinless character of Jesus. We meet with another strange thing here. Mr. Newman [1] represents it as moral suicide to sit in judgment on the claims of Jesus, and then to submit our judgment to his authority, first to criticise and then to cease our criticism, first to exercise free thought and then to abandon it. We say, that to yield the mind up to Christ, after having been convinced of the divinity of his claims, is alone worthy of the name of free thought. And we ask, Do you act thus in common life —in selecting a friend, for example? You criticise at first. Do you go on with your criticism? Mr. Newman would have us believe that it is with pain he gives up "sentiments toward an historical person, which have been tenderly cherished as a religion." [2] But, with his book before us, we refuse to do so.

In concluding the "Phases," he deems himself warranted, from his previous "passages," to consider it as a settled point that the external revelation is in collision with the moral sentiments. We have here Spiritualism *versus* Christianity. "If the spirit within us," says he, 'and the Bible (or Church) without us are at variance, *we must either follow the inward and disregard the outward law; else we must renounce the inward law and obey the outward.*" [3] Matters have been brought to no such pass. The child has not received "discordant commands" from his father and mother, and is not reduced to "the painful necessity of disobeying one in order to obey the other." Mr. Newman, throughout his book, has given such representations of the atonement and the doctrines connected with it, not

[1] Phases of Faith, p. 210. [2] Ibid. p. 214. [3] Ibid. pp. 227, 228.

to speak of the old-refuted objections which he brings against many parts of the sacred record, as to remind us of the coarseness and unfairness of the school of Paine. He has first perverted the outward law, and then set over against it the inward. He has exalted the one to the judgment seat, and then brings the other, blackened and deformed, before it, to be condemned. And what, after all, does he mean by "the spirit within us," but individual feeling? One man's spiritualism may differ widely from another man's. Judging from some recent manifestations, the inward oracle is far from being harmonious in its utterances. "The authoritative unity claimed for it is a fiction. Newman's Personal Spiritualism, in place of being a center of rest, must be a perpetual battle-field between the claims of feeling and the claims of the understanding."[1] And then what willful blindness to, or ungrateful reading of, the world's history, to speak of the world's religious progress as having been intercepted or turned back by *the claim of Messiahship for Jesus.* And what a miserable delusion to anticipate that, if the world was swept clear of intellectual creeds and an historical Christianity, and men were thrown on their own inward sentiments, having no doctrine in common but the vague thing called "God's sympathy with individual man," the race would move steadily onward![2] But for the historical Christianity which he contemns, Mr. Newman's religion, most assuredly, would not have differed in the degree that it does from the religion of the Greek and Roman philosophers. The "progress" would not have been quite so "spiritual."

Mr. Mackay's "Progress of the Intellect," though differing in many respects from Newman's "Phases" and Parker's "Discourse," is a production of the same school, and assumes a like hostile attitude toward the doctrines of

[1] British Quarterly, No. XXIII. [2] Phases of Faith, pp. 225, 234.

the Christian redemption. These doctrines, with him, are "a petty sanctuary of borrowed beliefs." And he has much more admiration for the times when men saw "serious meaning in the golden napkin of Rhampsinitus, nay even in the gush of water from the jaw-bone of Samson's ass," than for our age with its doctrinal articles and creeds.[1] A floating, ever-changing sanctuary of faith is, in his view, more beautiful than a fixed one. If the Bible would only submit to be regarded as a part of this shifting cloud-land, one of the many phases of our ideal creations, it would, like the other "playful mythi," be attractive to Mr. Mackay and his school; but it cannot be tolerated in its claim to be the law and the testimony. The ancients, with their mythical legends, "were as the eagle intently gazing on what he wants strength to reach;" we, with our Bible creeds, are the owls blinking at the first daylight, which, however, we are slowly learning to support."[2]

Our author places the polytheistic systems of the Greeks and the Jewish and Christian Scriptures on the same plane, both, according to him, being the mind's own weaving, the results of investing the inward conceptions with an outward and divine authority. He assumes that all religion is a form of symbolism; Christianity and material idolatry being in this respect on the same level, only the one is deemed a higher product of the intellectual law of development than the other. Like Mr. Parker and his fellow disciples, he holds that Christianity has two aspects. The first is "the moral conception, which, as eternally good and true, is not so much its own peculiarity as an essential part of all civilization." And secondly, its "special dogmas and forms," such as the atonement and Spirit's influences, "which, making up its accidental expression or clothing, have never ceased to accompany its development, though often threat-

[1] The Progress of the Intellect, vol. i, p. 7. [2] Ibid. vol. i, p. 12.

ening to obscure or supersede the vital meaning connected with them."[1] This is something like taking a man's soul for his clothes, or depriving him of reason and intelligence in order to reduce him to the mere animal. Mr. Mackay, in short, like his fellow on the other side of the Atlantic, is a resolute disciple of what is called "absolute religion"—"an eternal, never-failing principle," of which all religious symbols or dogmas are but the temporary livery.[2] By this eternal, indestructible principle, we are to understand some such vague thing as a sense of dependence, or a feeling of divine sympathy, which, as an ultimate fact, is supposed to underlie all the religions that the world ever saw,— a sort of universal soul pervading all systems,— Pagan, Hebrew and Christian,— a kind of pantheistic element, to which all "artificial forms of ritual or creed" bear the same temporary relation that the leaves of the forest, or the grass of the field, bear to the principle of life that pervades the universe. Mr. Mackay would, without scruple, indorse Mr. Parker's statement, "There is but one religion, as one ocean; though we call it faith in our church, and infidelity out of our church."[3] And he would shake hands with brother Newman in affirming, "Religion was created by the inward instincts of the soul: it had afterward to be pruned and chastened by the skeptical understanding."

The pruning and chastening process goes on; and Mr. Mackay is resolved, in relation to Christianity, that spare the knife who will, he will not. The Bible doctrines of the fall of man, atonement by Christ, and regeneration through the Spirit, are, according to his theory, excrescences threatening to obscure or supersede the vital element, and he lops them off The work, of course, required no little daring, and something very different from shame-

[1] The Progress of the Intellect, vol. ii, p. 393 [2] Ibid. vol. i, p. 17.
[3] Parker's Discourse, p. 6. [4] Newman's Phases, p. 232.

facedness. It did not consist with the humility professed in the first sentence of his preface. And, accordingly, Mr. Mackay, on entering the temple, instead of leaving his shoes, after the eastern manner, at the door, left his humility.[1] And then the fall and the atonement, not denied to be in the Bible, are dismissed as mere "tricks of fancy," "ancient superstitions," "subjective facts in the writer's mind," in short, only a projection of the inward consciousness into the outward world.[2]

Dr. Strauss, in dealing with the evangelical histories, has been spoken of as without an equal in the *nil admirari* vein, but we warrant our author, in his manner of treating Jesus and Paul, to match him. He admits that there existed the notion of atonement in the Hebrew mind, but he "cannot admit the atonement doctrine to have been authorized by Jesus as part of his religion."[3] He is aware, however, that the teaching of Christ had something to do with the doctrine, and that the evangelists in recording his sayings are not altogether silent in reference to it. But the "foolishness" cannot be tolerated, the "stumbling-block" must be removed, though it be at the expense of Christ's character and the credit of the sacred record. Jesus, accordingly, is represented[4] as having eventually been influenced, contrary to his original intentions, by the prevailing idea of meritorious suffering, in order "to uphold his sinking cause." "He used the terms and symbols of his age." These the disciples applied literally, "thereby creating a superstitious mystery never deliberately contemplated by their master."[5] That there are "distinct announcements by Jesus of his propitiatory death," recorded in the gospels, Mr. Mackay does not venture to deny. But he easily disposes of them. Just as Mr.

[1] The Progress of the Intellect, vol. i, p. 18. [2] Ibid. vol. ii. pp. 396, 465, 466.
[3] Ibid. vol. ii. p. 464. [4] Ibid. vol. ii, p. 395. [5] Ibid. vol. ii, p. 46[illegible].

Newman, after putting the fifty-third chapter of Isaiah on the rack, and failing to extort a confession to his liking, settled the matter by saying that he "had no proof that the narrative had not been strained by credulity,"—so Mr. Mackay declares that none of the distinct announcements referred to "can be relied on as authentic;" or, lest this should be going too far, "it seems needless to ascribe to them more than the figurative sense."[1] Miracles are impossible, says Strauss. The doctrine of atonement is incredible, says Mackay. And nothing remains but to falsify the record, or to bring myths or symbolism to account for them.

Mr. Mackay does not say, with Mr. Newman, that the atonement might be dropped out of "Pauline religion" without affecting its quality, any more than he says, with Mr. Foxton, that in the teaching of Christ there is not the slightest allusion to the doctrine. On the contrary, this doctrine is made an essential part of the "Pauline development"—a development very different indeed from the scriptural one which took place in the minds of the apostles after the resurrection and ascension of their Lord. Christianity, according to him, had now shifted its ground. "The Christianity of Paul differs from that of Jesus as an imparted influence from without differs from moral effort from within."[2] In other words, Christ is represented as, on the whole, discouraging the idea of vicarious atonement, though using its symbolical terms; and pleading simply for amendment, sincerity and moral purity. While Paul is spoken of as having been the first to make the necessity of atonement felt by proving the inefficacy of the law for justification, and then as having supplied it.[3] Thus it is, according to "The Progress of the Intellect,"

[1] The Progress of the Intellect, vol. ii, pp. 394. 463.
[2] Ibid. vol. ii, p. 391. [3] Ibid. vol. ii, p. 396.

that "the Hebrew Palladium" has been "inherited by Christians."[1] The atonement then, even in the estimation of Mr. Mackay, could not be spunged out of Paul's religion without affecting its quality. He scorns it, however, as an excrescence, a special dogma that loads and obscures the moral conception or the simple element called absolute religion. The atonement, which in Scripture is represented as the brightest manifestation of God's love to our fallen race, and which has ever been regarded as such by the Christian world, is consequently made hideous, and spoken of, after the Parker fashion, as "practically giving to Christianity a character, which, though it have an ill sound, it would be vain as well as dishonest to dissemble, that of a religion of Moloch."[2]

Had we been reviewing Mr. Mackay's work as a whole, we would have felt ourselves called upon to show the untenableness of his mythical theory, the baselessness of his assumption that all religion is and can only be a form of symbolism. He accounts for the origin of Christianity, as we have already noticed, in a way somewhat similar to that of Strauss. His "Progress of the Intellect" is just the reproduction among us of what has had its day elsewhere. So that the answer to Strauss is substantially the answer to be given to his notions of the Messianic development.[3]

[1] The Progress of the Intellect, vol. ii. p. 465. [2] Ibid. vol. ii, p. 466.

[3] We should also have taken Mr. Mackay to task in regard to a considerable number of his Scripture references. It was truly difficult to account for many of these references, or to see how they bore out his statements, till we reflected that he had beforehand warned us of his intention to be guided more by German (neological) criticism than by the English version of the Bible. For example, it serves Mr. Mackay's theory, to maintain that Christ "was unconscious of his own mission" till he was baptized of John; and for proof he refers us to John i, 26, 33; vii, 27. Why did he not tell us how the ignorance of the Baptist and of the people proved unconsciousness on the part of Christ? Again,—as an evidence that the "ancient Hebrew God" was only one of the many gods, and that He acknowledged their existence, we are referred to Deut. xxxii, 17–21. On the same principle, it might be maintained that missionaries acknowledge the real existence of the gods of the heathen and are jealous of them.—Vol. ii, pp. 315, 416.

But it is only with what bears on the atonement that we have at present to do. And here his development theory is at fault. History is opposed to it. And it is only by the most gross assumptions that the conflicting evidence of history is set aside. Any writer who should deal with the Hebrew Scriptures as he has done, could not be expected to feel much scruple in twisting the New Testament record. It serves his theory of symbolism to make out idolatry or Moloch-worship to have been the practice of the early Hebrews. The ancient Hebrew God, according to him, was only one of the many gods of the nations, and cannibalism was associated with the rites paid to him by the people. The sacred record is at open conflict with this, the fact being that in the earliest Hebrew writings we have some of the sublimest descriptions of the glory of the one God that are to be found in the Bible. Mr. Mackay feels this. But in order to preserve his theory, he is forced to come out with the assertion that the Bible writers have transferred to olden times improvements of newer date,—ancient Moloch practices having been cleansed by modern whitewash, and then impressed with the stamp of antiquity.[1] And if we ask for evidence in support of this "borrowed belief," we receive no better answer than that it must have been so, because his development theory requires it. Having in this way made out a Hebrew development from mere nature-worship up through polytheism to the recognition of a personal and independent God, it could not be difficult for him to make out a Christian development in which Christ and Paul stand at antipodes — a development, however, according to his own showing, in a contrary direction, from better to worse.

But this is no more the development of the New Testament than the other is of the Old. There was

[1] The Progress of the Intellect, vol. ii, pp. 406–445.

development throughout the period embraced by the New Testament record, but it was like the morning light which shineth more and more until the perfect day. Men must presume very much upon the unreasoning unbelief or intense hatred of our age in regard to evangelical religion, who can say, either that there is not the slightest allusion in the teaching of Jesus to the evangelical doctrine of atonement, or that He on the whole discouraged the idea of it. That the doctrine is not so fully enunciated in the discourses of Christ as in the letters of his apostles must be admitted. But this is just what might have been expected. In the one case, the work of atonement was unfulfilled; in the other case, it was finished and had become matter of history. Besides, the strain of Christ's teaching pointed to the time when the germs of truth which He had thrown out among his disciples would be fully unfolded, when, under an increased effulgence from on high, they should see the truth enshrined in his sayings which their prejudices prevented them from now doing. The atonement *was* embraced in Christ's teaching. What can be more explicit than his own words — words which are felt to be a difficulty even by Mr. Mackay — "The Son of man came not to be ministered unto, but to minister, and to give his life a ransom for many." The "Pauline development" was not different from this, nor anything added to this, but it was this very truth more fully unfolded, and made, as it was designed to be, the grand central fact of the Gospel of Christ. The progress of the New Testament was no more "the Progress of the Intellect" than was the progress of the ancient Hebrews. And Mr. Mackay fails in giving us anything more than assumption for his bold denial that the doctrine of Paul's epistles is countenanced by the prophets and the Great Teacher, as completely as he does in finding a basement for his assertions that idolatry was the established religion in Israel up to the reign of Josiah — that the prophets then, in adaptation to the wants of the age, remodeled the system, made Jehovah, who had hitherto been only one among the many Gods, now the Universal Power, and then represented this better religion as the religion of Moses and the early Hebrews. We are constrained to say that Mr. Mackay, in thus dealing with history, is guilty of the very deception which he would charge upon the "holy men of God," and our wonder is how he can attempt to palm it upon the world. But the atonement must be got rid of. The gospel doctrines must be deprived of their historical basis. And, since the attempt to expel them from the sacred page has confessedly failed, nothing remains but to resolve them into the conceptions of a past age, to bring them before the chancery of the mind's own decisions, and to dismiss them as unfit for this stage in "the Progress of the Intellect."

In noticing Mr. Morell in this connection, we wish to be understood as indicating the tendency of his speculations on religion rather than their actual results. Wide indeed is the difference between the spirit in which he treats of such matters, and that of Messrs. Parker, Newman and Mackay. And yet the "School of Progress," as if conscious of some links of sympathy between him and them, regard him as advancing on the same path, only keeping a little behind. He, in common with them, resolves religion into a peculiar mode of feeling. And though not, like them, seeking utterly to demolish the objective element, he reduces it to comparatively little value. The subjective or intuitional consciousness has in his speculations a province assigned to it that can scarcely consist with the claim of Scripture to be accounted the law and the testimony. It is not what history has attested to be authentic that we are to receive, but what we feel to be morally and religiously true. "The Philosophy of Religion" is but a form of spiritualism.

Mr. Morell attaches much importance to the philosophical groundwork that he has laid in the first two chapters of his book. And it is found to influence all his subsequent speculations on the subjective nature of religion. Into a minute examination of that groundwork it would be out of place for us here to enter. With much of it we find no fault. But the broadly prominent principle that runs throughout it, is, in our apprehension, unsound and mischievous. We refer to his development of the "principal points of distinction between our logical and intuitional faculties"— a distinction, as he says, of vital importance, and which he carries along with him when arguing on the relation of philosophy to religion. He says,[1] "There is one state of our intellectual consciousness by virtue of which we define terms, form propositions, construct reasonings, and perform the whole office that we usually attribute to a mind that acts *logically:* but there is also another state of our intellectual consciousness, in which the *material* of truth comes to us as though by a rational instinct — a mental sensibility — an intuitive power — a 'communis sensus,' traceable over the whole surface of civilized humanity." These two classes of phenomena are denominated the logical and the intuitional consciousness. That there is a distinction between these two states of consciousness — a distinction recognized before the times of Mr. Morell — we readily admit. But we demur to the way in which he disparts the one from the other, exalting the power of intuition at the expense of the understanding, and assigning it an independence and efficiency which do not belong to it. "With regard to higher truths and laws," he tells us, "the

[1] Philosophy of Religion, p. 33.

understanding furnishes *merely* the subjective forms, in which they may be logically stated, while intuition brings us face to face with the actual matter, or reality of truth itself."[1] We open our eyes, and we see at once the blue heavens and the green earth In like manner, Mr. Morell would have us to believe, the mind by its simple spontaneous power of intuition looks out, "and the absolute stands before us in all its living reality." Now we maintain, in opposition to this, that the understanding has much to do in enabling us to reach the mount of vision, and that it is not restricted to the humble function of giving logical expression to the supersensual truth we gaze upon there. Mr. Morell would kick away the ladder by which he had been helped upward, and then refuse to admit that it had rendered him any assistance. "It is not enough for our author to say, as all sensible men have ever said, that our knowledge of 'the *true*, the *beautiful* and the *good*,' comes to us in part from our intuitions; he is peremptory in asserting that it comes to us *only* from that source — a doctrine which can never be made to harmonize with anything deserving the name of philosophy; and which must prove eminently hostile to the purity of religion."[2] *

In applying this philosophy to the fundamental questions involved in his subject, Mr. Morell very naturally

[1] Philosophy of Religion, p. 19. [2] British Quarterly, No. XIX, p. 149.

* The author of "The Eclipse of Faith"— a work that carries very destructive fire into the enemy's camp — in commenting "on a prevailing fallacy," thus addresses our modern "spiritualists": "You do not sufficiently regard man as a complicated unity; you represent, if you do not suppose, the several capacities of his nature — the different parts of it, sensational, emotional, intellectual, moral, spiritual — as set off from one another by a sharper boundary line than nature acknowledges. . . . What can be more obvious than that, whether we have a distinct religious faculty, or whether it be the result of the action of many faculties, the functions of our 'spiritual' nature are performed by the instrumentality, and involve the intervention of the very same much-abused faculties which enables us to perform any other function? . . . Religious *truth*, like any other truth, is embraced by the understanding — as indeed it would be a queer kind of truth that is not; is stated in propositions, yields inferences, is adorned by eloquence, is illus-

considers, in the first place, what is the peculiar essence of religion? He here treats the matter subjectively—not as a system of truth or form of doctrine, but simply as a fact or phenomenon in human nature. He lays down the position "that there are just *three* great and fundamental forms of man's inward consciousness expressed by the terms *knowing*, *willing*, *feeling*."[1] And, in determining to which of these generic forms of consciousness religion belongs, he, of course, fixes on feeling. The great error in his philosophy in parting off the intuitional from the logical consciousness, has here its counterpart in the separation between religious knowledge and religious feeling. It is not enough for him to say, "that there may be many gradations of religious intensity in men, whose amount of knowledge is as nearly as possible *identical*; and on the other hand, that there may be about an equal manifestation of religious intensity where the degrees of knowledge are immensely at variance." No sane mind denies this. But he concludes that "religion is really cradled in some phenomenon lying *without* the region of what we may term intellectual activity;" and, "that although the coöperation of knowledge may be necessary to the perfection of our religious life," yet it does not necessarily enter into the "essential germ" of religion.[2] We do not much object to the statement, that religion, subjectively considered, consists in the feeling of dependence upon God; but we deny that any emotion worthy of the name of religion can exist without some knowledge of divine things. Mr. Morell obviously felt himself entangled here by his philosophy, for while the drift of the chapter is to assert the independence

trated by the imagination, and is thus, as well as from its intrinsic claims, rendered powerful over the emotions, the affections and the will. . . . Hence we see the dependence of the true development of religion on the just and harmonious action of all our faculties. They march together; and it is the glorious prerogative of true religion that it makes them do so."—*The Eclipse of Faith*, p. 305, etc.

[1] Philosophy of Religion, p. 66. [2] Ibid. p. 69.

and exclusive importance of feeling as he had done that of the intuitional consciousness, he yet asserts that the coöperation of knowledge may, "in a subordinate sense," be necessary to the very existence of our religious life. If the scholastic and many of the rationalistic theologians made too much of the mere form of knowing, Mr. Morell assuredly makes too much of the mere form of feeling. It results, as we have seen in such men as Parker and Newman, in attaching no importance whatever to an objective revelation; and, as we will see, in the case of such as Morell, in assigning a very subordinate place to it.

In treating of the Essence of Christianity, which is done in the next chapter, the subjectivity of our author becomes more and more manifest. We reckon this chapter a complete misnomer. It is as if an astronomer were to give us an historical description of the thoughts and feelings awakened within him during his surveys of the heavens, and to designate it a treatise on astronomy, instead of giving us a discourse on the magnitudes, distances and revolutions of the planets. The Essence of Christianity is a phrase which conveys to an English reader the idea of those grand doctrines which distinguish it from all other forms of religion. But Mr. Morell generally here puts the effect for the cause, and sometimes plays on the two different senses of Christianity as objective and subjective. He says, "The only mode in which we can assign the true nature of Christianity, *relatively* to all other religions in the world, and show wherein its essential and distinguishing feature consists," is to consider "what is the distinguishing feature of man's religious nature, when it has come properly under the *Christian* influence."[1] He denies that what are esteemed the prominent facts and main doctrines of Christianity determine the essence of Christianity itself. This, he tells

[1] Philosophy of Religion, p. 100.

us, "does not consist in any development of thought, but in the flow of holy affections."[1] The outward revelation, according to this system, is not Christianity, it is only a means to awaken it. The Gospel is viewed rather as an external provision for cultivating certain states of feeling, than as an authoritative communication from heaven, designed to build us up in the knowledge of divine things. Christianity, as a distinct spiritual life, is made to occupy the place of Christianity as a body of inspired truth by which the spiritual life is organized. The true state of matters is completely reversed. And this Philosophy of Religion tends, like the systems of Parker and Newman, to make everything of the feelings within, and to reduce to little or almost nothing the objective truth that lies without.

Mr. Morell, though chiefly engrossed with the subjective point of view, does not, however, ignore the objective. He defines Christianity, viewed as an outward condition of the religious life, to be "that religion which rests upon the consciousness of the redemption of the world through Jesus Christ."[2] He very properly notices two great and essential points here—"the *exclusiveness* of Christianity as the sole appointed means of human recovery and the concentration of the agency for such recovery in the life and person of Christ, historically considered."[3] But beyond this we have no explanation. He does not say what is implied in the redemption of the world, or what was the nature of the moral expedient devised for its accomplishment. And he is silent also as to the truth about the personal Redeemer. This is unpardonable even in a philosophical discussion of the essence of Christianity, and while professing to look at the objective side of the question. Mr. Morell knows very well that the redemption of the world through Christ is about one of the vaguest expressions current in modern

[1] Philosophy of Religion, p. 256. [2] Ibid. p. 118. [3] Ibid. p. 119.

times. It would cover the whole "school of progress." Under its ample shade would come multitudes of teachers in Germany, America, England, and elsewhere, whose ideas of redemption and the Redeemer are as far apart from the Christian doctrines as the east is from the west. This vague and brief allusion to the objective element can only be explained on the principle, so dear to our modern sentimentalists, of unduly magnifying everything within man and lessening whatever comes to him in the shape of religion from without. What Mr. Morell's views are of the process through which the redemption of the world has been effected, and of the personal constitution of the Redeemer, we know not. But he has laid himself open to the suspicion of making the essential elements of the Christian life independent of those grand peculiar doctrines which have been generally understood to be the truth as it is in Jesus.[1]

It is foreign to our purpose to review the whole of "The Philosophy of Religion." We only point out some of its strongly marked tendencies toward that philosophic spiritualism which is so destructive of the essence of Christianity. These are, indeed, to be found in every chapter of the work. In passing on, for example, to speak of the method by which Christianity was first communicated to the human mind, he defines revelation to be "a process of the intuitional consciousness gazing upon eternal verities."[2] He denies that the Bible, strictly speaking, is a revelation,

[1] "No philosophy of religion that assumes to embrace Christianity can be complete if it does not show that salvation was effectuated by a process alike congruous with the Divine character, and with man's constitution and moral necessity. It may be replied, that this is the province of Christian theology, and not of internal subjective Christianity. We incline, however, to the opinion that the idea of 'a just God and a Savior,' through the atonement of Christ, is the meeting-place, the point, where Christianity as a theology *loses itself* in Christianity as a religion."—*Mr. Morell and the Sources of his Information*, p. 38.

[2] Philosophy of Religion, p. 141.

"since a revelation always implies an actual process of intelligence in a living mind."[1] And he asserts, that "the power which that book possesses of conveying a revelation to us, consists in its aiding in the awakenment and elevation of our religious consciousness." We have here, as throughout the whole treatise, a systematic undervaluing of objective truth. Christ and his apostles are represented as giving no exposition of Christian doctrine to the understanding, but as seeking to awaken man's power of spiritual intuition; and since it cannot be denied that Paul gives such a systematic inculcation of truth, we are reminded that "his writings were designed not so much to be a revelation of truth, as a farther explication of it."[2] He would make Paul the theologian, and John the intuitionist. Now, in reply to this, it might be said, in the first place, that it is not true that Christ and the apostles gave no systematic exposition of doctrine. The sermon on the mount, and the discourse on the way to Emmaus, when "beginning at Moses and all the prophets, he expounded unto them in all the Scriptures the things concerning himself," not to mention other discourses, contradict the statement in so far as the Great Teacher is concerned. The book of Acts falsifies the statement in reference to the apostles. And, in the logical expositions of Paul, we have as many new ideas revealed as in John, which proves that truth may be given first in a systematic or theological form. Besides, it is a mere play on words to say that the revelation was made in the mind, not in the Book. The Bible is the actual revelation imparted to the minds of the sacred writers. It brings us in contact with knowledge which, in its origin, lay beyond both the intuitional and the logical consciousness; and in conveying the truth to us, it addresses the understanding, and, through it, rises higher into the region of

[1] Philosophy of Religion, pp. 143, 144. [2] Ibid. pp. 139–141.

actual experience. God disclosed the revelation originally in the minds of Isaiah and Paul, and the inspiring Spirit so guided them that the oracle came forth unchanged to us. What Mr. Morell, then, calls special and divine arrangements for elevating the religious consciousness, we persist in calling the revelation of God.

The preceding remarks have prepared us for considering what our author's views are as to the true bond of religious fellowship, and as to the true basis of religious certitude. And here, also, the man of mere feeling appears very prominent. Things which God hath joined together are here put asunder. "The ground of all true union amongst Christians," he tells us, "is to be found, not in the common consent of the understanding to certain theological definitions, but in the common development of the intuitional consciousness as regards man's religious life."[1] It is not enough for Mr. Morell to say that no system of theological doctrine can of itself secure religious fellowship, he must maintain that the latter is independent of the former. He reasons on the assumption that if the basis of fellowship be moral in its character it cannot be theological, or that if it be theological it cannot be moral. We have always thought that the moral power of Christianity lay in its doctrines understood and believed, and that Christian fellowship, or a true evangelical alliance, must depend upon unanimity of religious feeling and adoption of common doctrines combined; and not only so, but that the influence of the two things would be reciprocal, the belief in the common doctrines strengthening the common feeling, and the common feeling strengthening the belief in the doctrines. But "The Philosophy of Religion," in accordance with its previous speculations, separates the one from the other.

[1] Philosophy of Religion, p. 288.

Mr. Morell's first reason for rejecting a fixed theological test of fellowship, is the want of authority for it in the apostolic church. "The bond of union," he says.[1] "amongst the early churches was, the powerful awakening of the religious consciousness, originating in and maintained by an intense belief of the great facts connected with the life, the death, and the resurrection of Christ." And what, we ask, were these great facts but a doctrinal basis? His second reason, which he anticipates will startle us, is, that theological statements do not contain any *essential* element of Christianity.[2] This arises out of the false principle that the essence of Christianity is only cognizable directly by the intuitional consciousness, and is supported only by telling us of persons who "take the sign for the thing; the counter for the money." But his principal objection, "and one which admits of historical verification," is, that a fixed logical or doctrinal basis, "tends inevitably to the gradual extinction of all that is *positive* in Christianity."[3] Mr. Morell's historical evidence only proves that churches, despite their doctrinal standards, have often lost the life of true religion, a thing which no one denies, but against which the mere flow of feeling, irrespective of objective truth, affords no guarantee. He appeals, among other places, to Geneva and Scotland,[4] and so do we. And we tell him that there is a church in Geneva — though it be little among the thousands of Judah — possessed of life and power which adheres firmly to a doctrinal basis; and that no country has ever enjoyed more of the religious life than Scotland, which has always attached much importance to theological doctrines. We have as little sympathy as Mr. Morell with lifeless forms and barren orthodoxy. But the idea that men, or communities, can be knit together in

[1] Philosophy of Religion, p. 271.
[2] Ibid. p. 273.
[3] Ibid. p. 278.
[4] Ibid. pp. 284–286.

holy love, while at variance on great essential doctrines, is perfectly utopian. There is much in this talk of leaving doctrinal matters undetermined in view of a broad and general fellowship, that reminds one of Parker's "absolute religion" and Newman's "doctrine of divine sympathy," over each of which might be inscribed, "Wide is the gate and broad is the way, and many there be which go in thereat."

Mr. Morell's basis of religious certitude accords with his basis of religious fellowship. He removes it from the Bible page to the religious consciousness of humanity which it awakens. "The basis of certitude," he says, "lies in the *essential characteristics* of the intuitions themselves — in their distinctness, in their uniformity, and, under due influences, in their universality; not in their symbolical representation upon the sacred page."[1] The test is thus shifted from the inspired Book — the law and the testimony — to a comparison of inward experiences. The ultimate appeal is not, What saith the Scripture? but, What is the catholic feeling and thinking of the Christian community? Such an appeal may, in certain circumstances, serve to corroborate, but can never afford a sure criterion. And then, how could it be applied in cases where the teachers of Christianity have stood almost alone, their intuitions of spiritual things being very partially experienced by others? Besides, how are distinct, uniform and universal intuitions to be secured, except through a living faith in the great Christian doctrines as revealed in the Bible? So that the catholic feeling and thinking of the whole Christian community must fall back on the Scriptures as at once a ground and test. The want of uniformity in the results of Biblical interpretation, is urged by our author as a formidable objection against making the Scrip-

[1] Philosophy of Religion, p. 337.

tures the basis of religious certitude; and the doctrine of private judgment is falsely represented as if rationalism were its inevitable landing-place.[1] It were easy to retaliate the charge of want of uniformity, and to show that we have no security for it in mere inward experiences; but the charge is unduly exaggerated. There is a wonderful harmony in the several sections of the Christian church, in regard to the bearings of Scripture on the great doctrines of salvation; and our complacency in that harmony is not disturbed, any more than our confidence in the principle of private judgment is shaken, by pointing us to such reckless unbelieving interpreters as Paulus and Strauss. We deny that the doctrine of private judgment necessarily cuts us off from the Christian consciousness of mankind, while we assert that its legitimate exercise is in searching the Scriptures, to see whether or not these things are so. But the "Philosophy of Religion" will not allow "that the data of Christian theology lie before us fixed and complete in the Bible,"[2] And intimations are given as if Christian ideas were subject to the same laws of development as the truths of astronomy. It is a fallacy to speak of Christian doctrine as a germ which received its first great unfolding in the apostolic age, and which goes on receiving other unfoldings. The Christian doctrine is not more fully unfolded in the mind of a believer now than it was in the days of Paul. The progress made from the day of Pentecost till the apostles finished their course, does not find its parallel in the progress subsequently made in the church. In the former period, the revelation was going on; the latter period received it complete. And the only kind of progress that awaits Christianity is the glorious one of seeing nation after nation coming to this "sempiternal source of truth divine," and all the sections of the church deeply

[1] Philosophy of Religion, pp. 334, 335.  [2] Ibid. pp. 375, 376.

influenced by, and united together in, the belief of the "common salvation." Mr. Morell's hopes for the world, and for unity and peace to the church, rest, however, on the power of the intuitional consciousness, and on the development of a new philosophy which shall smite all our theological dogmas and elevate us to the region of catholic feeling. The spiritualism of Mr. Morell wants the bold offensiveness of Parker and Newman, but it has this feature in common, that it unduly magnifies everything within man, and leaves little or no authority to the objective truth lying without.[1]

---

Such speculations as the above, surrender Christianity into the power of mere sentiment. That, as we have seen in the case of Parker, Newman, and Mackay, is made the test and arbiter of truth. And the tendency of much in the "Philosophy of Religion," is to bring matters to the same standard. Mr. Morell imagines that, under such custody, we would be led "from the barren region of mere

[1] It is with this principle of subjectivity that the Evangelical Church in Geneva has now to contend. There is much in Scherer's letter to D'Aubigné that reminds us of some of our own spiritualists, all of whom have drunk of the philosophy beyond the Rhine. He says "The Scriptures are the productions of great saints or of great religious heroes." "The inspiration of the apostles is purely religious." "For the simple believer, the Bible is no longer an *authority*, but it is a *treasure*." "*Biblicism* is not merely a theological error, but it is a plague upon the Church." Calvin, Beza, and the other Genevese theologians, had to combat the same errors three centuries ago. The President of the Theological Institute, who is now fighting the same good fight, says, in his well-timed treatise: "I dread this subjective tendency in our times. I dread it, convinced that it cannot fail to have the same developments, and the same consequences, that it had in the sixteenth century. You have remarked the sad progression of this opinion. Châtillon simply taught the doctrine which substitutes the authority of the individual spirit for the authority of Divine Scripture. But every seed bears its fruit. This doctrine, soon after professed by Socinus and Servetus, first overthrew all the doctrines of faith; then, interpreted by Coppin, Pocquet, Gruet, and the libertines, overthrows all the precepts of morality. It thus brought forth great heresies and frightful irregularities. The progression is terrible, but inevitable. . . . *The foundation of Christian dogma and Christian morality, is involved in these opinions*."—*The Authority of God*, by D'Aubigné, (pp. 189, 190.)

logical forms into the hallowed paths of a divine life." The men of the "School of Progress" know full well what these paths are, and hence their complacency in his speculations. He has not urged the moral argument against the evangelical doctrines, nor do we charge him with denying them; but those who do urge it are disposed to look upon him as an auxiliary in the same warfare. It is this argument that runs throughout, or underlies, many of the writings of our philosophical spiritualists. It extends, like a broad belt, through Parker's "Discourse," and Newman's "Phases." It is involved in very much of Mackay's "Progress." And, in some other productions, it is supposed to receive a tacit, if not an avowed, support. Texts of Scripture, involving the obnoxious doctrines of redemption, which will not bend before a neological exegesis, are reduced under the weight of what is called the moral argument. We shall scrutinize it for a little.

The argument is grounded on the supposed contradiction between men's moral sentiments and the peculiar tenets of the evangelical creed. God is the author of our moral nature, and his revealed will must harmonize with its utterances. The voice of the Immutable One within the breast, pronouncing decisively on right and wrong, can never be falsified, or disputed, by the voice speaking in the word. Man's reason and moral consciousness, it is alleged, are opposed to much of what currently passes for the Christian theology. In the latter, views are given of God and man so dark and awful as to be repulsed by the former. There is a collision, it is maintained, between the dark creed of depravity, the vindictive justice of God as exhibited in the atonement, and the indestructible judgments and feelings of the human heart. Christ has revealed unto us the Father, and it sufficeth us. He has taught us to look up to heaven, and, inspired with filial confidence, to say, "Our Abba, our Father." He has inculcated love to our enemies, that we may be the children of our Father in heaven, who maketh his sun to rise on the evil and on the good. He has bidden us behold God as a Father feeding the fowls of the air, clothing the lilies of the field, and much more caring for men, his own children. These are sentiments which meet with a welcome response in every human bosom, and they proclaim themselves divine. They are in unison with those genial currents of thought and feeling which flow through the soul of every man of sensibility, when looking on the shining heavens and the green earth, and which move him to say, "My Father made them all." It is in this endearing character that we must view Him as presiding over the universe, pitying men even as a father pitieth his children, and making all things to work together for their good. And it is in this character that we would expect to meet Him, in making a special revelation of Himself to the world. But the doctrines of what is called evangelism, continues the objector, conflict with such sentiments as these. Man is therein represented as a most wretched object, a creature shapen in iniquity, and a child of wrath. The God of mercy is exhibited as incensed against his own offspring, making a heavy exaction for their guilt, and being appeased only by the interposition of his well-beloved Son. Repentance does not suffice to procure forgiveness, as, from the fatherly character of God, we would have been led to suppose. But an atonement must first be made to turn away God's wrath, and a supernatural power must be exerted to raise man up from his degradation.

These are strong statements. There is in them much gross misrepresentation. But it is in some such way as this that the religion of the moral sentiments and the orthodox creed are arrayed against each other. It is not, as in the old rationalistic controversy, a warfare waged on the ground of critical exegesis. But it is an attempt to set the moral nature of man over against what the general mind of Christendom has pronounced to be the Revelation of God. Are, then, the doctrines of redemption irreconcilable with the paternity of God? and do the persons who urge the moral objection give a view of the Divine character that is adequate, and consistent with the nature of things? We trow not; and we assign our reasons.

1. This argument is *unsupported by analogy*. Although urged by professed theists, it is as applicable to natural religion as to revealed. If it has any bearing against the great facts of the scriptural record, it has not less against the great facts of the book of providence. The argument is an old and by no means an invincible one. The answer is old also, and, in our estimation, a truly satisfactory one. The gist of the argument is, that God must always act in accordance with the simple idea of his paternal character; and that the doctrines of redemption, militating, as is alleged, against that idea, cannot in their orthodox sense be true. Carrying along with us, then, the simple and exclusive idea of paternity, suppose that from the date of our creation we had dwelt in another reign of God's empire where sin and misery were unknown, where knowledge of the most delightful kind was diffused wide as the light, and where all the inhabitants were perfectly holy and happy. Suppose, farther, that we had known nothing, by report or otherwise, of the moral and physical condition of this earth, but that at a certain period we alighted on its soil and mingled with its children, would we not have found much in the condition of mankind irreconcilable with the simple and exclusive idea of the paternity of God? We are far from believing that there is any part of the wide universe, however sinless and happy, the in-

habitants of which have no other idea of the Eternal than that of a Father. The idea of paternity is of all others the most delightful, and, in such a province of the Creator's dominions as that supposed, will be most vivid; but it is not all-comprehending. It is a glory that blends with other glories in the Divine character, and the idea will consequently be associated with other ideas in the minds of those beings who have the most enlarged and correct knowledge of God. But, for the sake of argument, we suppose ourselves to have lived in some remote happy region, and then, bringing along with us the exclusively vivid idea of paternity, to have come into this world; and we ask, How much in its condition would we not have found apparently at variance with it?

There is the palpable fact of moral evil meeting us at every step, a fact which, however much men may attempt to disguise or mitigate it, cannot be denied. The existence of this, in any part of the earth, would be to us a monstrous anomaly, and conflict mightily with our exclusive idea of the Divine paternity. Much more would this happen, when we ascertained that it was neither local nor temporary, that traces of it were to be found wherever man set his foot, and that it had been perpetuated from generation to generation ever since the existence of the first family. *Here*, we might say, is a phenomenon, which, judging from our notions of the paternal character of the Divine dispensations, we would never have expected. And how account for the permission at first, and for the prevalence hitherto, of this dreadful evil in a world under the supreme control of Him whom we have been accustomed to regard as the Father of his creation, the wisest and best Father of his people?

Then, again, there is the moral nature of man, speaking clearly, by its primitive judgments, on behalf of truth and rectitude, and yet ever in love with error and swerving from the right path. The human soul declaring, by the wondrous natural powers with which it has been endowed, that it is celestial in its origin; and yet making it evident, by the manifestation of these powers, that it is allied to the dust. *This* is what we never would have anticipated under the government of Him who is the Father of spirits. And, as we traveled through this world, or read its history in past ages, and became acquainted with the ignorance, the irreligion and suffering that prevailed, our preconceived notions would be the more scattered, and our exclusive idea of paternity be brought the more into conflict with actual realities. Here and there, we would perceive a few minds, like tall trees studding at intervals a level tract of country, rising by their intelligence and attainments above the crowd, while the greater part of that crowd were groveling, ignorant, sensual. The perplexities would increase, and the gloom thicken upon us, as we proceeded to consider the religious condition of mankind in general. Here, on an insignificant spot of the world's map, would we behold a small portion of the race possessing anything like worthy conceptions of God; and, even among these, an ever manifesting tendency to corrupt that knowledge and to depart from Him; while, in reference to the rest, we would find the description of the sacred oracle to be by no means exaggerated, "darkness covered the earth, and gross darkness the people."

The darkness would become the more visible, and the anomalies the more bewildering, on noticing the moral and physical suffering that prevailed. What a vast and varied amount of mental and bodily distress meets the eye in this direction and in that! The thirst for happiness is insatiable, the cry is deep, earnest and incessant, "Who will show us any good?" The yearnings and strivings of the human spirit indicate that happiness is "our being's end and aim,"—and yet men in general fail of attaining to it. The moral viciousness of individuals and communities has its counterpart in dreadful and complicated sufferings. *Here*, we see physical ills following moral transgressions with something like the certainty of fixed laws; and *there*, we behold ever and anon in history terrible special interpositions, in the form of famine or flood, pestilence or war, proclaiming to those who have ears to hear, that there is verily a God that judgeth in the earth. The innocent are involved in these calamities, as well as the guilty. The sins of the fathers are visited upon the children. The good and beneficent are not unfrequently overwhelmed in the same national judgments that come upon the evil-doers and the profane.

This is a state of matters, a complicated scene of ignorance and irreligion, of moral and physical suffering, which the inhabitants of a sinless world, having a vivid idea of the paternity of God, would have found on their arrival (until the explanation was given) to be awfully and distressingly embarrassing. And, had it been possible for such intelligences to have had no other idea of God but the paternal one, they would have learned that some other must be embraced, and that between them there was the most perfect harmony. Here, then, we meet the objection against the doctrines of the Christian redemption, urged on the ground of their supposed contrariety to the paternal character of God. The objector says, the atonement and the system of which it forms the center are utterly at variance with what we, judging from his character as a father, would have supposed God to have done had He interposed on behalf of the human race. We ask the objector, Is that world without and around you such as you would have supposed it would be? Had you come from another sphere, with no other idea about God in your head than the paternal one, would you have expected to have found that mysterious and mighty thing, moral evil, at the heart of humanity, perpetuating and diffusing itself from age to age, and bringing in its train such an amount of moral and physical wretchedness as has inscribed on the world's history mourning and lamentation and woe? We ask you to reconcile that fact, which is patent to every eye, with your preconceived notions of the paternity of God; and we tell you, that you could no more ward off the objection which the supposed visitant might bring against the condition of our world, than, as you suppose, it can be warded off from the doctrines of the Christian redemption.[1]

2. The view of the Divine character taken by this argument, is *one-sided and partial.* It embraces a delightful and important truth, but it is not the whole truth, nor the whole of the most important truth. God is the common father of all his creatures. "Have we not all one father, hath not one God created us?" And it is in this character, that He opens his hand, and satisfies the desire of every living thing. The child feels the sweet power of this truth, when with bended knee and uplifted heart and look, he says, "Our Father which art in heaven." The man of feeling, casting his eye over the varied face of nature, is moved,

[1] Harrington, the skeptic, who had been prevented from taking refuge in the "half-way houses" between the Bible and religious skepticism, says: 'If I acquiesce, on Mr. Newman's grounds, in the rejection of the Bible as a special revelation of God, I am compelled on the very *same* principles to go a few steps farther, and to express doubts of the absolutely divine original of the *World* and the administration thereof, just as he does of the divine original of the Bible. If I concede to Mr. Newman, however we may differ as to the moral and spiritual faculties of man, that these are yet the sole and ultimate court of appeal to us; that from our 'intuitions' of right and wrong, of 'moral and spiritual truth,' be they more perfect according to him, or more rudimentary and imperfect according to me, we must form a judgment of the moral bearings of every presumed *external* revelation of God; I cannot do otherwise than reject much of the revelation of God in his presumed *Works* as unworthy of him, just as Mr. Newman does very much in his supposed *Word* as equally unworthy of him."—*The Eclipse of Faith*, p. 147.

and justly so, at the thought of that immense paternity which embraces heaven and earth, and the whole empire of animated being from the seraph to the reptile. And the Christian has been taught, by the holy oracles, to look upon God as being in the highest sense his Father, and as thus making all things work together for his good. But the regal character pertains no less to the Divine Being than does the parental; and nature and revelation teach us to regard Him as a Sovereign no less than a Parent. The two ideas blend together, and are realized, in the utmost perfection, in the Divine nature; and so should they blend in our conceptions of what God is, and of what are his relations to our world. He is not only the best and wisest of fathers, but the most righteous, benignant, and powerful of kings. The same dispensation of Providence may bring impressively before our mind this two-fold view of the Divine relation. Afflictions, in one sense, are sovereign judgments; and, in another sense, they are fatherly chastisements. In one view, they are punishments for sin; and, in another view, they are tokens of a father's love. They manifest at once the righteous Sovereign and the benignant Parent. Justice has been defined to be goodness regulated by wisdom, and the sovereign relation may be said to be the parental controlled by the same attribute. It would, however, be a very defective view of the Divine character, to exclude the idea of justice, and adopt the bare idea of goodness, as comprehensive of the whole truth about God. And it is the very same defect in that theory which regards Him simply and exclusively as the Parent of all. It is a gross misrepresentation of the Christian atonement, to speak of it as if the fatherly character of God was there overshadowed or shut out. "Go to my brethren," said the Apostle and High Priest of our profession, "and say unto them, "I ascend unto my Father and your Father; and to my God and your God." It is, indeed, in the atonement, that we see the paternal relation in its richest elements and loveliest manifestation, not dissociated from or shrouded by the regal, but the majesty of the one rendered attractive by the love of the other, and the love of the one appearing the more grand and costly in union with the other. "Mercy and truth meet together, righteousness and peace embrace each other." We behold at once, "the just God and the Savior." The theology of the natural religion is no less meager and contracted than that of the revealed, and the view of the Divine character as the God of providence, is no less partial than the view of Him as the God of redemption, which does not embrace the twofold relationship of Jehovah as the King and Father of his people. Whether we contemplate Him as seated on the circle of the universe, presiding over the movements of the spheres, and magnifying the affairs of men; or, as manifested in the cross, magnifying his law and bringing redemption to a lost world; we do not contemplate Him aright, unless it be in the blended relations of the righteous Sovereign and the benignant Parent. "The Lord reigneth; let the earth rejoice; let the multitudes of isles be glad thereof. Clouds and darkness are round about Him; righteousness and judgment are the habitation of his throne."

3. The *doctrine of depravity*, as stated in Scripture or implied in the atonement, is not a whit more aggravated and mysterious than the *actual condition of man*. The Bible doctrine, on this subject, has been denounced as dark and perplexing; but it is not more so than the palpable facts that come under observation and experience. To hear some men speak about the dark and mysterious doctrines of Scripture, you would imagine that, without the pale of Christianity, difficulty and darkness were unknown, that all was unclouded sunshine, comprehensible and plain.

Whereas, it is just because there are mysteries in nature, that there are mysteries in revelation. No one disputes the existence of sin in the world. The mountain stands before us, however different may be the estimates formed of its origin and size. But some would represent its existence in nature, and account for its presence in the human soul, in such a way as to set the natural religion over against the revealed. The conflict takes place at two points. The Bible teaches that sin is an element of positive evil in the heart, consisting in the corruption of the will, and that, as a depraved force, it affects all the mental powers, and manifests itself in the outward conduct. Opponents consider sin as a negative thing, consisting rather in the defect of a positive good than in the presence of a positive evil. The Bible traces all human transgression up to the inward depraved principle, which is strengthened and developed by outward circumstances. The objectors maintaining the original goodness of the heart, regard sin as an accident, and the product of external forces acting upon man's constitution. *There* it is, however, in the heart of humanity, account for it as you will.

The first thing we affirm respecting it is, that it is not represented more darkly in Scripture than it exists actually in the world. There is not a darker picture of depravity in the Bible than that which is drawn by Paul in his epistle to the Romans. He there proves, by an induction of evidence, that mankind are deeply and universally depraved. And the testimonies of historians, who were by no means friendly to Christianity, may be appealed to in proof that the apostolic description is not darker than the outward reality. Experience and observation are in perfect harmony with scriptural representations on this point. The book declares that all have sinned, and the world sets its seal to the statement as true. The book declares that the heart is deceitful, and what man of self-reflection will deny it? The plague raged not less fearfully in the city, than Daniel Defoe describes it. The desert is not less arid and cheerless, than it appears in the pages of the traveler. And the actual state of the moral nature of man, before better influences came down upon it, is no less dark and depraved than it is represented in scriptural statements, or implied in the doctrine of atonement.

But we assert, farther, that the Bible account of the origin of sin, however mysterious, is more in accordance with fact than the view given in the opposite argument. The doctrine of Scripture is, that all men have been involved in the fall of their common parent, and that, in consequence of the first sin of the first man, they have inherited a depraved nature. Not that men actually sin without the concurrence of their own will, but that the principles of depravity are inherent within them. This we hold to be more philosophically true than the explanation that sin is an accident, the result of external agencies, a thing not proceeding from the soul within, but coming to it from without. It is true that we cannot detect depravity till some time after the birth of an individual, but neither can we detect reason or the rudiments of a moral nature. The child, in the process of time, however, gives signs of the existence of the reasoning faculty, and of the moral constitution, and contemporaneously therewith does it manifest tendencies to evil. Now, as has often been remarked, we never ascribe the existence of reason and the moral sense to education or to any external influences. They may develop them, but they do not produce them. Men, in all circumstances, manifest reason and a moral nature; and this is to us a proof that they are inherent in the human constitution. Men, in all circumstances, manifest depraved affections. These circumstances may call them forth, strengthen them, or even counteract them, but they do not originate them, and this we take to be a proof of an original depraved propensity. The uniform occurrence of moral actions is not a stronger evidence of a moral nature, than the uniform occurrence of wrong moral actions is an evidence of a corrupt moral nature.

It is somewhat strange, that certain reforming projectors, who persist in maintaining that inherent depravity is to be found nowhere but in the "dark creed" of the Gospel, and that all the evils which afflict man are to be traced to external circumstances operating on his mental and physical constitution, should, on the supposition of their theory being true, never have succeeded,— in those genial climes whither they have removed, and amid those favorable circumstances by which they were surrounded,— in rearing up plants without spot or wrinkle or any such thing. They have had their Utopias, their Icarias, and Harmony Halls. But old Adam has always proved too strong for young Melancthon. The power of inward evil has sported with all their fondly-cherished schemes to subdue it, and shown such schemes to be visionary and vain. And, it is not less strange (on the supposition of the truth of the theories of Parker and Newman), that, notwithstanding the alleged virtue of the "absolute religion," and the "spiritual faculty," which are said to render the Gospel unnecessary, men, uninfluenced by that Gospel, should have everywhere continued corrupt and corruptors. But it is not strange on the belief of the Scripture doctrine, that man is radically depraved, that the principle of evil is within, and that out of the heart come the things that defile the man. This doctrine, as we have admitted, is dark and mysterious, standing boldly forth as it does on the Bible page. But it is not a whit more so than the actual condition of man in the world. The account of the astounding phenomenon as given in the inspired volume, is, however, vastly more in accordance with observation and experience, than any opposite theory. And we ask, when are men of philosophical pretensions to cease assuming, or how long is the world to tolerate their assumption, that darkness and mystery belong only to the theology of the Gospel which they disown, and that these horrible things have no place in the theology of nature of which they profess themselves the disciples and friends?

4. *The doctrine of pardon on the ground of an atonement is neither unreasonable nor inconsistent with the Paternity of God*, as is supposed. We assent to the remarks of the eloquent preacher,[1] "that there is in this doctrine something extremely remote from ordinary apprehension, apart from the instruction derived from Holy Writ. That one of the human race, by submitting to an ignominious and painful death, should be the moral source of the salvation of an innumerable multitude of mankind, and, if duly improved, a sufficient source for the salvation of all, is surely one of the most extraordinary of the Divine proceedings with regard to man. Nothing like this has ever existed. It seems to stand by itself, an insulated department of Divine Providence, to contain within itself a method of acting which was never seen before, and will never be repeated." It was a mysterious exigency, altogether unprecedented, that had to be met, and the expedient devised by Infinite wisdom has a height and depth that pass knowledge. And yet, notwithstanding the unique and unparalleled nature of this distinctive act of moral mediation, the idea of moral substitution has a foundation in nature, and pardon through a mediator is a principle not unfrequently exemplified in history. Some men speak under a kind of horror at this doctrine, because it represents the God and Father of mankind as inflicting

[1] Robert Hall.

punishment on the innocent, and thus reversing all our ideas of moral rectitude, that where there is no sin there should be no suffering. But,— not to dwell on the assumption involved in this objection, that the objector knew all the ends God had in view in the work of atonement, or that these ends are not better secured by the sufferings of Christ than they could have been in any other way,— does it not frequently happen in God's providential administration that persons are involved in sufferings in consequence of the sins of others, in the commission of which they had no part; and that men possessed of little or no virtue in themselves, have much respect shown to them, and many benefits conferred upon them, solely on account of the virtues of others? Some of the most direful calamities that ever fell on individuals or communities, have been the consequences of the wrong-doings of others, of which they themselves were innocent. And some of the richest blessings that ever descended upon families or nations, may be traced to the merit and suffering of those who, for righteousness' sake, perished in the field, at the stake, or on the scaffold.

In such cases as these, we see the existence of a principle, which is manifested, in a manner altogether unparalleled, in the Christian redemption, the principle of moral substitution, the principle of conferring benefits on individuals or communities from a regard to the merits of others, and of the innocent suffering in consequence of the deeds of the guilty. And that this principle is in harmony with the general sentiments of mankind, is abundantly testified by their religious observances even in lands where the Gospel is unknown. It is altogether unphilosophical to ascribe any permanent and universally diffused feeling and sentiments to what have been considered a few interested classes of the community. "To affirm, as some have done," says Isaac Taylor,[1] "that priests are the authors of religion

[1] Man Responsible, p. 8.

and moral sentiment, is a sort of upside-down logic, not easily understood. Surely it were more philosophical to invert the terms of the proposition, and to affirm that religion and moral sentiment are the authors of priests.' The altars which have been reared and the sacrifices which have been offered, in every age and quarter of the world, show that the idea of vicarious interposition has its foundation in the constitution of nature. And the same principle is evinced in cases, unconnected with religious rites and observances, of the good and great in history suffering for the unworthy, and the virtues of such illustrious sufferers being so reckoned to others as that on account of them undeserved favors have been bestowed. We never look, in anything among men, for a parallelism to the amazingly grand fact of salvation by the interposition and sacrifice of the Son of the Highest. But, in such cases as those to which we have adverted, we see, be the actions blameworthy or commendable, that the notions of vicarious suffering and of treating the undeserving kindly for the sake of the deserving, are not so strange and unnatural as some persons, in objecting to the atonement, would seem to suppose.

It was one of the unworthy expedients of the old deistical writers, and the same is not unfrequently resorted to in more modern times, to misrepresent and disfigure the atonement, and then hold it up to the execration of mankind. The following is a specimen from Bolingbroke: "Let us suppose a great prince, governing a wicked and rebellious people,—he has it in his power to punish, but thinks fit to pardon them. But he orders his only and well-beloved son to be put to death, to expiate their sins, and satisfy his royal vengeance. Would this proceeding (asks the writer) appear to the eye of reason, and in the unprejudiced light of nature, wise, or just, or good? No man dares to say that it would except it be a divine."[1]

[1] Leland's Deistical Writers.

No person deserving the name of a divine but would cry out on the monstrous injustice as loudly as the philosopher himself. But is such a case parallel to the Christian atonement? Far from it. It fails in two things, and failing in these, the whole is vitiated. In the first place, the highest injustice would have been done to the substitute, in the case supposed; whereas, no injury whatever was done to Christ, for, with a perfect knowledge of what he would have to endure, his undertaking was entirely voluntary. He is represented in the ancient oracle as saying, when about to enter on the work of mediation, "Lo! I come, I delight to do thy will, O my God;" and, on earth he declared, "No man taketh my life from me. I have power to lay it down and I have power to take it again." In the second place, no sentiment is more derogatory to the Divine character, and more opposed to the declarations of Scripture, than that which represents God as naturally implacable toward the human race, and as being appeased by the interposition of his beloved Son. The sacred penman, and the adherents of the doctrine of redemption, always speak of the mission and death of Christ, not as the cause, but as the effect of the Father's love, not as rendering Him merciful toward us, but as the divinely appointed way of manifesting his self-moved benignity to the guilty. What can be plainer than the golden passage in John, "God *so* loved the world as to give his only begotten Son, that whosoever believeth in Him should not perish, but have everlasting life." The paternal theory, as we have seen, embraces only one aspect of the twofold relation in which the Supreme Being stands to men; it separates the glories that blend in the Divine character, and overlooks one of them as if it had no existence. Whereas, it is the pre-eminent excellence of the Christian doctrine of atonement, that it is comprehensive of the whole. In it, we see at once the righteous Governor of the world maintaining the integrity of his just and good laws, and the benignant Parent, in perfect consistency with the holiness of his character and the honor of his administration, extending mercy to his rebellious children. We behold in the theory of the atonement, what we fail to perceive in the paternal theory, a high regard to the cause of moral right and to the general interests of the universe, and an altogether extraordinary manifestation of Divine benevolence to guilty man. It speaks loudly in behalf of its truthfulness, that it harmonizes so wondrously the Divine relations of sovereign and parent; exhibiting in the world's great exigency, righteousness inviolable and uncompromising to be the girdle of God's throne, and love, unexampled and ineffable, going forth from his heart. The angels embraced the blended glories of king and father, when they sung over the plains of Bethlehem, "Glory to God in the highest, and on earth peace, good-will toward men."

But this is mysterious doctrine! As if, by crying up mystery as a bugbear, men are to be scared away from it. We reply to the taunt by saying, there is a mystery no less inscrutable and astounding before your eyes, a mystery which has called this other forth — the mystery of moral evil. Solve that mystery, or deny it, before you urge mystery as an objection against the Divine provision that has been made to meet it. It is the mystery of man's fall that has occasioned the mystery of man's redemption. "Without controversy, great is the mystery of godliness; God was manifested in the flesh." But, "herein he hath abounded toward us in all wisdom and prudence."

5. The *doctrine of Divine influence* as indispensably necessary *to regenerate the souls of men, is a reasonable doctrine;* at variance neither with the dictates of nature

nor the principles of sound philosophy. It deserves notice, that while the earlier unitarians shrunk from boldly impugning this article of the evangelical creed, their successors generally ridicule and deny it; or, in accordance with the "School of Progress," merge it in the very commonest natural influence. Men may think to construct a religious philosophy without it, but it requires little consideration to see, that of all philosophies it is the most unphilosophical. It has been already shown, that, to be thoroughly consistent in denying the intervention of God in preserving and ruling the universe, men must take up their position in atheism and deny the existence of God Himself. And it may as justly be affirmed, that, to be thoroughly consistent in denying a Divine influence on the soul, men must either hold that the soul exists independently of God, or is placed beyond the reach of his operations. The possibility, not to say the probability or actual certainty, of the Almighty Maker exerting an influence on the material worlds, in accordance with the laws and properties which He has impressed on them being granted; it cannot, with any pretensions to philosophy, be denied that God may exercise an influence on the souls which He has formed, so as not to interfere with their free agency and responsibility. No one will venture to assert that it is more difficult to conceive how the spirit of God operates on mind, than how He operates on matter. Yea, we will venture to say that it is more easy to conceive the action of mind on mind, than the action of mind on matter. Many of the ancient Greek and Roman philosophers, as has often been shown by quotations from their writings, admitted not only the possibility but the necessity and reality of Divine influences on the mind for the attainment and practice of virtue. Seneca declares, "It is God that comes to men; yea more, He enters into them, for no mind becomes truly good but by his assistance." Plato has remarked, "that virtue is not to be taught but by the assistance of God." And he introduces Socrates as declaring, "that wheresoever virtue comes, it seems to be the fruit of a divine dispensation." These considerations show, not only that the exercise of a Divine influence on the mind is possible, but that the want of it has been felt, and the reality of it admitted, by the greatest men living under the glimmering light of nature. This augurs something in favor of its reasonableness and accordance with sound philosophy. And surely, if we admit a supernatural intervention in revealing Christianity at the first, it is more in accordance with right reason to believe that it makes its way through this world, rife as it is with powerful principles that are hostile to it, accompanied with an influence from on high, than that it has been left to struggle alone, unaided by the spiritual energy which gave it birth.

But the objection is, that it interferes with the moral freedom of man. As if an influence coming from without could not but destroy or impair the freedom of the will within. It is a sufficient reply to this objection, that the operation of such an external cause no more implies interference with human liberty than the operation of any other external causes. One man exerts an influence upon another by his speech or example, without it ever being supposed that the moral freedom of that other is interfered with. The orator in the senate, or from the pulpit, influences men to change their opinions and follow a different line of conduct, and no one ever imagines that the responsibility of men is thereby lessened. We are thrown into society, or brought into contact with the scenes of external nature, and passively receive impressions from the objects that surround us, but we, nevertheless, feel that our free will is not interfered with in avoiding or pursuing any train of thought or course of conduct to which they would lead us. And why should it be thought to be otherwise with an influence coming not from earth but from heaven, not from objects that are natural but divine and spiritual? Men, it has been remarked, are passive in receiving natural light and bodily strength from God, and yet free and active in making use of them. And so it may be conceived that men derive spiritual light and strength from the same source, and enjoy their moral freedom in like manner. If it be objected that the cases are not parallel, we answer that they are perfectly parallel in the point for which they have been adduced—viz., non-interference with man's moral liberty. We are conscious that the influence exerted on our minds by human spirits is according to the laws of our moral constitution. We feel that influence, and nevertheless we are conscious that we are morally free. In like manner, the subjects of Divine influence know that it is God that worketh in them, and yet they feel, too, that they are free to choose the good and avoid the evil.

Such are the aspects in which the doctrine is presented in Scripture, and in that orthodox creed which is objected against. It is obviously implied in those inspired statements which speak of men resisting and quenching the Spirit's influences, that these influences do not in the least interfere with man's free agency, nor diminish but rather increase his responsibility. David, conscious of his moral freedom, meditated on his comparatively small and dark Bible, while he lifted up his heart to the heavens and said, "Open thou mine eyes, that I may behold wondrous things out of thy law." Paul gave the exhortation, "Work out your own salvation with fear and trembling, for it is God that worketh in you both to will and to do of his good pleasure." At this point, then, the Scripture doctrine, however inscrutable otherwise, accords with human consciousness, and with the principles of sound philosophy. We attempt not, and wish not, to strip it of its mysteriousness. But mystery here is not mystification. And, as Dr. Vaughan remarks,[1] "The mystery is, that men should be in a condition to need regeneration, not that, such being the fact, the Spirit of the Lord should be sent to regenerate them."

In farther confirmation of the reality and reasonableness of this doctrine, we appeal to three unquestionable facts. The first is, that where the Gospel is unknown, men are morally degraded and vile. Whether we look at the ancient or modern heathen world, the testimony given is the same, that men, without Christianity, are unregenerate and destitute of moral loveliness. Let any one read Tholuck's admirable treatise "On the Nature and Moral Influence of Heathenism, especially among the Greeks and Romans," and he will be convinced, if unconvinced before, of the truth of the proposition which he seeks to demonstrate,—that "heathenism as such, did not restore, but profaned the image of God in man." "History," observes Maclaurin,[2] "showeth the weak and contemptible efficacy of the sublimest philosophy of the heathens, when it is encountered with inveterate corruptions or violent temptations. How many of them that spake of virtue like angels, yet lived in a manner like brutes: whereas, in all ages, poor Christian plebeians, unpolished by learning, but earnest in prayer, and depending upon grace, have, in comparison of these others, lived rather like angels than men; and shown such an invincible steadfastness in the practice of virtue, as shameth all the philosophy in the world." Plato represents Socrates as saying, in his discourse with Alcibiades, "Methinks, as Homer says, that Minerva removed the mist from

[1] The Age and Christianity, p. 299.

[2] Maclaurin's Works, p. 78 (Collins' Edition).

the eyes of Diomede, in order that he might well distinguish God from man, so it is needful that He (the heavenly teacher), first removing from thy soul the mist which is now present, should then impart means by which thou shalt know good and evil; for *now thou dost not appear to me capable of this.*" And the absence of life in modern heathenism to renovate and raise up man, and the presence and power of it in the Gospel, are strikingly illustrated in the veritable records of Christian missions. "Why do you believe in the Divine origin of Christianity?" said an officer of a British ship to some converted islanders of the South Sea. "We look," replied one of them, "at the power with which it has been attended in effecting the entire overthrow of idolatry among us; and which, we believe, no human means could have induced us to abandon."[1] If, over against all this, men will set the corruptions which have existed in the presence of Christianity, and assert that the moral pollution within the pale of the church has not been less than within the province of heathenism, we reply, in the words of Tholuck, that, "The question is not, in what the Christian, who is merely baptized with *water*, is better than the heathen, but the one who is baptized with the Spirit and with fire. . . . Vain would be the task of him who would prove that the mass of weeds which have luxuriated within the pale of the Christian church from the beginning might have sprung from the root of the Spirit of Christ."[2] It can be shown that the Divine life has been wanting wherever a native or baptized heathenism prevails, but it cannot be shown that a spiritual deadness has been prevalent where the Gospel, in its purity and simplicity, has been believed and obeyed. This of itself is a strong presumptive proof that a Divine influence accompanies, in a

[1] The Bible not of Man. By Dr. Spring, p. 156.

[2] Nature and Moral Influence of Heathenism, pp. 6, 7.

greater or less degree, the truths of Christianity among men.

The second fact to which we appeal is, that where Christianity is exhibited stripped of all its grand distinctive peculiarities as a system of atonement and spiritual regeneration, and reduced to a kind of religious philosophy, it is seen to be destitute of life, and morally impotent to regenerate men. It is "Christianity in the frigid zone." It contains no elements of truth fitted to arouse the conscience of the ungodly, or to interest the heart of the virtuous. In so far as doctrinal truth is concerned, it is negative rather than positive; and Christianity in its hands, having dwindled down to little more than a code of ethics, is supplied with no power to counteract the stubborn principle of depravity, and to infuse a holy, heavenly life into the soul. Having shorn the Gospel of its mysteries, it has, in a great measure, deprived it of its strength and left it to move a cold, meager, uninfluential thing among men. Let it be carried, accordingly, into the lanes and hovels of our cities where ignorance and vice hold their ancient reign; or let it, if it has the zeal, cross the seas and be brought to bear on the malignant and inveterate forms of heathenism; — and it is alike powerless in reclaiming the vicious, and in turning men from idols, to serve the living and true God. It is by their fruits that we are to judge of systems as well as of men. And may it not be asked, (without breach of charity,) is the power of godliness manifested, does a lofty, unearthly piety prevail, are the duties of religion generally attended to, do works of faith and labors of love begin and progress, do real conversions to God and a radical reformation of heart and life take place, under a system of religious teaching that expunges from its creed the doctrines of atonement and Divine influence? Is there not rather a great congeniality of spirit between this system of an impoverished Christianity and the skepticism and indifference of men who wish to retain an outward form of religion, while destitute of its inner life? Dr. Priestley honestly acknowledged that infidelity and unitarianism were not very far from each other. The little state of Geneva, under the predominance of such principles — the progress of which afforded such delight to D'Alembert and Voltaire — was characterized by its depravity, its neglect of public and domestic religion, and the dissoluteness of its manners in general. And though the system, in the hands of some of its chiefs, has recently begun to assume a more spiritual aspect, and "*to represent the progress of man in theology*," it is not the spiritualism of the revelation that has come from above, but that of the idealistic philosophy; and, being as destitute as ever of the great distinctive elements of the Gospel, it is as ineffectual to make men holy and happy. But it is of little consequence what shape systems may assume, or what name their abettors may take,— go forth as they may, avowing themselves to be religious teachers, so long as they have the corruptions of the heart to contend with, they will be seen to be visionary and powerless, and will leave the race, as similar systems have left it, depraved and unrenewed, because they have not the Spirit. And this we take to be another presumptive proof of the reality and reasonableness of the doctrine of Divine influence.

The third fact to which we appeal is, that wherever the Gospel has been influential in working a radical change on masses of men, or in adorning the individual character with the beauties of holiness, strong faith in the doctrine of Divine influence has existed in the minds of its teachers and disciples. It was so in the beginning of the Gospel age. The whole machinery of means had been completed, the atonement had been finished, the apostles had been chosen and instructed, the Lord had risen from the grave and ascended up on high,—but life in the wheels was wanting, and no remarkable success followed the movements of the moral machinery, till a supernatural influence came down from heaven. The first teachers of Christianity waited in expectation of such an influence. It descended according to the promise of their Lord, and they had power in converting, sanctifying, and saving men. Paul and his fellow-laborers never failed to acknowledge, in any distinguished success that attended their preaching, the presence and power of the Spirit of God. And a similar devout recognition of the regenerating Spirit has been made in every succeeding epoch of revival and missionary achievement. It was so at the Reformation, when the Gospel trumpet sounded anew and awoke the nations. It was so in the times of the good and brave Puritans, men of whom the world was not worthy, and who were instrumental in bringing about an age of strong faith and reviving earnestness. It was so in the age of Whitfield and Wesley and Romaine, men born to summon the dead to life, and quicken again the things that were ready to die. It has been so in the brilliant successes that have crowned modern missions, and in the times of refreshing that have ever and anon come upon the church of God. The most honored instruments in advancing the world's regeneration have been persons who had firm faith in the doctrine of the regenerating influences of the Holy Spirit. And a like testimony is obtained, on perusing the memoirs, or in mingling in the society, of eminent private Christians. The choicest spirits of our race, whether in the public or retired walks of life, whether standing forth before the world and battling with its vices and errors, or shedding noiselessly a hallowed influence in the domestic circle, have been men who looked up to God for the high life of the soul, and for success to their benignant labors.

This doctrine has often been stigmatized as chimerical and visionary. But such epithets are misapplied, unless they are kept to brand projects and systems which count on the world's regeneration while unaccompanied with a power that can overcome the world's depravity. "Their work," says John Foster,[1] "is before them: the scene of moral disorder presents to them the plagues which they are to stop, the mountain which they are to remove, the torrent which they are to divert, the desert which they are to clothe in verdure and bloom. Let them make their experiment, and add each his page to the humiliating records in which experience contemns the folly of elated imagination." The world's regeneration meanwhile goes on; and it must go on, with the same system of moral means, and accompanied by the same heavenly energy, (though it may be with greater potency,) as it has proceeded hitherto, until the glorious consummation shall have come, when voices in heaven shall be heard saying, "The kingdoms of this world have become the kingdoms of our Lord, and of his Christ."

6. The *charge of gloominess* which opponents bring against the *doctrines of redemption is unfounded.* Some men are incessantly speaking of these doctrines as if they tended to hang the world in mourning, and to repress every genial impulse of the soul. They taunt us, in no measured terms, with the "dark and horrible creed of depravity," as if this article were a shade darker in the Gospel than in the book of nature. The hideous thing has its origin in the world, not in the Scripture, and it is dark in the one just because it is dark in the other. They taunt us with the doctrine of sacrifice and atonement as if it clothed the Divine Being with the most unamiable attributes. But we repel the taunt as a gross misrepresentation, and maintain

[1] Foster's Essays, p. 173.

the atonement of the Gospel to be the most illustrious manifestation of Him who is at once inflexibly just, immaculately holy, and inconceivably kind. They taunt us with the doctrine of Divine influence as implying that man is unequal to his duties and destiny, as interfering with his moral freedom, and tending to unnerve all his energies. But we reply that man's moral impotency is a fact that lies within the range of observation and experience, that Divine influences no more necessarily interfere with his moral freedom than other external influences, and that the doctrine, scripturally understood, instead of unnerving, rouses and quickens the energies with which man has been endowed. And not only do the doctrines of redemption, abstractly considered, falsify the charge under consideration; but the fact is undeniable, that persons in every age who have yielded themselves up to the influence of these doctrines have generally been the best and happiest of men. The tree is known by its fruits. In rebutting the charge of gloominess, then, we appeal to palpable testimony. The power and character of principles are especially manifested in circumstances of fierce opposition and severe trial. In such circumstances were the early Christians placed, men who were of one heart and of one soul in reference to the doctrines of redemption, and to them we appeal for evidence of their power to elevate man above his depraved condition, and to assimilate him to the holiness and happiness of heaven. They gladly receive the word — the word about the person and work of Him who had suffered and died the Just One in the room of the unjust — they continued daily with one accord in the temple, and did eat their meat with gladness and singleness of heart; they departed from the councils, whither they had been summoned, rejoicing that they were counted worthy to suffer for Christ; in the prisons into which they had been cast, they prayed at midnight and sung praises to the God of heaven; and, of the generality of primitive believers, Peter could say, when speaking of their Lord, "whom having not seen ye love; in whom, though now ye see him not, yet believing, ye rejoice with joy unspeakable and full of glory." Paul was no dreaming visionary, no weak enthusiast, but a man of towering intellect and acute powers of reasoning, and yet who ever grasped these doctrines more firmly; and what a well of joy sprung up within him under their influence! "I would to God," said he to king Agrippa, "that not only thou, but also all that hear me this day, were both almost, and altogether, *such as I am*, except these bonds."

There have been, and may be, many melancholy Christians, but, passing over the fact that all the melancholy in the world is not to be found within the pale of the church, it requires little philosophy to perceive that that melancholy is no part of their Christianity. It may be resolved into a natural gloomy temperament, into weak faith, into partial views of divine truth, or into a want of devotedness in the life; but the Scripture says, and the cross says, "It is not in me." Solemnity is not to be confounded with gloom; seriousness and joy are quite compatible. Hume, sporting on his death-bed, was liker a fool than a philosopher. The world in which we dwell is fitted to make men grave and thoughtful. But, it may be unhesitatingly affirmed, that the believers in the atonement are not less sensible to the grand and beautiful in nature, and not less capable of appropriating to themselves the good that is to be found in the world, than any other class of men. Yea, we go beyond this, in asserting that the truth as it is in Jesus is better fitted than any other to expand every intellectual power and to purify and strengthen every moral feeling, and that, in the view of the mind in whom it dwells, creation is the more radiant and lovely, and God, even our own God, "sits enthroned on the riches of the universe." The recorded experience of Jonathan Edwards has, in some degree, been the experience of many, who, being originally endowed with susceptibilities to receive impressions from external nature, have had the eyes of their understanding enlightened at the foot of the cross. But we appeal specially to it as an illustration of a mind, second to none in acuteness and vigor, holding with a strong faith the doctrines of redemption in what some men count all their repulsiveness, and yet sunning himself, as it were, amid the light and beauty of God's world. "The appearance of everything," says he, in speaking of the influence produced on his mind by the clearer views which he had obtained of the work of Christ, "the appearance of everything was altered; there seemed to be, as it were, a calm, sweet cast, or appearance of divine glory, in almost everything. God's excellency, his wisdom, his purity and love, seemed to appear in everything; in the sun, moon and stars, in the clouds and blue sky; in the grass, flowers and trees; in the water and all nature; which used greatly to fix my mind. I often used to sit and view the moon for a long time, and in the day spent much time in viewing the clouds and sky, to behold the sweet glory of God in these things: in the meantime singing forth, with a low voice, my contemplations of the Creator and Redeemer."

"He looks abroad into the varied field
Of nature, and, though poor, perhaps, compared
With those whose mansions glitter in his sight,
Calls the delightful scenery all his own.
His are the mountains, and the valleys his,
And the resplendent rivers. His to enjoy
With a propriety that none can feel,
But who, with filial confidence inspired,
Can lift to heaven an unpresumptuous eye,
And smiling say — My Father made them all!"

# CHAPTER V.

## THE DENIAL OF MAN'S RESPONSIBILITY, OR INDIFFERENTISM.

A diluted kind of skepticism — Not necessarily implying open hostility to the generally-received body of truth — A weakened sense of responsibility, or an actual denial of it, lies at the bottom of indifferentism — Indifferentism on the Continent — Remarks of Dr. Krummacher — Continental Churches — Characterizes much of our own literature — Man's responsibility for his dispositions, opinions and conduct maintained; — A matter of consciousness — Rests on the fact of man's free agency — Measured by ability and privilege — Remains indestructible amid all objections from original temperament and external influences — Phrenology — Case of Alexander the Sixth — Men individually, and societies in general, advance morally in proportion as the sense of responsibility is high.

IN this case, no hostile attitude to the generally-received body of truth may be taken. The doctrines respecting the Divine existence, personality, providential government and the Bible redemption, may theoretically be admitted, but there is a want of stern fidelity to these doctrines. The truth is not, like a fortress, stoutly assailed and bravely defended. But it happens, either that those who are without pass by and turn toward it a look of indifference; or that some of its professed guardians would shake hands alike with friends and foes, persuade them that their variance is a mere trifle, and receive the one as well as the other within the citadel. The man does not go forth before us fully equipped and boldly defying the armies of the living God, but he shouts for a truce, alleges that mere matters of opinion are not worth contending for, and that a man is no more responsible for his belief than he is for the color of his skin or the height of his stature. This diluted kind of skepticism is large in its toleration. Not attaching much importance to any kind of religious belief, it is indulgent toward all. It cares not to assail by argument, or otherwise, this creed or that; and it cares as little about defending what it may have adopted as its own. It says, Leave me alone to the indulgence of my opinion, and I will leave you to the indulgence of yours. Different forms of religious belief are much the same, in its estimation, as the different shaped or different colored coats which men wear. And it is disposed to think that the one sits with as little responsibility on the conscience as the other does on the back. It will stand up resolutely for a political creed, and unsparingly denounce its opposite; it will have its favorite theory in science, and argue keenly for it against every other; it will be engrossed with its land or merchandise, and suffer nothing to interfere with the most intense devotion thereto. But it has no zeal to spend on religious opinions, it has no article in theology so dear as to muster up an argument in its defense, and it will suffer itself to be engrossed with anything or everything rather than with the system of truth which it professes to believe. It is indifferent itself toward religion, and it cares little what quiet shape it may assume in others. Gibbon, speaking of the paganism of ancient Rome, says, "The various modes of worship which prevailed in the Roman world were all considered by the people as equally true, by the philosopher as equally false, and by the magistrate as equally useful." The comment of some one is, "After eighteen centuries of the Gospel, we seem unhappily to be coming back to the same point."

A very weakened sense of responsibility, or an actual denial of it, lies at the bottom of that indifferentism which is so extensively prevalent in the present age. On the Continent, especially in Germany and France, not only are opinions destructive of the sense of responsibility widely diffused among the masses, but in the case of vast multitudes, who would not wish to be counted the foes of

Christianity, there is an utter absence of anything like the religious obligation of belief. This state of matters — the showing a kind of civil deference to religion while utterly heedless of the obligation which rests upon the individual conscience in reference to religion itself — exists among all classes from the higher ranges to the low levels of society. "We find especially," says Dr. Krummacher, speaking of Germany, "an indifference to all that is called religion in that mass of people with whom care and anxiety for daily bread exists. In this so-called *proletariat*, particularly in large towns, this indifference often borders on animal stupidity; the material wants fill the whole soul. . . . The number of the indifferent are, however, unhappily not less in the circles of the well-instructed, and particularly among State functionaries. Besides that time which is necessary for the fulfillment of their official duties, they have but barely sufficient left for the more trivial dissipations which they find in literary and political lectures, and in social intercourse. In regard to all higher interests, Pilate's question reigns — 'What is truth?' They believe that they are able to infer from the religious controversy, by which they are on all sides surrounded, that in the region of supernatural things nothing certain is to be learned. They therefore consider it wiser not to enter upon their consideration, and passively to await what is once to be revealed as truth or as a lovely dream."[1] This picture is too true a description of other parts of Europe besides Germany. It is obvious that such a state of things can only consist with an avowed rejection or with the very faintest recognition of the principle that man is responsible for his religious belief.

Indifferentism as to the real import of evangelical truth — the result, it may be, of an indiscriminate recognition

[1] The Religious Condition of Christendom (1852), p. 423.

of widely-differing churches by the political powers—is sadly prevalent in some of the continental religious bodies at the present day. It is no uncommon thing, to find men of all shades of opinion, from simple deism up to the dry skeleton of an orthodox creed, blended together as parts of the same professedly Christian church. Recent events have shown an unwillingness, on the part of the ecclesiastical authorities to moot the subject of a confession grounded in its details on the law and the testimony, and to insist on a personal adherence to the articles of evangelism as an indispensable condition of membership The liking of some of the continental Protestant churches for a coat of many colors, has long been evinced; and the same ecclesiastical robe is made to cover the man whose Christianity consists merely in a bare recognition of the New Testament and a respect for Jesus as a better moral teacher than Socrates, and the man who professedly holds the divinity of Christ, the atonement and the regenerating influence of the Spirit. This state of things indicates an enfeebled sense of responsibility, or the existence, somewhere, of the notion that religious belief is not a matter of personal obligation for which we are accountable to God. It was against such indifferentism that Arndt, Spener, Bengel, Franke, and others, lifted up their voice in the two preceding centuries. And on the side of a spiritual Christianity, of a sound doctrinal faith, and man's responsibility for the same, have their illustrious successors, Tholuck, Hengstenberg, Müller, Neander, D'Aubigné, Monod, and others, fought valiantly in our own times.

This vague sort of infidelity, sometimes associated with a professed respect for Christ and the Scriptures, and, at other times allied with unbelief in some of its bolder forms, is often to be met with in the workshops, and in the higher circles of our own land. It has not lacked advocacy on the part of some whose position and talents give them influence. It is stated or implied, in much of our current popular literature, that a man's creed does not depend upon himself. This dogma pervades the writings of Mr. Emerson.[1] Napoleon, one of his "representative men," of whom he tells "horrible anecdotes," must not, in his view, "be set down as cruel; but only as one who knew no impediment to his will." He depicts him as an "exorbitant egotist, who narrowed, impoverished, and absorbed the power and existence of those who served him;" and concludes by saying, "it was not Bonaparte's fault." He thus condemns and acquits in the same breath, sends forth from the same fountain sweet water and bitter. Mr. Theodore Parker makes each form of religion that has figured in the history of the world, "natural and indispensable." "It could not have been but as it was." And, therefore, he finds truth, or the "absolute religion," in all forms; "all tending toward one great and beautiful end."[2] Of course, the idea of the religious obligation of belief resting upon the individual conscience, is here quite out of question. Mr. F. W. Newman, who is so fond of parting off things that most men connect together, would persuade us that there may be a true faith without a true belief, as if the emotional part of our nature was independent of the intellectual. "Belief," says he, "is one thing, and faith another." And he complains of those who, on religious grounds, are alienated from him because he has adopted "intellectual conclusions" different from theirs—"the difference between them and him" turning merely "on questions of learning, history, criticism, and abstract thought."[3] The philosophy is as bad here as the theology. In the view of common sense and Scripture, a living faith is as the doctrine believed. But Mr. Newman,

[1] Emerson's Representative Men, pp. 144, 127.

[2] Parker's Discourse, p. 81.

[3] Phases of Faith, Preface.

in common with Mr. Parker and others, can lay down his offensive weapons when he wills, and take up a position on the low ground of indifference as to religious belief. *Then*, creeds become matters of mere moonshine, and responsibility is regarded as a fiction invented by priests. This is part of the bad theology of Mr. Bailey's "Festus," as we formerly noticed. The hero of the poem is made to say:

> "Yet merit or demerit none I see
> In nature, human or material,
> In passions or affections good or bad:
> We only know that God's best purposes
> Are oftenest brought about by dreadest sins.
> Is thunder evil, or is dew divine?
> Does virtue lie in sunshine, sin in storm?
> Is not each natural, each needful, best?"[1]

And, to come down to the lower levels of our literature, it is an avowed principle of the Owen or Holyoake school, that a man who does wrong is not to be blamed but pitied; and, if restraint be necessary, he must be restrained like a wild bull, merely that society may be uninjured. Man is thus degraded, in the attempt to set him free from the Divine moral government. And these philosophers are every day acting an absurdity, in speaking of "wrong" or "bad" actions; since, in their view, men cannot help performing them, and these actions are but parts of one harmonious whole.

But, to rise up in the scale, a greater name than any yet mentioned has, in an "inaugural discourse," lent his authority to the pernicious doctrine of non-responsibility for belief. Many of our ingenuous academic youth were startled, some years ago, on hearing it given forth, with something like oracular authority, from the halls of science, as a great truth, that man has no control over his belief,

[1] Bailey's Festus, p. 49.

that he is no more responsible for his opinions than he is for his color or his height, and that an infidel or an atheist is to be pitied but not blamed. This, we are persuaded, is a piece of flimsy sophistry, which no man durst utter, and which would not be listened to for a moment in connection with any other subject but that of religion. It would be condemned in the senate and at the bar, it would be drowned in the tumult of the exchange and the market-place. Common sense, and a regard to worldly interests, would rise up and hoot down the traitor. Unfortunately, however, in the province of religion, the natural indisposition of the mind to things unseen and spiritual, allies itself with the pleadings of the sophist, and receives his doctrine of irresponsibility with something like flattering unction. Nothing more than this is requisite to undermine the foundation of all religious belief and morals, to let open the floodgates of immorality, and to make the restraints of religion like the brittle flax or the yielding sand. In opposition to such latitudinarianism, we maintain that man is responsible for the dispositions which he cherishes, for the opinions which he holds and avows, and for his habitual conduct. This is going the whole length of Scripture, but no farther, which affirms that every one of us must give an account of himself unto God. And this meets with a response from amid the elements of man's moral nature, which sets its seal that the thing is true.

1. Our first remark, then, on this subject, is, that *responsibility is a matter of consciousness.* A sense of moral responsibility naturally springs up in the mind of man. It does not depend upon processes of reasoning, nor does it arise originally out of the truths of revelation. But it is itself a fundamental truth in moral science, a primary principle of our mental and moral constitution. Like the doctrine in physics of the existence of a material world, or that in

metaphysics of the free agency of man, it is not to be brought to the bar of reason, but it is a simple question of fact to be determined by observation and experience. Revelation takes it for granted, and reasons and exhorts upon it. And we often find it healthy and vigorous in men whose reasoning powers are feeble and little exercised. Every man knows and feels that he is a moral agent, that he is placed under a system of government which takes cognizance of right and wrong, and that he is accountable for his dispositions and conduct to his fellows here, and to the Supreme Being hereafter. We may be told that travelers have described savage nations so degraded and brutalized, as to have no such consciousness as that of which we speak. We may be pointed to individuals living and moving amid civilized society, so besotted and sunken in vice as apparently never to be disturbed with the idea that they are the subjects of invisible government and accountable to God. Yea, we may be directed to those few philosophers who stood out from the crowd in persuading themselves, and in endeavoring to persuade others, that the notion of moral responsibility is a mere chimera invented by priests and fanatics for frightening and enslaving men. And we may be asked, how, in the face of all these exceptions, we can maintain that the consciousness of responsibility belongs to all mankind. Why, suppose that a man with a jaundiced eye were to hold that the fleecy clouds which float over the face of the sky, or the pure snow that covers the sides of the hills, or the white paper on which he looks, were yellow. What would that prove? Not that these objects, which everybody else believed to be white, were of a different color; not that men's eyes were organs which in general conveyed false impressions, but that the eyes of the individual himself were diseased. We would never think of going among savage nations which have become brutalized by a long course of sensuality and ferocity; we would never appeal to this individual or that individual, who, by vicious indulgences, has sunk himself below the level of the brutes; nor would we sit at the feet of skeptical philosophers, in order to obtain any very strong proofs of the universality and force of those moral convictions which we assert to be fundamental principles in man's nature. But we would make our appeal to minds where conscience sits invested with some authority, and where she is listened to with some degree of deference; where the moral sense, so to speak, is not drowned in sensuality, nor bewildered and led astray by a false philosophy; and, in such minds, we would find that the consciousness of moral responsibility springs up naturally and is strong. We are not disposed, however, to exclude these exceptions, as they are called, altogether. We might appeal to these very savage tribes, and amid their brutal degradation, and in their cruel and superstitious rites, discover the rudimental principles of man's moral nature. We might follow the man whose conscience seemed seared, and whose heart seemed reprobate, whose perceptions of right and wrong were severely blunted, and who appeared never to be troubled with the idea of responsibility — we might follow him into his retirement, and, in his hours of calm reflection, we would see conscience asserting her supremacy and avenging her wrongs, the banished idea of responsibility returning in its vividness, and the dread of a Supreme and Omniscient Being forcing itself upon the soul. We might appeal to the sophist himself, and, notwithstanding all the refinements of his false philosophy, we would see that at times he could no more divest himself of his moral nature, than he could of his belief in matter and a material world, when he walked the streets, jostled the crowd, or came in contact with the pillars that stood by the way. Men are responsible, they know it and feel it, and it is only by a long-continued process of vicious indulgences, or by the refinement of an unreasonable philosophy, that their sense of accountability is deadened or subdued.

Now we affirm that men are responsible for the dispositions which they cherish, and that this is a matter of consciousness. Look at that man who is ever and anon hurried into scrapes and calamities by a proud, ambitious, and hateful temper. And you will see that, when the storm of passion is passed and reflection has succeeded to fury, the individual blames himself, and suffers keenly in his own bosom. His own unsophisticated mind never tells him that over his temper he had no control, that it was as purely the result of physical causes as the swollen river that chafes and fomes in its bed, or as the ebbings and flowings of the sea. No. The consciousness of responsibility rises naturally on his bosom, and, under its influence, he bewails his folly and condemns himself. We affirm, too, that men are responsible for their opinions, and that this also is a matter of consciousness. Men's opinions are generally very much influenced by their dispositions, their belief on most subjects is in a great measure controlled by their inclination. And of this every man is conscious. We feel that we cannot believe otherwise than that two and two make four. And were an individual, without jesting, stoutly to maintain that two and two make five, we would set him down for an idiot, and pity — not blame — him for the aberrations of his understanding. But we know that we may, if we will, reject or receive this and the other moral truth; and we not merely pity, but blame the man, who, in spite of the strongest and clearest evidence, refuses to believe. Now, it may be asked, How is this fact to be accounted for — a fact in the natural history

15

of man — that men feel they can embrace or reject this opinion or that opinion if they will, and that they commend or condemn others for embracing or rejecting it, except on the principle that God has made man a moral and responsible agent, and that man himself is conscious of it? "His creed may be his crime; and surely none ought to see this more clearly than the writers who deny it; for why their eternal invectives against 'dogmas,' — and especially the tolerably universal dogma that men are responsible for the formation of their opinions,— except upon the supposition that men *are* responsible for framing and maintaining them? If they are not, men should be left alone; if they are, they are to be thought of as 'worse and better' for their 'intellectual creeds.'"[1] We affirm, too, that men are responsible for their conduct in general, and that this also is a matter of consciousness. Our conduct is very much the result of our dispositions and opinions. So that, if it be admitted that we are responsible for the one, it must be admitted that we are responsible for the other. But it is not so much with the philosophy of the fact, as with the fact itself, that we have at present to do. There is the feeling of remorse bearing witness to this truth. "Remorse," says Isaac Taylor,[2] "is man's dread prerogative, and is the natural accompaniment of his constitution as a knowing, voluntary agent, left in trust with his own welfare and that of others. Remorse, if we exclude the notion of responsibility, is an enigma in human nature, never to be explained."

It will not do to say, as has been said, that these feelings are altogether factitious, that they have been instilled into our minds by our fond mothers who have spoiled us, or by the ministers of religion who, from policy or self-interest, would frighten us; and that, but for such artificial

[1] The Eclipse of Faith, p. 115.

[2] Man Responsible, p. 25.

training, the spendthrift, the sensualist, and the criminal, would never shrink from the fear of a present God, and the anticipation of a future reckoning. For, besides remarking with the author of the "Natural History of Enthusiasm," that, "nothing can be more unphilosophical than to attribute any permanent and universally diffused modes of feeling to the influence and interested teaching of some one class of the community"— we ask, How comes it that men who never crossed the threshold of the sanctuary, and never sat at the feet of the teachers of religion, who have despised a good mother's counsels, and whose lives have run contrary to the parental example — how comes it that they, in their calm moments of reflection, cannot divest themselves of the unwelcome idea of responsibility, of an invisible Power, and of a coming account? It is a fact, then, in the natural history of man, not to be proved by reasoning, but to be decided simply by observation, that the consciousness of responsibility attaches to him. Independent of all external teaching, the conviction is naturally produced in his mind that he has, in a great measure, a control over his opinions and conduct, and that for these he is accountable here and hereafter. And it is only when he has unmanned himself, as it were, by vicious indulgences, or been led astray by a corrupt philosophy, that he becomes dead to the feeling that he is the subject of moral government and responsibility to God.

2. Our second remark is, that *Responsibility rests on the fact of man's free agency.* The ground has been denied. But what has not? We appeal to every man's conscience and unsophisticated sense in proof of it. "It moves for all that," said Galileo, after signing his memorable recantation. And endeavor to persuade men as you will that they are driven on by irresistible physical causes, they declare, in spite of all your reasonings, We are free after all. Now, it

is obvious, on the slightest reflection that our will, and our will only, is the proper object of command; and that we are no otherwise responsible or susceptible of moral government, than as we are the subjects of moral powers. Man is accountable because he is a free agent. And the dispositions which he habitually cherishes, the opinions which he holds, and the conduct which he pursues, are, in a great measure, under his control, and as he wills them to be. The distinction between moral and natural inability is a sound and useful one. Moral inability lies in the want of disposition, inclination, or will, to do that which a man has natural faculties to perform. Natural inability, on the other hand, arises from the want of natural faculties and means to do that which the individual, it may be, would very gladly do. This distinction is before us, when we notice that man is responsible for his dispositions, his belief, and his conduct, in so far as they are the result of his own free agency.

Man is responsible for his dispositions, because the Creator has endowed him with faculties in the right exercise of which he can bring them under his control. We make all reasonable allowances for original temperament, or peculiarities in the organic structure of individuals. These, however, are not altogether beyond the reach of moral culture. On the contrary, it is a chief business in education to study these peculiarities, to bring proper motives to bear upon them, and thus, in some measure, gain a mastery over the original temperament. In asserting that man can, to a considerable extent make himself master of his dispositions, and that for their state he is responsible, we do not mean to say that he can, at any given moment, by a direct volition of his mind, call forth this emotion or that emotion, this kind of temper or that kind of temper. But what we mean to say is, that he can, at his will, attend to those truths, or come in contact with those objects, the natural influence of which is to excite certain emotions, and produce such a disposition of the mind and heart. Take an example in illustration of this principle. Benevolence toward the suffering poor is an excellent disposition of the soul. I may not be able by a direct effort of the mind, to call up this emotion at any time or in any place. But I can, if I will, listen to the honest tale of distress which the virtuous poor have to tell; I can, if I will, visit the fatherless and widows in their afflictions. And thus, by a voluntary exercise of my own power, place myself in circumstances that will excite or strengthen compassion and benevolence toward the wretched. The frequent repetition of this voluntary process of attending to and impartially examining scenes of distress, results in the production of the man of feeling and of a benevolent disposition. Whereas, in the case of a man who meets every suppliant with a surly look, and refuses to listen to the tale of the stranger, who, like the Levite in the parable, coldly and unconcernedly passes by the sufferer on the wayside; that callous and unfeeling disposition is forming which is not only proof against compassion, but which even delights in producing scenes of woe

It is just in like manner with the devout emotions. One man moves day after day amid the glories of earth and sky, without a pious sentiment or feeling toward Him who stretched out the heavens like a curtain and clothed the grass of the field, because he does not attend to them as manifestations of the wisdom and goodness of God. Another individual, of no greater strength of intellect, it may be, directs his attention to these evidences of the character and presence of the Divinity, habitually meditates on them, and feels that —

> "These declare
> God's goodness beyond thought, and power divine."

In these and similar cases, men are responsible for the moral state of the heart, because they have the power of attending to those truths and objects which are fitted to produce such impressions on the soul. We say to the ferocious man, to the avaricious man, to the sensualist, and the revengeful, and to the man all whose mental tendencies are away from the absolute good, that for these dispositions you are responsible, because you voluntarily sought and familiarized your minds with those objects and scenes that produced and strengthened them, and turned away from those other objects and scenes that would have counteracted them, and produced dispositions of a different and nobler kind. It is thus that a man is brought in responsible for those ungodly emotions and dispositions, which, having grown with his growth, and strengthened with his strength, have carried him captive, and hold him in fetters which nothing but a mighty spiritual influence can rend asunder.

It is on the very same principle, that we hold man to be responsible for his belief. Our opinions, in so far as they are influenced by our dispositions, our beliefs in so far as they are controlled by our inclination, are legitimate subjects of responsibility. Inclination has nothing whatever to do in believing that two and two make four, or that the three angles of a triangle are equal to two right angles. A man in his senses could not believe otherwise. But inclination has much to do in receiving or rejecting moral and religious truth. All enlightened belief depends upon evidence, the effect of the clearest and strongest evidence depends very much on attention, and attention is a mental exercise over which we have a complete control. This being the case, it is very obvious that a man may contract deep moral guilt, by neglecting to attend to evidence in support of a subject of intrinsic magnitude and bearing on man's highest interests. The case of the Jewish people is in point. When Jesus of Nazareth appeared among them, He claimed to be the Son of God and the Messiah of promise. In support of these claims, He openly wrought miracles of surpassing grandeur and benevolence. He did not call on them to believe on the ground of his own bare assertions, but He pointed them to his mighty deeds in proof that He had come from God. He said, If ye believe not me, believe the works. Now, we do not assert that the Jews were under a moral obligation to believe at the very first that Jesus was the Messiah, but we do assert that they were morally bound to attend to that clear and strong evidence, to weigh it fairly, and to let it have its full influence on their minds. Those of them that did so, hailed Him as the deliverer and consolation of Israel; while the vast majority of them, because his doctrines thwarted their fondest wishes and frowned on their groveling expectations, ridiculed his pretensions, ascribed his works to Satanic agency, and treated Him as the vilest of impostors. That inclination had much to do with this, is evident from the fact that the multitudes, at his first appearing, would, on the ground of his miraculous deed, have made Him their king; and it was not till they saw his designs to be running counter to their wishes, that they rejected Him and cried out, "Crucify him." It was in their refusal honestly and impartially to attend to that evidence, that the Israelitish nation incurred deep moral guilt in the sight of heaven.

A messenger from majesty arrives in the condemned cell of some gaol, and presents the doomed criminal with a document containing a full and free pardon, to which is affixed the royal seal. He is skeptical at first as to the truth of the document. But he carefully examines the seal. He is convinced that it is the sovereign's, and on that evidence he joyfully and gratefully receives the pardon.

The Bible is such a document. It claims to be divine. It contains important statements on subjects of vast magnitude. It presents itself to our notice under the highest of all authority. It declares that on its reception or rejection depend our greatest interests in time and eternity. And, in support of all these claims and assertions, it exhibits an amount of evidence which, for weight and clearness, can be produced by no other book in the world. It says, Attend to that evidence, look at it fairly and impartially. And it dreads not the consequence. We do not say that a man is morally bound to believe the volume, on the naked assertion that it is divine. But we do say that he is responsible for whatever opinions he forms in reference to it, be these opinions friendly or hostile. He can, by a voluntary effort, examine the evidence; he can search the book, he can look at the seals, he can question the witnesses. This he can do, and must do honestly. And, in this intellectual process over which he has a direct control, in this effort of the attention which he has at his will, lies his responsibility for his belief. The very fact that the book, irrespective altogether of its truthfulness, claims to have come from the throne of the Eternal, the very fact that the subjects of which it treats are of vast moment, the very fact that it presents such a brilliant array of evidence in proof of its divinity,—these place all men, among whom it comes, under a moral obligation to attend to it, and, in the face of the evidence, impartially to form their opinions regarding it. One man may refuse to do this, because his mind is habitually so listless and indifferent as never to care about having any settled opinions on such subjects. Another man may be so profligate and sensual as, like the beast in his lair, to be unwilling to be disturbed by the approach of the light. While another man, from pride of intellect, or station, or self-sufficiency, may never bend his mind humbly and fairly to consider whether or not the Gospel is the truth of God. Hume, the celebrated infidel, tells us that his readings in the New Testament were but scanty. Voltaire and Paine betrayed gross ignorance of the Christian system which they thought to banish from the world. But whatever be the specific moral cause that keeps men from attending to the Gospel testimony, or induces them to examine it in a frivolous and prejudicial manner, it is in the attention, over which they have a direct control, that lies their responsibility for their belief.

This point being established in reference to dispositions and opinions, nothing need be added to show that the principle holds good in reference to actions. Our conduct, as already said, is very much the result of our opinions and dispositions. I cherish such dispositions and form such opinions in reference to my neighbor and the Supreme Being, and I act accordingly. If I have a control over my dispositions and opinions, and am responsible for them, I have a control over and am responsible for the actions that proceed from them. This is never questioned in the sphere of worldly concerns. It is only when you venture within the sphere of religion that skepticism is thrown over it. Some men who talk and act rationally enough in their ordinary intercourse with the world, would doff that rationality and play the fool, when they touch upon man's relation to things unseen and eternal. They assail and condemn men of a different political creed from their own for the opinions which they advocate, and the thought never occurs to them that it is folly so to do, because over their belief they have no control. But no sooner does the politician become a moral teacher, than (as in a well-known instance, not, we trust, to be repeated) he announces it as a great truth which has gone out through all the earth, that man has no control over his belief, and that an atheist is to be pitied but not blamed. True philosophy and man's unsophisticated nature, common sense and revealed religion, tell us that we have such a control, and that for our sentiments and conduct we are responsible to God.

3. Our third remark is, that *responsibility is to be measured by ability and privilege.* Responsibility springs, as we have seen, from the structure of the human mind as endowed with faculties, in the exercise of which man can direct his thoughts to a given subject, compare all the facts and considerations bearing upon it, and thus arrive at an honest and impartial decision regarding it. But the measure of responsibility, in the case of particular communities or individuals, is to be estimated by such things as the following: the capacity of their understanding, the means and opportunities of information, and the force of evidence. The poor, harmless idiot, who fancies himself a king, and declares the reigning monarch a usurper; who talks day after day of raising armies, and marching on to London to take possession of the crown; is never accounted a traitor, tried and condemned as such. The man whose intellect is naturally so imbecile as scarcely to comprehend the ideas of a God, of his own moral relations, and of a future life, occupies a vastly lower position in point of responsibility (if he occupies any position on that ground at all), than the man whose intellect is naturally sound and vigorous, but who, in reference to moral and religious truth, is a child in understanding.

It is, in like manner, with the means and opportunities of information. No one would ever say that the Bechuana of the desert, who had lived like his forefathers, remote from civilization, who had never seen the face of a missionary, nor heard a word about the Savior of mankind, is responsible in the same degree as a Briton living in this land of light and liberty, where knowledge runs to and fro and is increased.

Responsibility takes its measure, not only from the capacity of the understanding, and the means and opportunities of information, but also from the force of evidence. This is strikingly illustrated by Paul in the first two chapters of his epistle to the Romans, and the inspired illustration accords with uninspired testimonies and man's moral sentiments. Look abroad, then, upon the ancient heathen world, upon the seats of intellectual refinement, Egypt, Greece and Rome. And what do we witness? Men professing themselves to be wise,—claiming to be philosophers,—worshiping images in the shape of men and birds and beasts and creeping things; debasing and dishonoring God, and debasing and dishonoring themselves. But some will say, They were not responsible for this; over their dispositions, their opinions and their conduct in this matter, they had no control. They were to be pitied, not blamed; no more to be blamed than for the color of their skin or the height of their stature. Yes, says Paul, they were to be blamed; they were responsible in this matter, they were guilty in cherishing these vile affections, in holding these erroneous opinions, and in manifesting such degrading conduct. They had evidence which, if they had duly attended to it, would have led them to feel, to think and to act differently. There was a sufficiency of evidence in the works of creation, in the shining heavens above them, and in the fruitful earth around them, to have convinced them that one almighty and all-perfect Being had made and presides over the whole. It is not the want of evidence, but the want of relish for the truth about the Creator, that accounts for their idolatrous opinions and practices. "For the invisible things of him from the creation of the world are clearly seen, being understood by the things that are made, even his eternal power and godhead; so that they are without excuse."[1]

The heathen, then, were responsible; and that responsibility took its measure from the means of information, and the force of evidence which they possessed. But the measure of our responsibility is vastly greater than theirs. We walk amid a clearer light than what is emitted from these resplendent heavens, we hear louder, fuller and more impressive voices than any which proceed from the hills and the valleys, the woods and the waters. The revelation which has come to us direct from the throne of the Eternal, containing, as it does, ample information on subjects of supreme importance,— information which none of the wisest of the heathen could have evoked from the material heavens and earth,—this places us on a ground of responsibility higher far than that occupied by the most gifted sage of the Grecian schools, who had no other light but the glimmering light of nature. This is what the apostle means when he says, "As many as have sinned without law (that is, without a special revelation of the divine will), shall also be condemned without law (or by a different standard); and as many as have sinned in the law shall be judged by the law."[2] All who, without a divine revelation, have erred from the truth and done wrong, will be condemned by the evidence afforded by the light of nature; and all who have sinned under the revelation of God's will shall be judged by that revelation. Reason and Scripture thus unite their testimonies in establishing the position that responsibility is in proportion to the means of information and the weight and clearness of evidence.

An individual may be very unwilling to avail himself of these means, and to look calmly and impartially at that evidence; but this indifference only adds to his guilt, and

[1] Romans i, 20. [2] Ibid. ii, 12.

does not, in the least, lessen the measure of his responsibility. Responsibility takes its measure not from an individual's inclination, but from an individual's capacity of understanding, his opportunity of arriving at the truth, and the sufficiency of evidence which he enjoys. Were an individual to hold that responsibility takes its measure from the inclination, or what is called moral ability, he would be landed in the very strange position that a man is under an obligation only to do that which he is inclined to do. In other words, he would tear up responsibility, root and fiber, and cast it to the winds. Suppose that, in reference to some disturbed district, a royal proclamation were issued forbidding the inhabitants, under severe penalties, to go abroad after sunset. The proclamation is read aloud at the market-cross, it is posted up on the church doors and all other places of public resort. None who wished to become acquainted with the purport of the royal decree could remain ignorant of it. But some individuals who gave no heed to royal proclamations, and would not trouble themselves to ascertain the meaning of this particular one, venture abroad in the time prohibited, are captured, charged with breaking the law, and put upon their trial. Would any judge, knowing the capacity of the men, and the means of knowledge within their reach, listen for a moment to the plea, We never heard the proclamation, and were utterly ignorant of the law in this matter. No. The judge would say, You are persons who can read and understand; this proclamation was published in your streets, and placarded in the most frequented places; you were indisposed to become acquainted with it, you are responsible for the consequences, and must endure the stated penalty. Now, it is on this principle, we hold, that men, having available means of coming to the knowledge of the truth, and yet indisposed to avail themselves of them; having the Bible within their reach, and yet refusing to read it; having the Gospel at the very threshold of their doors, and yet unwilling to come out and hear it — it is on this principle, we maintain, that their responsibility is little less than if they knew that Bible, and understood the truths of that Gospel. A man may say, I did not know that the Book prohibited such a course of conduct, and threatened such penalties against those who pursued it. I did not know that it prescribed such a path to be followed, and promised such blessings to those who entered upon and prosecuted it. There would be force in such a plea coming from an individual so situated as that it was physically impossible for him to have access to the divine record, to read and understand it. But the answer to an individual having access to ample means, and urging such a plea, would be: You had the volume near you and could have read it, you had the Gospel within hearing and could have listened to it, you were indisposed to come to the knowledge of the truth, sin lies at your own door, your responsibility is to be measured not by your inclination but by your privileges. "Unto whomsoever much is given, of the same much shall be required."

4. Our fourth remark is, that *responsibility remains indestructible amid all objections from original temperament and external influences.* It is not necessary that we here pronounce any judgment on the claims of phrenology to be regarded as a system of intellectual philosophy. We would only say, that as long as any of the results of comparative anatomy disagree with it, and physiologists of the first rank can urge some strong objections against it, so long must we regard it as far from being a fixed and settled science. But assuming that the physiological facts upon which it is grounded are correct, that the feelings or faculties of the mind are in proportion to and determined by the protuber-

ances in the cranium, human liberty and accountability are not, as some have alleged, affected thereby. Mr. George Combe, who advances such high claims for the science, obviously thought it consistent with responsibility, when he says, "To the animal nature of man have been added, by a bountiful Creator, moral sentiments and reflecting faculties, which not only place him above all other creatures on earth, but constitute him a different being from any of them, a rational and accountable being."[1] But some men, with the phrenological map of the human skull before them, and knowing it to be a fundamental principle of the science that mental dispositions are determined by the form, size and constitution of the brain, leap at once to the conclusion that an individual's character is made for him, not by him, and that for it he is not responsible. It were vain to deny an original difference of temperament and organization in different individuals, or to underrate the difficulties arising thence in reference to man's moral agency, but the admission of these can be made while firmly holding the doctrine of responsibility. *That* is a matter of consciousness, a fact in the natural history of man, of which it were needless to seek any further explanation, and it consequently must harmonize with all the other facts and principles of the human constitution. But this is not all. Some men have originally, it is admitted, powerful tendencies to certain vicious dispositions and practices. Such propensities may be said to ally them to the brutal tribes; and, were they not possessed of a higher order of faculties, they would stand on the same level of irresponsibility. But man is distinguished from the lower animals by the possession of faculties, and a susceptibility of motives, of which they are destitute and incapable. These raise the worst of men above the level of the brutes, place them within the

[1] Constitution of Man, p. 2. (People's Edition.)

sphere of moral agency, and give them a power of counteracting or controlling an original bad temperament. We take an extreme case for illustration. It was said, by Spurzheim, of Alexander the Sixth, the most infamous man that ever sat on the Papal chair, that his "brain was no more adequate to the manifestation of Christian virtues, than the brain of an idiot from birth to the exhibition of the intellect of a Leibnitz or a Bacon."[1] Here were great difficulties arising from original temperament and organization; but these difficulties were not of the same kind, nor insuperable in the same manner, as the difficulties that beset the mind of the idiot. Alexander was endowed with mental faculties, and a susceptibility of moral motives, which gave him a power counteractive of the evil propensities, and rendered him, in some measure, the trustee of his own well-being, and responsible for his moral character. It may have been a vastly more difficult thing for such a man to manifest Christian virtues than it was for Philip Melancthon; but conscience must have been torn wholly out of his breast, and he must originally have been utterly incapable of moral sentiment, before he could have been divested of the character of a moral and responsible agent. The pontiff, though carried along in a vicious course by powerful depraved tendencies, was doubtless conscious of his moral freedom; and unless given up to a reprobate mind, must at times have had a sense of his responsibility. It is as natural for such men, amid all their depravity, to have a sense of desert, before the process of searing the conscience has been completed, and for others to hold them responsible for their dispositions and conduct, as it is for the idiot to be undisturbed by such a feeling, and to be accounted guiltless of the evil that may arise out of his actions.

[1] Combe's Constitution of Man, p. 42.

The remarks made in reference to organization are substantially applicable to external influences. Both may modify human responsibility, but neither of them destroys it. The temperament and situation of one man may be much more favorable for manifesting whatsoever things are lovely and true than the temperament and situation of another, but responsibility is an attribute of the character and circumstances of both. If there is power on the side of individual organization and outward influences, so that some men are less favorably situated in a moral point of view than others, there is power also in those energies supplied by the moral world which are counteractive of evil and productive of good, and which men are under an obligation to study and employ. They may refuse to acquaint themselves with these moral forces, or to avail themselves of them, and thus be carried away without a struggle on the current of depraved propensity or external vicious influences; but in that refusal lies their guilt, as in the availableness of the moral power lies their responsibility. It is an easy thing to muster up arguments against human liberty. Let the doctrine of the Divine prescience and foreördination of all things be asserted, and some men at once conclude that no room is left for man's moral freedom. The doctrine does not paralyze their energies in the workshop or in the field, and they never dream that it renders them irresponsible for the operations of their hands. And yet the objection is as tenable in the one case as in the other. In like manner, let the force of original temperament and external circumstances be admitted, and man, by some, is represented as helpless and destitute of moral freedom, as a raft carried irresistibly down the river on which it floats. It is not so easy, however, to destroy the argument grounded on the facts that man is possessed of faculties and susceptible of motives that give him, in some measure, a control over original temperament and external circumstances. Far less easy is it to destroy that consciousness of moral freedom which every man possesses, whatever be his mental conformation, and the influences that are brought to bear upon him. If, then, the sense of responsibility cannot be destroyed, without falsifying the testimony of all our primitive beliefs, it may be said to remain truly indestructible.

5. Our fifth remark is, that *men individually, and societies in general, advance morally in proportion as the sense of responsibility is high.* No one doubts the absolute necessity of a belief in this doctrine in the daily business of life. The dealings of the shop and the exchange could not be carried on without it. We would not intrust a servant with a letter, or admit a professed friend into the confidence and hospitalities of the domestic circle, if they avowed themselves to be irresponsible, and acted on the avowal. From the first minister of an empire who kisses the hand of majesty on receiving office, down to the private soldier who takes the oath of allegiance on entering the ranks, the necessity and reality of responsibility are acknowledged. And not only so, but it is just in proportion as the notion of responsibility in individuals, or in societies, assumes a decidedly religious aspect, that it is powerful for good. France, a country where experiments on human nature, on a large scale, have often been made, gave, at the close of the last century, a fearful illustration of what the social system becomes when it loses its hold of moral obligation. The philosophers and wits of the Voltaire school jestingly cried out, "What is truth?" declared the moral system to have been superseded, ridiculed the notion of responsibility as an antiquated fiction, taught that the only causes in the world are physical and irresistible, and that men are the offspring of an invincible necessity. It was

this doctrine of irresponsibility, propounded by the Encyclopædists, countenanced by statesmen, and propagated throughout the masses, that was expressed in the torrents of blood that flowed during the reign of terror. Men being looked upon as creatures of physical necessity, were no more accounted of than stumps of trees or ruined houses when they stood in the way of the revolutionary movement. They were leveled to the ground and torn up by the roots. The principle, laid down by Diderot, was acted upon,—a principle that rose out of the ruins of man's moral agency,—that those who encumbered the social system should summarily be destroyed. And what more is necessary to let loose the reins upon fury, corruption and massacre, than to instill into men's minds the notion that they are the creatures of fate, and no more responsible for their belief than for the color of their skin and the height of their stature!

It is very much with the doctrine of man's responsibility as it is with Sabbath observance. Public men in our country generally acknowledge the moral and physical advantages of the weekly day of rest, just as they recognize the utility and necessity of a sense of accountability being diffused throughout the state. But, as by far the most valuable benefits of the Sabbath result only from its religious observance as a day sacred to the memory of the resurrection of Christ; so the real and high advantages of responsibility are only experienced when the doctrine is felt to link earth with heaven, man with his Maker, and the judgment of conscience with the judgment of the great white throne. "This practical doctrine of responsibility," says Isaac Taylor,[1] "can rest on no fulcrum short of the center of the universe — the throne of God. Rest it at any intermediate point, and though it may bear *some* stress,

[1] Man Responsible, p. 63.

it will not bear every stress; and it fails where most it will be needed." Take an individual or a community, in which the sense of responsibility is weakened, or associated merely with worldly calculations; and take another individual or community, in which it is religious and vivid; and it will be found that while the one is unstable as water, the other is steadfast as a rock; that while the one is ever in danger of sacrificing principle to selfish gain, the other counts nothing dear that comes into competition with principle itself. It is the man deeply imbued with the religious sense of responsibility that stands firm amid all temptations, while another is driven with the wind and tossed; and it is in the former that even men, who have no vivid sense of religion themselves, prefer reposing confidence.

It will also be found that in societies professedly religious, where the dry skeleton of a creed remains,— but where men nominally adhering and others avowedly opposing are gathered under one ecclesiastical organization around it,— the doctrine of responsibility, in its high import, is either denied or fluctuating and feeble. Wherever religious belief comes to be regarded as an accident of the mind just as color is of the hair of the head, or wherever responsibility, though admitted, is languid,— doctrinal articles are counted as of little worth, the standards are either deserted, or friends and foes proclaim a truce, and shake hands around them; and the distinction between the church and the world,— a distinction so much insisted on in the New Testament,— disappears and is lost.

Individuals of the brightest moral excellence have been those who were influenced by a high and religious sense of responsibility. Men, to whose instrumentality the world owes its reformations, and the church its life and purity, would never have struggled as they did, and could never have effected the regenerations which they have effected, had they not had firm faith in the truth that we are responsible to our fellows here and to God hereafter. And those communities in which the truth shines conspicuous as a star, and who have faithfully guarded the church from the abomination of desolation, have been mightily influenced by the idea of their stewardship and the prospect of rendering an account. Is, then, a doctrine so influential for good both on individuals and societies, on churches and states; a doctrine that has been the guardian of so much that is true and holy, and the spring of so many grand and benignant enterprises; a doctrine that is beneficent in proportion as it is believed and acted upon,— is it to be regarded as a beautiful and useful fiction, necessary for the well-being of society, but having no foundation in truth? This were something like yielding to the tempter, and falling down and worshiping him. But it cannot be. It is written upon the heart—and nothing but a long process of vicious indulgence can cover or efface it; it is written upon the social system under which men live safely and happily; and it is written more legibly and impressively in the inspired page,—that every one of us must give an account of himself unto God. Happy the individual or the community, who moves under a felt sense that the Great Searcher of hearts is in the heavens and looks down upon men, and that He will hereafter judge the world in righteousness, and render to all according to their works.

# CHAPTER VI.

## THE DENIAL OF THE POWER OF GODLINESS, OR FORMALISM.

**Not infidelity in theory, but in practice — Nature of formalism — Prevalency of it — Philosophy of formalism — Religions of ancient heathen world generally of this description — Many of our men of taste and science chargeable with it — Remark of Foster— Strong tendency to formalism in the ancient Hebrews — Pharisees of the Christian Age — Formalism in the Christian Church — Result of Romish theory of fellowship —The Oxford Ritual — Remarks of Morell, D'Aubigné and Taylor — Formalism not peculiar to Romanism or Tractarianism — General remarks on it: Its utter worthlessness to satisfy the great wants of human nature —The pleasure found in spiritual religion not experienced — Its tendency to intolerance — Diametrically opposed to the spirit and precepts of the Gospel.**

HERE we advance from the region of speculative into that of practical infidelity. All the body of truth previously noticed, which some men have denied wholly or in part, is supposed to be admitted; but the grand influence of that truth on the conscience and conduct is virtually disowned. The primal truth that God *is*, the self-existent, independent, and all-perfect One,— is unhesitatingly assented to; but the practical testimony to that truth which is given in enduring as seeing him who is invisible, is withheld. The proofs of the being and character of God, drawn from the phenomena of mind and matter, convince the understanding; but, amid all the light that beams from these phenomena, the heart is alienated and darkened. That God is really a Person — not a merely infinite substance — a Person related to us as Father and Lord, Savior and Judge, is not questioned; but there is no devout recognition of Him as being, in these relations, the glorious and gracious One with whom we have to do. The no less well-attested truth that God is ever-present with, and exercises a minute inspection and control over his creatures, has a place willingly assigned to it among the things believed; but there is an utter absence of the manifested power of that truth, in (as Scripture significantly expresses it) walking with God. The Bible doctrines of redemption, including and presupposing, as they do, the guilt and depravity of man, the atonement of Christ, and the regenerating influences of the Spirit, are essential parts of the creed; but that creed is like the dry, lifeless skeleton, the body without the spirit. The man never thinks of questioning the dark doctrine of sin, but he is not penitent and humble under the conviction of his own sinful character. He musters up no argument against the work that expiates and the influences that sanctify, he no more doubts that they are truths in the Bible than he doubts that the sun is in the heavens; but he is not found standing on that work, or living under the power of those influences, any more than if their existence and efficacy were restricted to some distant world. He would no more think of denying that man is responsible for his dispositions, opinions and conduct, than of denying that he thinks, feels and acts. Words implying moral agency and accountability are ever flowing over his lips, and yet his habitual sentiments and conduct are such as could only be formed under an habitual forgetfulness of Him whose eyes behold and whose eyelids try the children of men. There is no infidelity in theory, but there is abundance of it in practice. In so far as the mere letter of a creed is concerned, all may be evangelical and correct; but the inner and outer man are as little influenced by it as by the abrogated notions of the Ptolemaic system. There is religion, but it is merely professional and verbal. "The sign is taken for the thing, the counter for the money." The structure is complete as regards shape, size and bones; but the flesh and blood, the sparkling eye and the agile limbs are wanting. This is what the Scripture means when it speaks of men having the form of godliness, but denying the power thereof.

Formalism is the tendency of the mind to rest in the mere externals of religion, to the neglect of the inner life of religion itself. It is just as when a child runs his lesson rapidly over without heeding the import of the story which he reads. It is just as if our knowledge of a man was confined to his stature, to the shape and color of his coat; so that, when his name is mentioned in our presence, we immediately think of his size and dress, but nothing more. It is the folly of valuing the tree for its bark, instead of its goodly timber; the folly of choosing a book for its binding, irrespective of the nature of its contents; the folly of delighting in painted windows and adorned walls, regardless of the character of the society and accommodation within. It is the very essence of formalism to set the outward institutions above the inward truths, to be punctilious in going the round of ceremonial observances while neglectful of those spiritual sacrifices with which God is well pleased, to substitute means in the room of ends, and to rest in the type and symbol without rising to the glorious reality. It will stand up for the skeleton creed, though the life be as little influenced by it as by a mummy; it will, in the strength of its zeal, put on armor, brandish weapons, guard the courts of the sanctuary from unhallowed intrusion, and shout lustily, "The temple of the Lord, the temple of the Lord are we;" while it lacks heart for fighting the good fight of faith, and wrestling with spiritual wickedness. The church and the sacraments, the symbol and the lettered creed, fill the sphere of its vision, and draw forth its devotion, to the almost utter exclusion of those grand spiritual objects that are unseen and eternal. Such, in general, is the character of formalism.

It is not a thing peculiar to any age or country, though

it may be more prevalent at one time and in one place than in another. Wherever there is a field, we meet with weeds or thorns; and wherever humanity dwells, we witness, to some extent or another, formalism. We may travel over a large tract of inhabited country, and find there no such monster as absolute atheism; we may meet with large masses of men among whom pantheism, or naturalism, has scarcely a local habitation; we may enter into one crowded congregation after another, and hear the doctrines of Socinianism, of a false spiritualism, and of irresponsibility, repudiated; but formalism is a thing at hand as well as afar off, it lies everywhere about us, many colored and many shaped, sometimes gorgeously decked and at other times meanly clad, sometimes prominently manifested and at other times scarcely perceptible. Man will worship. It seems to be as natural for him to have something in the shape of religion as it is for him to have a place to dwell in. And there may not be a greater variety in the habitations which he constructs than in the religions which he adopts. The gradation, in the one case, varying from the gorgeous palace to the hole dug in the earth, may not be more than the gradation in the other,— varying from a purely spiritual Christianity to the lowest form of fetichism or nature-worship. And not more true is it that man will have a religion, than, if left to himself, he will choose a corrupt one, or corrupt a spiritual one into a system of formalism.

There is a principle in man which leads him out of himself to worship and perform religious services. That principle, in a holy being, would fix his thoughts and affections on the most excellent glory, and the forms which he employed would only be used as symbols of eternal realities, or means by which to rise up to the Supreme Good. But that principle in man, as he now is, participates in the depravity of his nature; and while it goes forth after a religion, it is one which, though demanding much bodily service, lies very lightly on the conscience and heart; one which says, Go this round and that, but seldom or never summonses the soul to an earnest conflict with the power of evil. Man will have a religion, but depraved man will have a formal instead of a spiritual one,—one consisting in mere outward observances, in preference to one requiring the homage of the heart and the consecration of the life. The philosophy of formalism is, therefore, easily explained. It is the result of two opposing forces. The one of which will not let man live without a religion, and, if undisturbed by hostile influences, would lead him spiritually to worship God who is a Spirit. The other is of the earth earthy, and, by its greater potency, prevents the former in the natural man from rising above rites and ceremonies, above the symbol and the lettered creed. An adjustment or compromise of the claims of two rival parties takes place. The one pointing the thoughts and affections upward to God, and the other seeking to draw them away from Him. Both are persuaded to meet and shake hands over a religious form, and thus the former is hoodwinked while the latter triumphs.

Our object, more especially, is to notice the formalism that lies within the domain of revealed truth, or that is thrown up within the pale of the visible church. But before doing so, we may glance at some of the formalism that lies beyond. In fact, that is formalism, be it baptized pagan or Christian, natural religion or revealed, which, though bearing the name of a religious belief, exerts no influence in transforming the character, and produces no love and likeness to God. The religions of the ancient heathen world were generally of this description. What were the creeds and rites of Greece and Rome, but splendid and imposing systems of formalism? Objects of religious worship met the Greek or Roman wherever he turned his eyes. Every street down which he passed, every house into which he entered, every fountain at which he drank, and the summit of every little hill on which he stood, reminded him of the divinities that he was to adore. Religion blended itself with almost every piece of daily business that he performed, with almost every journey that he took, and with nearly every amusement that he witnessed. There were numerous and magnificent temples into which he could enter. There was a gorgeous and attractive mythology with which he was familiar. There were statues and paintings everywhere, on which unrivaled art depicted to his view things sacred and divine. And there were rites and ceremonies of the most engrossing description which he was ever called upon to observe. But, amid all this sensible pomp and grandeur, there was no provision for the wants of the inner man. Heathenism had no line to reach the depths of human depravity, and no power to raise man up from his degradation, to break the spell by which he was bound to sensual objects, and to set his spirit free. It had no object of religious worship fitted to call forth love, veneration, gratitude; and no body of truth that could be instrumental in purifying and ennobling man's mental powers, in connecting him with the higher world and renewing him after the image of God. It was a system every way fitted to gratify and strengthen the tendency in human nature to rest in mere external symbols, regardless of spiritual and invisible realities. The heathen duly went his round of religious observances, but it was merely a round of formalism.

Much of the same thing constitutes the religion of many of our men of taste and science. We give forth no sweeping condemnation against philosophers as a class.

Not a few of them have been, and are, spiritually-minded men — men who, while prosecuting enthusiastically their researches into nature, have held high converse with nature's God. But against a large proportion of them must be brought the charge of formalism. They are conversant with, and have much admiration for, the material types; but there they rest. As if afraid of being counted pietists or fanatics, they guard their researches effectually from the intrusion of the living God, and shrink from having their language imbued with anything approaching to a deep devotional feeling. In the case of such individuals, the existence and providential agency of the Holy One may be admitted, but the admission is only formal, not elevating and consecrating. There would be no difficulty in getting them to acknowledge that the Great Eternal Spirit sits behind all those wondrous creations that meet their eye, that the heavens are bright with his glory, and the earth full of his praise; but there is a difficulty in getting them to allow that truth to occupy its legitimate position in their minds, and to exert its legitimate influence over their thoughts and speculations. There is in them no lack of sensibility to the grand and beautiful assemblage of natural phenomena. They may feel a kindling of fancy, and an aggrandizement of thought, in looking, from some eminence, over a magnificent region, rich in all the elements of sublime and graceful scenery, or in taking a telescopic view of the innumerable worlds that move harmoniously throughout the fields of space; but there is apparently a sad want of the capacity of rising from the grandeur and loveliness of creation up to the infinitely greater grandeur and loveliness of creation's God,— a sad want of being moved and subdued under the impression that He who is supremely good reigns over all these scenes, is present in every star and atom, witnesses every thought and feeling, and will one day call us to account. The world has tolerated not a few books in the shape of travels and journals, in which the writers have been more careful to tell us how many miles they passed over in a day, how they slept and were fed, than to make us acquainted with the moral and physical aspects of the country and people where they sojourned. These writers are not more chargeable with a want of good taste and natural sensibility, than are those philosophers and men of genius to whom we have alluded chargeable with being insensible to the glory of the Divine character, while impressed with the loveliness and grandeur of the Divine works. We would not have our men of science and cultivated taste to turn theologians, and mingle doctrinal discussions and prayers with their descriptions of mental and material phenomena; but we would have them to rise up from the magnificent symbols that meet their eye to the High and Holy One, whose perfections they shadow forth. "It is unfortunate," says John Foster,[1] "I have thought within these few minutes,—while looking out on one of the most enchanting nights of the most interesting season of the year, and hearing the voices of a company of persons, to whom I can perceive that this soft and solemn shade over the earth, the calm sky, the beautiful stripe of cloud, the stars, and the waning moon just risen, are things not in the least more interesting than the walls, ceiling, and candle-light of a room." But it is still more unfortunate that there are men of genius fascinated and elevated by the grand scenes of earth and sky, and yet unattracted by the excellency of God, of which all that material grandeur and gracefulness is but a type. It is sad to think that the thought of nature's magnificence should so often fail, in the case of men in whom that thought is vivid, to bring in its train the more ennobling thought of the unrivaled glory of the Author of Nature himself.

[1] Foster's Essays, pp. 16, 17.

"These are thy glorious works, Parent of good,
Almighty! Thine this universal frame,
Thus wondrous fair: Thyself how wondrous then,
Unspeakable!"

It is not of such a writer as the author of "Cosmos," who has given us a great picture of nature without any reference to the living God, that we are now speaking. He has, at least, in this melancholy exclusion, been consistent with his own established belief, "that the forces inherent in matter, and those which govern the moral world, exercise their action under the control of primordial necessity." But it is of those of our men of taste and science, who, while acknowledging the truth about God as the Creator, Preserver, and Moral Governor of the universe, seem to rest in the mere natural phenomena; to concentrate there all their thoughts, and spend there all their feelings; and can carry on their researches, and give us graphic and useful descriptions of the material world, without being led themselves, or attempting to lead others, to the contemplation of Him who has set his glory above the heavens. This, whatever other epithet may be applied to it, must be denounced as mere formalism.

The tendency, in the domain of revealed religion, to halt in mere forms, was strongly evinced by the Hebrew people. The Levitical economy, containing a large machinery of divinely-appointed rites and ceremonies, though cumbersome compared with the dispensation of the Gospel, was admirably adapted to the state of the Israelites, in conveying to their minds, and preserving in the midst of them, those elements of Divine truth which have been fully developed in all their simplicity and majesty in the Gospel age. But their history, as faithfully recorded in Scripture, shows that their besetting sin was to idolize the symbol, instead of rising from it to the thing signified; to go the mere round of external observances, neglectful of the cultivation of the heart and that spiritual worship which God requires. And it deserves notice that, in the same record where the typical and ritual system is so fully and minutely detailed, the most strict cautions are given against resting in it; and the most terrible denunciations are uttered against those who substitute the symbol in the place of the invisible reality. The burden of prophecy, while leading the mind forward to the glory of the latter days, and seeking to concentrate the thoughts in Him who was emblematically represented in every lamb that bled on the Hebrew altars, contained often a strong rebuke to the hollow formalism that prevailed. The divinely-appointed rites were repudiated as worthless, when men converted them into idols, and failed to be led by them to the high spiritual realities. "Hath the Lord," said Samuel to Saul, "as great delight in burnt-offerings and sacrifices, as in obeying the voice of the Lord? Behold, to obey is better than sacrifice, and to hearken than the fat of rams." "To what purpose is the multitude of your sacrifices unto me?" was the question which Jehovah addressed to the punctilious formalists among the ancient Hebrews. This system of religious ceremonialism appeared in all its odiousness in the Pharisees of the Gospels. And it was against the men who were scrupulously exact in paying tithe of mint, and anise, and cummin, while regardless of the weightier matters of the law,—judgment, mercy and faith,—that the meek and lowly Savior pronounced the most tremendous woes. Rigid adherence to bare rites went hand in hand with the most gross corruptions. Men would stand up and stoutly contend for the mere letter of the law, while shamelessly violating its spirit. The formalism of the system was complete, and the Amen, the faithful and true witness, denounced the hypocrisy of its worshipers.

The new economy is distinguished from the old by its greater simplicity and spirituality. It has no gorgeous and imposing ritual. The schoolmaster, necessary for the instruction of the Jews, has been dismissed. The shadow has vanished away and given place to the substance. And the hour has come when neither in this mountain exclusively, nor yet at Jerusalem, men should be required to worship the Father, but when the true worshipers should worship Him in spirit and truth; for the Father seeketh such to worship Him. But under the shadow of Christianity, formalism soon grew up, and extended its cold, withering influence for ages over the church. Judaizing teachers — the masters of forms — insinuated themselves into the first Christian societies, and insisted on the observance of abrogated ceremonies as indispensable to salvation. Apostolic vigilance and zeal, in a great measure, thwarted their pernicious efforts, and preserved the truth of God, pure and unclogged. But, soon after the apostles had fallen asleep, and the spiritual energy which they had infused into the church had diminished, the tendency to exalt the material above the spiritual, and bind up the living element of truth in a system of forms, appeared almost unchecked. The symbols were aggrandized, and occupied the place of the grand realities. The inherent efficacy of the sacraments was preached, instead of the doctrine of the cross. And that deadly dishonoring system of pinning men's faith to the priest and the mere external rite, of identifying baptism with regeneration, and of making the tithe of mint and anise and cummin, a substitute for the practice, and a plea for the omission, of the weightier matters of the law, almost everywhere prevailed. History bears witness to the fact, that the darkest period in the annals of the church, when the question might have been put, Were the Son of man to come, would he find faith in the earth? was the period when

Christianity was ritual bound, ministers and people as intent on mere forms as the heathen on idols.

Such is the result of the Romish theory of fellowship. Instead of making the church, as the apostle Peter did, a *living* body, composed of faithful men, who "as lively stones, are built up a spiritual house, an holy priesthood, to offer up spiritual sacrifices, acceptable to God by Jesus Christ," it has set up a lifeless, artificial system of mosaic work, the essential qualifications to a name and place in which are, *not* the faith of the truth and the love of the Savior as manifested in a life of moral loveliness, but a strict attention to rites and ceremonies. It matters not, according to this theory, how much glorying there may be in the cross of Christ on the part of individuals, and how brightly in them the features of the new creature may shine, if the party watchword cannot be pronounced, and the party rite cannot be submitted to, there is no recognition of them as belonging to the Israel of God. It is in accordance with this theory that some Romish missionaries have baptized large companies of the heathen in a mass, pronounced over them the name of Christ before they really knew who Christ was, set them down as children of the truth before the truth had gained an inlet into their minds and reported them as accessions to the Holy Catholic Church,—which is just like the swelling of a body with diseased flesh. "We find," Mr. Morell truly remarks, "as the result of this theory, multitudes of the most debased, most unscrupulous, most antichristian of mankind, standing in due right and order, as channels of Christian truth to the world; while, on the other hand, we find multitudes of the humble, the holy, the self-denying, hopelessly thrust out beyond the pale of brotherhood, as *not* being in the legitimate succession of official validity. If the fellowship of the faithful is to depend upon such principles as these, then, to make it all intelligible to the reason or consistent with the moral sense of mankind, we need altogether a different interpretation of the whole nature and design of Christianity from what we have in the life of Christ and the writings of the apostles."[1] There are, doubtless, not a few spiritually-minded men in the Romish Church, but they are spiritually-minded in spite of her theory of fellowship. As a whole it is a gigantic system of formalism.

Formalism has not, however, been restricted to the ample and imposing shades of Popery. It has taken root, also, grown up and been carefully fostered in the bosom of Protestantism. The Oxford ritual, as it has been called, makes a very near approach to that of Rome. And the doctrines propounded by the Tractarians, viewed as a whole, come in direct antagonism with those grand spiritual principles of the Reformation, which have been so happily expressed by Merle D'Aubigné: THE WORD OF GOD ONLY; THE GRACE OF CHRIST ONLY; and THE WORK OF THE SPIRIT ONLY. Their theory of the church, and of the efficacy of its rites, is the very theory that quenches spiritual life, dries up the goodly sap, blights every green thing and superinduces a dark and leaden system of formalism. The church and the priest come between the soul of the sinner and the Savior; and the church and the sacraments are made to dispense those spiritual influences for which we, as Bible-taught, look to the church's Head. Let men be instructed, as multitudes of our fellow-countrymen are, that the sacraments are the wells of Divine grace, that they are efficacious only as administered by the hands of episcopally-ordained men, and that perishing souls can find the bread of life only in this particular fold,—and, within the pale of the Protestant Church, will soon become rampant a system that will eat out the very life of the Gos-

[1] Philosophy of Religion, p. 268.

pel — a system having the form of godliness but denying the power thereof. "If we be Christians *ecclesiastically*, it is enough; all besides is illusion,"— is the ingrafted word which thousands of cultivated and uncultivated minds have in our day received within the church of Cranmer. "And such, in fact," says Mr. Isaac Taylor, "are every day seen to be the products of the ecclesiastical theory, which we denounce as, at this time, the antagonist of Spiritual Christianity. In its recent revival it has shed a cold arrogance into many bosoms that once glowed with Christian affection; and at the same time, it has drawn such aside (in how many sad instances!) from an enlightened regard to the substantial truths of the Gospel; while they give all their cares to frivolous and servile observances."[1]

The snake is to be found creeping among the grass, as well as displaying its sinuous form under some stately plant or tree. And formalism is not a sin peculiar to Romanism or to a Romanized Protestantism. It is to be met with, not only under the imposing shade of the cathedral pile, clad in white vestments, kneeling before the altar, clasping to the bosom a crucifix, and going punctiliously the prescribed round of gorgeous ceremonies; but it often has a place in the plain-built chapel, and on the low wooden form where no sacramental theory has even been propounded, where a creed thoroughly evangelical has been adopted, and where nothing but the pure spiritual Gospel of Christ has been heard. It may have a much more ample shelter, and be much more countenanced amid great architectural splendor, venerated altars, and a rich ceremonial; but it can and does exist in the absence of everything external that is fitted to rivet the eye, regale the ear and engross the heart. Men may place a false dependence on the simplest observances as well as on the most artificial

[1] Spiritual Christianity, p. 100.

and splendid, and there may lurk as deadly and hateful a spirit of self-righteousness under an appearance of Puritan meekness, as ever did in the bosom of the ostentatious Pharisee who, in the temple and before God's throne, boasted of his fast-days and the regular payment of his tithes. It matters not whether the forms be few or many, bald or costly decked,— if they are unduly confided in, shifted from the position which they may lawfully occupy as means, to that which in God's sight they never can occupy as a ground, and if the observance of them is made a substitute for piety and holy obedience,— the system must be branded as mere formalism.

1. Our first remark on such a system is, its *utter worthlessness to satisfy the great wants of human nature.* The wants of man, in a religious point of view, are obvious. He is guilty before God, and needs expiation. He is the subject of depraved principles, and needs to be regenerated. Formalism, whether gorgeous or naked, can no more remove the condemning sentence from the head, and root out depraved principles from the heart, than saying to a destitute brother or sister, Be ye warmed and filled, can profit, if we give them not those things that are needful to the body. To look amid a mere ceremonial for some power to atone and purify, were as foolish and vain as to seek the living among the dead. And yet this is a folly which multitudes of cultivated and uncultivated minds are repeating every day. Forms are necessary, in this world at least, to display and maintain the power of godliness. But it should never be forgotten that in the forms the Divine efficacy is not inherent. The internal religious sentiments and emotions must express themselves in some outward shape, and neither reason nor revelation forbids that the external institutions of piety should be imposing and graceful. But as man cannot feed upon flowers, nor

his natural life be sustained by the most enrapturing music; so, amid the most strict observance of even divinely-appointed rites, he will, if halting in them, remain, in the scriptural sense of the expression, dead in trespasses and sins. The use of a ladder is to ascend by it to some lofty eminence; but if men were merely to run up and down the steps, and imagine that they had reached the height to which it pointed, and that they had beheld the view which the summit commanded, they would be regarded as under a strange hallucination. The hallucination is not less real, and infinitely more dangerous, in the man who goes the round of religious observances, stops short at them, builds upon them, and deems himself all the while to have attained to the position and character of a child of God and an heir of heaven. It betrays a littleness of conception in reference to the character and law of the great I Am, to suppose that, by mere outward rites and ceremonies, men are to be pardoned, sanctified, and saved. It manifests a great lack of spiritual discernment, to regard a punctilious attention to a ritual, and a reliance on forms, as occupying the place, and answering the ends, of faith and repentance, holy love and spiritual obedience. It is acting as if the reverse of the proposition — and not the proposition itself — were true: man looks upon the outward appearance, but God looks upon the heart.

The worthlessness of such a reliance, in reference to the two great wants of human nature,— deliverance from guilt and from the dominion of evil,— is attested by observation and experience. Men have run, countless times, round the circle of prescribed observances, leaning on the symbol without rising up to the thing signified; and it has either been, in their experience, a round of anguish, or a dead tread, in which they were destitute of a sense of reconciliation and peace with God. Sacrifice after sacrifice has been offered, the yoke in a thousand forms has been borne, words of what seemed holiest prayer have been daily uttered, hymns of sweetest harmony and devout fervor have been chanted; and, after the excitement, produced by the pomp of ceremony, by a religion of refined ceremonial, or a religion of primitive simplicity, has subsided, the soul has been, like a stricken deer, ill at ease, and panting again for the excitement of the chase. The splendid ritual and the plain, the divinely-appointed institute and the human, the sacrament stamped with heaven's authority and that bearing only man's, have, each and all of them, declared, the merit that atones and the grace that pardons are not to be found in them.

The inefficacy of the system to regenerate, and assimilate men to the likeness of God, is as manifest as its powerlessness to remove the burden of guilt. Be it in the shape of a court ceremonial, of things appealing to refined taste and sentiment, or of the common sacred decencies of the Sabbath-day, if it be a religion merely formal, men will observe its rites, and pass through its forms, without throwing off any more of their impurity and receiving any more of the beauties of holiness than if they paced to and fro the floor of a gallery amid cold marble statues. The man of taste has stood amid some glorious amphitheater of nature, and felt his soul elated by the majesty of the hills, the green loveliness of the valleys, the splendor of the setting sun, and the concert of the rejoicing creation. He has witnessed the same magnificence and felt its power over and over again. But when the excitement of the imagination has been subdued, and the charm has passed away like a dream, and the man has fallen back upon himself, or mingled with the world, his heart has been found without God, and his life reflecting not a ray of the Divine image. Thus making it manifest that the formalism of taste, gratified though it be by the grand and graceful in scenery, has, in itself and independent of influences from above, no efficacy whatever to purify the heart and clothe man in moral beauty. The formalist has gone up, demurely and punctually, to the temple at the hour of prayer, and, whether it has been amid the architectural splendor of the cathedral, where the pealing organ carries the soul aloft, and gorgeous ceremonies are observed; or whether it be in the humble meeting-house, where psalms are plainly sung, and the Gospel is plainly preached, he has felt himself attracted and regaled as with a lovely song. But it has been a mere round of formal excitement, which has never moved the depths of the heart to harmony with the will of God, and thrown no hallowed comeliness over the life: thus showing that the ritual of a sanctuary, be it splendid or simple, can of itself no more regenerate the soul of man, than the ritual of material nature. Men may speak of the efficacy of the sacraments, but daily observation makes it too palpable, that multitudes who are baptized and received to the Lord's Supper, even by those claiming to be the successors of the apostles, differ little or nothing in their temper and conduct from the ungodly world around them. And the same thing is evinced in the observance of other forms, when these are made halting-places on which the mind unduly leans. Whatever observances men may substitute for the finished work of the Son of God and the regenerating influences of the Holy Spirit, be they costly or mean, imposing or simple, appointments of heaven or appointments of earth, their worthlessness to satisfy the wants of man's moral nature will be made evident.

2. Our second remark is, that, *in mere formalism, the pleasure found in spiritual religion is not experienced.* It is impossible that it should. The creation is not so joyous and full of life when a mass of dark clouds intercepts the

rays of the sun, as when that sun beams brightly forth on hill and valley, and covers heaven and earth with light as with a garment. God is a sun. He is the infinite good. Nothing but a living, sensible communion with Him can displace heaviness from the heart, and shed a holy happiness over the life. Formalism interposes thick shadows between the fountain of light and the human soul. It is as when a man halts on the somewhat bleak and rugged borders of a lovely region, without ever entering into the beautiful territory itself. Forms were designed, by Him who knoweth our frame, to be the means by which we might ascend to the enjoyment of Himself. But when the mind halts in the symbol, instead of rising from it to the thing signified; when the man runs up and down the ladder, instead of reaching the eminence which commands the glorious prospect, he loses the enjoyment inseparable from intercourse with the blissful reality. It has often been remarked, that, in those countries and ages where religion has appeared in her most gaudy trim,— ages characterized by the architectural splendor of churches, and by the observance of a gorgeous round of rites and ceremonies,— the spiritual element in worship has been feeble and scarcely perceptible. And there, too, the light, loveliness and joy inseparable from the Gospel truth have been wanting, and gloom and slavish fear have prevailed in their room. When one passes from a country that lies under the deadly grasp of civil and ecclesiastical despotism, to another where political and religious liberty is richly enjoyed, it is like making a transit from a region of thick gloom to one of joyous sunshine. And the difference is not less discernible between a religious community where the spiritual element is buried in the formal, and one in which the former pervades and gives life to the latter; or between an individual who has a feeling of the Divine presence and a relish of the Divine excellence, and one whose idol is the church he attends and the rites in which he engages. It is not the ritual in itself — at least, it is not the divinely-appointed ritual — that is incompatible with or obstructive of spiritual life and joy, but the substitution of it as means in the place of ends. David and Asaph, who lived under the Levitical economy, so full and minute in its provisions regarding forms, lost not sight of the spiritual element, and had a vivid experience of the joy inseparably connected with it. The mere formalist is a stranger to that life of godliness which enables a man to say,— when he looks abroad upon the fields of creation, or when he has entered into his closet, shut his door, and is conscious that no eye sees him and no ear hears him but the eye and ear of God,—"Whom have I in heaven but thee? and there is none upon earth that I desire beside thee." "There be many that say, Who will show us any good? Lord, lift thou up the light of thy countenance upon us."

Formalism may be found in all religious communities, for it is the besetting sin of human nature; but we look in vain, in the religion of the formalist, for those robes of fine linen, as joyous as pure, which clothed such men as Leighton and Doddridge, Baxter and Edwards, and thousands of others whom the world never heard of, and of whom the world was not worthy. There is a pleasure which a man of taste and sensibility enjoys in contemplating the grand and beautiful objects of nature, but the pleasure is poor and transient compared with what the same man experiences when, in filial confidence, he views them as the creations of his Father. Byron, amid the lovely scenery of the isles of Greece, never felt what the great metaphysician of New England felt, when, as he tells us, he "spent much of his time in viewing the clouds and sky, to behold the sweet glory of God in these things; in the meantime singing forth, with a low voice, his contemplations of the Creator and Redeemer." There is a pleasure, too, felt under the shadow of the cathedral pile, derived from the imposing splendor of the place, the enrapturing music, and the rich ceremonial; but it is a pleasure different in kind, and vastly inferior in degree to what is experienced by the man, observant it may be of the same forms, who rises through them to divine fellowship with the Father of spirits, and the God of his salvation. And there is a pleasure, also, in going up to the humble chapel, amid the hallowed calm of the Sabbath morning, and bearing a part in the routine of its simple services; but that pleasure, likewise, may have little or none of the life and joy of godliness, and be as unlike the holy inward happiness of the man who worships God in spirit and in truth, as earth is unlike heaven. Men do not gather grapes of thorns, nor figs of thistles; neither do they experience that joy which is a fruit of the Spirit, in a religion which is merely formal and not spiritual.

3. Our third remark is, *that formalism ever has a tendency to intolerance.* Men, in proportion as they are imbued with the spirit of the Gospel, have enlarged hearts. Love is represented, in almost every page of the New Testament, as the characteristic of the Christian. It is not an attachment to men merely because they are members of this or that particular society, but because they belong to the church of the living God. It is not entwined around a man because he bears a humanly-devised name, but because he wears in his bosom, and shows in his life, the Savior's image. This holy principle looks beyond the outward appearance, and fastens its regard on that image, though it be found in a Lazarus sitting in rags and seeking to be fed with the crumbs of the rich man's table. Nor does it confine its regards to those who are united to the common Savior, and are made partakers of the common

salvation. It looks on the wide world with an eye of compassion, and feels toward it those stirrings of benevolence which seek to save that which is lost. It is like the sun in the firmament, which confines not his radiance to any little spot on the surface of the earth, but spreads it over the wide fields of creation. "Its going forth is from the end of the heaven, and its circuit unto the ends of it: and there is nothing hid from the heat thereof."

Formalism engenders a spirit the reverse of all this. It is sectarian. It is pent up within the pale of its own community; and whatever religious zeal it possesses is spent on its own creed and ceremonies. We see this in the Pharisees of the Gospels. They were proud, haughty separatists. Men who stood aloof from others on the ground of mere outward observances. They erected the banner of party distinction in the temple where all meet on a common level. They said to others, by their looks and actions, "Stand by yourself, come not near to me, for I am holier than you." We see this in that church which arrogates to itself the exclusive claim of being "Holy Catholic." The most massive system of religious formalism, it has ever been the most intolerant in theory and practice. Out of the Romish pale there is no salvation — is an infallible dogma which every good Catholic is bound to believe. It is instilled into the minds of youth by the Catholic school book. It is the vital element that pervades Papal decrees. It ever and anon drops from the priest's lips, in the hearing of young and old, of peasant and noble. And, in accordance with this monstrous dogma, members of other communions are consigned over to eternal perdition, though they may have been the most excellent ones of the earth, men of seraphic piety, the very salt of the earth, and the lights of the world. Sectarian exclusiveness is strikingly characteristic of Oxford Tractarianism. It refuses even the name of church to whatever Protestant body lies without the pale of its own communion, arrogates the commission to administer Christian ordinances to episcopally-ordained ministers only, denounces dissent as apostasy from the true church, and considers it sinful to have fellowship with any beyond the episcopal border. Hence the intolerance, which has sometimes been manifested in high places, in prohibiting the catholic-spirited men in that portion of the church from co-operating in good works with Christian men of other denominations. But it behoves us not to be unmindful that the same exclusively sectarian feeling may exist in persons, mere formalists, sitting side by side with each other in the same church pew. Whoever — instead of humbling his heart before God, and recognizing in the meanest worshiper a child of the same bountiful Father, and alike welcome with himself to a participation in the fullness of his house — assumes a conceited sentiment of his own superior sanctity, such as removes him in fancy to an elevation apart from other men, is filled with the same self-righteous and intolerant spirit which actuated the Pharisees, and which Jehovah, by the prophet, so strongly reprobates: "These are a smoke in my nose, a fire that burneth all the day!"

The transition from such separatism to a rancorous fanaticism is easy and natural. The full-blown separatist not only stands aloof from other men and disregards their claims, but he assumes toward them an attitude of scowling defiance. He carries his hateful spirit into the very exercises of the sanctuary, and utters his denunciations at the altar. The formalist, wrapped up in the robe of his own righteousness, feigns a "God, I thank thee," that he is not as other men are, extortioners, unjust, but that he fasts twice in the week and gives tithes of all that he has. With his tongue blesses he God, even the Father; and therewith curses he men, which are made after the similitude of God; out of the same mouth proceed blessing and cursing, and we behold in him a fountain sending forth at the same place sweet water and bitter. This odious system stings like a serpent, and bites like an adder, at every species of spiritual piety that crosses its path. It varies in the manifestation of its intolerance, from the man who, like a sentinel, goes the round of his own church observances, and inwardly says, "The temple of the Lord, the temple of the Lord are we," to the man who would erect the gibbet and kindle the faggot for schismatics and heretics, and persuade himself that in thus acting he was doing God service.

4. Our fourth remark is, that *such a system is diametrically opposed to the spirit and precepts of the Gospel.* It says, "Our fathers worshiped in this mountain." This is *the* church in which alone is given under heaven that name whereby we can be saved. The Lord and Master says, The exclusive system has ceased. "The hour is come when ye shall neither in this mountain, nor yet at Jerusalem, worship the Father. God is a spirit, and they that worship Him, must worship Him in spirit and in truth." Formalism says, We who fast so often, pray so fervently, and attend on the sacraments so punctually are God's people. Evangelism replies, "He is not a Jew, which is one outwardly; neither is that circumcision which is outward in the flesh: but he is a Jew which is one inwardly; and circumcision is that of the heart, in the spirit, and not in the letter; whose praise is not of men, but of God." The one says, "We have Abraham to our father," and are in the line of the true apostolical succession. The other says, "We are the circumcision," the true seed of Abraham, "which worship God in the spirit, and rejoice in Christ Jesus, and have no confidence in the flesh." The one

says, Perform this ceremony and that, go this round of observances and that, and ye shall be justified. The other, in holy indignation, exclaims, "If righteousness come by the law, then Christ is dead in vain; therefore by the deeds of the law there shall no flesh be justified." The one says, Baptism is regeneration; only be baptized, come to the sacramental table, and ye shall be saved. The other says, "Neither circumcision availeth anything nor uncircumcision, but a new creature." Formalism looks chiefly at what a man does, irrespective of his character and motives. It takes notice of his long and numerous prayers, while it winks at him oppressing the poor and devouring widows' houses. It approves of his strict observance of the decencies and rites of the Sabbath day, while it frowns upon him healing the diseased, raising an ox out of the pit, or performing any other works of mercy in the same sacred period. It is heedless of the state of heart in which a man approaches God's altar, while it is careful to see that his hands are washed, and that his raiment is tidy. It will furnish him with a reason for neglecting a moral duty, and throw an air of sanctimonious pretense over the violence done to natural affection, provided he his mindful of the claims of the temple treasury. It teaches him to say "Corban," it is a gift; and thus frees him from the obligation of relieving his father and mother. There is not less communion between light and darkness, than there is between such a system and the spiritual Christianity taught by Jesus and his apostles. "This people," said the Great Teacher, "draweth nigh unto me with their mouth, and honoreth me with their lips; but their heart is far from me. But in vain do they worship me, teaching for doctrines the commandments of men." Christianity does not overlook what a man may have done, but it looks more to what a man *is*. It gives no countenance whatever to despise sacred rites and seasons, but it says to the man who attaches an undue importance to them, while neglecting the weightier matters of the law, "These things ought ye to have done, and not to leave the others undone."

"There are two ways of destroying Christianity," remarks D'Aubigné, "one is to deny it, the other to displace it. To put the church above Christianity, the hierarchy above the word of God; to ask a man, not whether he has received the Holy Ghost, but whether he has received baptism from the hands of those who are termed successors of the apostles and their delegates; all this may doubtless flatter the pride of the natural man, but is fundamentally opposed to the Bible, and aims a fatal blow at the religion of Jesus Christ. If God had intended that Christianity should, like the Mosaic system, be chiefly an ecclesiastical, sacerdotal, and hierarchical system, he would have ordered and established it in the New Testament, as He did in the Old. But there is nothing like this in the New Testament. All the declarations of our Lord and of his apostles tend to prove that the new religion given to the world, is 'life and spirit,' and not a new system of priesthood and ordinances. 'The kingdom of God,' saith Jesus, 'cometh not with observation, neither shall they say, Lo here! or lo there! for behold the kingdom of God is within you.' 'The kingdom of God is not meat and drink; but righteousness and peace and joy in the Holy Ghost.' . . . Let us not, then, esteem the bark above the sap, the body above the soul, the form above the life, the visible church above the invisible, the priest above the Holy Spirit. Let us hate all sectarian, ecclesiastical, national or dissenting spirit; but let us love Jesus Christ in all sects, whether ecclesiastical, national, or dissenting."[1] "And as many as walk according to this rule, peace be on them, and mercy, and upon the Israel of God."

[1] Geneva and Oxford, by D'Aubigné.

# PART THE SECOND.

## INFIDELITY IN ITS VARIOUS CAUSES.

GENERAL CAUSE—SPECIFIC CAUSES—SPECULATIVE PHILOSOPHY — SOCIAL DISAFFECTION — THE CORRUPTIONS OF CHRISTIANITY — RELIGIOUS INTOLERANCE — DISUNION OF THE CHURCH.

## CHAPTER I.

### GENERAL CAUSE.

Causes of infidelity ethical rather than intellectual—The will has much to do with it — Moral evidence not irresistible — Existence of God does not admit of demonstration — Remark of Dr. Arnold — Pantheism and Naturalism traced to aversion of heart — Sufficiency of Christian evidences —Jewish unbelief originated in a moral cause — Speculative and practical infidelity have same origin — Bible account of the matter.

IT is evident that unbelief, generally speaking, can originate in only one of two sources; either in a deficiency of evidence, or in a state of mind and heart on which the clearest and strongest evidence has no power. The causes of infidelity, we are persuaded, are more ethical than intellectual. And this persuasion is greatly strengthened by the perusal of some of the productions of our modern infidel writers. "Nothing can be more contemptible," says Professor Garbett,[1] "than the *argumentative* resources of modern infidelity. *It does not reason, it only postulates;* it dreams

[1] Modern Philosophical Infidelity, p. 5.

and dogmatizes. Neither can it claim *invention.*" This witness is true. Indeed, we venture to assert, that the general strain of argument brought to bear against Christianity by its modern assailants would not be tolerated for a moment within the province of purely literary criticism. The strong determination to withstand everything in the shape of reasonable evidence, contrasts very much with the feeble argumentation by which many of the truths of religion are set aside. Be it atheism or pantheism, naturalism or spiritualism, indifferentism or formalism, the will has much to do with it. Moral evidence is the appropriate proof of moral truth. All moral evidence is cumulative, but however strong it may be, it is never irresistible. An indocile reason can ward it off.

The existence of God, for example, does not admit of demonstrative, but of moral certainty. And, though supported by a vastly preponderating amount of proof, room is left for the cavils of a strongly-prejudiced unbelief. The argument from design is one of great power, and though it does not of itself lead us to the High and Holy One, it points us very clearly thither. But the ground is by no means free from difficulties. Faith, supported by the immensely overbalancing amount of clear evidence, triumphs over these, whereas the unbelieving heart yields to them. Still stronger is the testimony to this primal truth given by our own inward consciousness — a testimony that outweighs all atheistical assumptions and arguments; but, in spite of it, man can befool himself, and say in his heart, There is no God. The disrelish of the truth that God *is*, strengthens itself in the comparatively small residue of phenomena that seems to conflict with it, and there repels the conviction arising from the irrefragable proof on the other side. Dr. Arnold, reasoning on the supposition that the intellectual difficulties are balanced, remarks, "Here is the moral fault

18

of unbelief,— that a man can bear to make so great a moral sacrifice, as is implied in renouncing God. He makes the greatest moral sacrifice to obtain partial satisfaction to his intellect: a believer insures the greatest moral perfection, with partial satisfaction to his intellect also; entire satisfaction to the intellect, is, and can be, obtained by neither."[1] The choice in such a case must be resolved into the inclination, or the wish to have it, that there is no God. But matters are not really so balanced. The difficulties greatly preponderate on the side of unbelief. And for a man to accept of the proposition that God is not, with the mass of monstrosities and difficulties that attend it, and thereby renounce the affirmative proposition that God is,— a proposition so well substantiated, and for which there is an intellectual necessity,— indicates very plainly the leanings of the heart. Lord Bacon says, "None deny there is a God, but those for whom it maketh that there were no God."

The personality of the Divine Being, irrespective of its being interwoven with the language of the Bible, and imparting to it a burning energy, is much more rational than the pantheistic doctrine. It does not admit, however, of strict demonstration. We may argue very conclusively in favor of it from our own personality, and maintain that, since personality is a perfection, God must possess it in the highest degree, otherwise He would be inferior to ourselves, and not only so, but we could conceive of God as a more glorious being than He really is, which is an absurdity. We may strengthen our proof by the consideration that men in general feel, in the most solemn and affecting moments of their lives, that God is a real person. And to this we may add that, without the idea of a personal God, "we cannot really explain the origin or the order of the

[1] Dr. Arnold's Life and Correspondence.

universe; and that it is a mere assumption to assert that personality is in its very nature finite — since it is the finiteness of man's attributes, and that alone, which gives the finiteness to his personality."[1] But the heart can repel all this proof; and bring to its aid, if not the force of argument, the language of the mystic and the principles of a dreaming philosophy. The reluctance to think of God as a living person, holy, just and good, and with whom we have to do, is greater than the incapacity. It is in the delirium of self-adoration, in the swellings of a pride-intoxicated heart, that men break loose from a sense of responsibility, ignore the existence of the Personal Creator and Judge, and yield to the temptation — Ye shall be as gods. No one can read the rhapsodies of such a man as Emerson without perceiving that the state of the heart,— a heart puffed up with the delusive notion of its own divinity,— lies at the bottom of his unbelief. And the appeal is made, not to men's sober judgment, but to their rebellious propensities, when they are told that they have the resources of the world in their own souls, and that all their actions are forms of piety.

Naturalism has its root in the same soil. In so far as argument is concerned, it has scarcely a leg to stand upon. The evidences of a Supreme Presiding Intelligence are as manifest as those of a Supreme Creative Power. The development hypothesis is nothing better than a wild dream, which is fast disappearing before the light of advancing science. Astronomical and geological researches are rapidly cutting away the ground on which any such theory is supposed to rest, whether as applied to the heavens above or to the earth beneath. The nebular hypothesis, which would remove God beyond the limits of the visible universe, and account for the changes, as well as for the

[1] Smith's Relations of Faith and Philosophy, p. 13.

orderly movements in the heavens, without his presiding agency, was merely thrown out as a conjecture at first, and is now being falsified by the discoveries of the telescope. And, as Professor Whewell remarks, "Science negatives the doctrine that men grew out of apes, that language is the necessary development of the jabbering of such creatures, and reason the product of their conflicting appetites."[1] Besides, it is doubtless more rational to suppose that God continues to govern the world which He has made than that He has abandoned it. "When a man," says Bacon, "seeth the dependence of causes and the works of Providence, then, according to the allegory of the poets, he will easily believe that the highest link of Nature's chain must needs be tied to the foot of Jupiter's chair." Having interposed in a miraculous manner at the creation of the world, it is reasonable to believe that God would interpose again, for an end worthy of his character, and bearing on the highest interests of the human race. The position taken up by Strauss, — that miracles are impossible, — is utterly indefensible. It may consist with his philosophy, but not with the common-sense truth that God is in the heavens, and that He doeth whatsoever He pleaseth. But the doctrine of the Divine Providential Government does not admit of demonstrative certainty. The facts lying without, and the voice of conscience within, speak loudly in proof of it. The evidence is sufficient to justify our faith, but it is not irresistible. There are other facts which seem to conflict with the doctrine. Darkness and difficulties, which have been felt by the best men in every age, beset us in this field of inquiry. But what is the darkness to the light? The difficulties arise from our limited capacity and knowing but in part. Our vision is restricted to a point of a universal system; and analogy warrants the con-

[1] Indications of the Creator, p. 8.

clusion, that, were our range of view widened, these difficulties would lessen, if not disappear. The difficulties are much greater on the side of naturalism, besides the monstrosities that are involved in the hypothesis. And when men choose the latter, and thereby extrude God from the throne of his natural government, or compliment Him out of it, there is reason to suspect that the thing is done with the view of excluding Him from his moral dominion. We must fall back on the state of the heart, in seeking for the great reason why men, in the face of such preponderant evidence for divine providence, will have it that 'God doth not know, and that the Almighty doth not consider."

Christianity is based upon evidence. The reason why evidence is necessary is to be found in our moral constitution as rational, discriminating, accountable agents; and in the fact that, from the existence of evil in the world, we were otherwise liable to deception in reference to our highest interests. It could never be a man's duty to believe in a revelation claiming to itself the authority of heaven, unless that revelation bore, legibly on its front, heaven's signature, or was in some way attended with heaven's evidencing power. The evidence that attests the truth of Christianity, vast, varied, and of great cumulative power though it be, is not, however, irresistible. No man is warranted to expect it to be so. Faith is a moral act, and while resting on a strong groundwork of proof, it must have some difficulties over which to triumph. Origen, speaking of the difficulties in the Bible revelation, and of those in the revelation of nature, says: "In both we see a self-concealing, self-revealing God, who makes Himself known only to those who earnestly seek Him; in both are found stimulants to faith, and occasions for unbelief." "There is light enough," says Pascal, "for those who sincerely wish to see; and darkness enough for those of an opposite description." Mr. Newman tells us, it "supersedes the authoritative force of outward miracles entirely," to say that "a really overpowering miraculous proof would have destroyed the moral character of faith." This, however, is not argument, but a foolish dogmatic assertion. The Christian miracles are of "a convincing and stupendous character," and yet not so overpowering as the axiom that a whole is greater than its part; and we lack sagacity to perceive where lies the contradiction between these statements. Evidence is obligatory on man, not because it is overpowering or irresistible, but because it preponderates. Indeed, on the former supposition, to talk of obligation were an absurdity. The judge on the bench is every day deciding important cases, not on the ground that the evidence is absolutely perfect, but because, notwithstanding objections, the proof on the one side preponderates; and no reasonable man questions the validity of his decision. The external and internal evidences of Christianity constitute a mass of proof fully sufficient to justify our belief in its truths; and, as if aware of the force of it, our modern infidels attack one part of it, and represent us as if resting on that, to the exclusion of the rest. Difficulties there are, both in the record and in the outward evidence. But what are these difficulties compared with the greatly preponderating amount of clear heavenly proof? The difficulties arise out of our ignorance. Analogy warrants us to conclude that they are so only relatively, not absolutely. And they are but as the small dust in the balance compared with the thousand paradoxes which a man must be prepared to swallow who denies that Christianity is an authoritative revelation from heaven. The infidel is reconciled to these paradoxes, on the alleged ground of objections which appear as nothing compared to them. And this furnishes a strong presumption that the will has much to do with infidelity, whether it be named deism or spiritualism. "Nor do we well know what multitudes, who neglect religion on account of the alleged uncertainty of its evidence, could reply, if God were to say to them, 'And yet on *such* evidence, and that far inferior in degree, you have never hesitated to *act*, when your own temporal interests were concerned. You never feared to commit the bark of your worldly fortunes to that fluctuating element. In many cases you believe on the testimony of others what seemed even to contradict your own senses. Why were you so much more scrupulous in relation to ME?'"[1]

The cause of unbelief among the Jews, for example, in the days of the Savior's flesh, could not be a want of evidence—for that evidence was numerous, varied and brilliant. Many, in our day, affect to despise the evidence from miracles, for no better reason, we are persuaded, than that it is against them. But the Great Teacher rested his claims on the fact of his miracles. "If I do not the works of my Father," said He, "believe me not. But if I do, though ye believe not me, believe the works; that ye may know and believe that the Father is in me and I in him." Their fathers had beheld the mighty works of the Lord in the wilderness, in the land of Ham, and at the Red Sea; but never did they witness such a visible agency multiplying, in quick and varied succession, its deeds of benevolent and miraculous power, as was daily beheld by their children. They bowed before the majesty of that evidence itself, they paid to it a willing homage, they were fully persuaded that Jesus was the Messiah, so long as the golden dream of an earthly monarchy remained unbroken; and, on the strength of that evidence, would have proceeded at once to make Him their king. It was not till they felt his doc-

[1] Rogers' Reason and Faith, p. 26.

trine thwarting their fondest wishes — not till they perceived that his kingdom had no battle for the warrior, and was unaccompanied with confused noise and garments rolled in blood — not till they perceived that his subjects were to be composed of the pure, the meek, and the poor in spirit — that they hid, as it were, their faces from Him. It was, therefore, a moral cause that produced Jewish unbelief — a state of mind that, relatively to itself, weakens evidence the most powerful, and darkens evidence the most brilliant. His religion ran counter to their moral tendencies, condemned their favorite pursuits, and frowned on their groveling expectations. And in this originated that carping spirit in which they ever after listened to his discourses, that deadly enmity with which they incessantly pursued Him, even when performing among them works of unparalleled grandeur and benevolence. It was because their deeds were evil, that they hated his light. When He was in the world, the world hated Him, because He testified of it that the works thereof were evil.

The same remarks are substantially applicable to the hostility which has been shown to the pure Gospel in every succeeding age. If, for convenience, we divide infidelity into the speculative and the practical, it will be found that both these forms, however different may be the specific process by which the mind in each case settles down in it, may be traced to the same moral cause — the repugnance in human nature to what is purely spiritual and divinely authoritative. Could we, for instance, have looked into the hidden chambers of imagery, and beheld the processes of thought and feeling in which many talented infidels investigated the Scripture testimony, our wonder would not have been that they landed in unbelief. The religion of Jesus, when summoned to the bar of their understanding, has met with such treatment as an innocent man meets with when he comes before a hostile jury. Rather, we should say, they never suffer themselves to behold Christianity in all its radiant glory, nor to mark its lofty towers and stable bulwarks; for, as they advance on their way to the temple of truth, they are ever and anon raising around them a thick cloud of dust and darkness. In most cases, we doubt not, Christianity and its evidences have never been examined by such men at all. In our times, it is fashionable, in many quarters, to ignore the evidences altogether,— to pass them over with a proud sneer as things antiquated and effete, and to judge the Gospel according to the conceptions of the individual mind. In other words, the case is prejudged, before the witnesses are examined, if examined at all. And in other cases, while an inquiry into the evidences has been entered upon, it has been with a lurking wish that the examination, after all, might prove unfavorable. In such circumstances, the wish biases the judgment, and the inevitable result is that the man can never believe to be true what he wishes may be false.

Now this process, which ends in unbelief, has its origin in the aversion of the mind to the high and holy principles of the Gospel. There is a demand, made in that Gospel, of every lofty imagination, and every high thought, being brought into captivity to Christ, which is repugnant to that reckless independence of mind in which such a skeptic glories. To such a mind, Christianity is too humbling; its meek and lowly and crucified Savior appears mean and uninteresting, and he easily turns from the thought of Him who has no form or comeliness to the contemplation of some stormy hero of romance. Its strict morality,— exercising a minute inspection over every movement of the inner man, and claiming to be a discerner of the thoughts and intents of the heart,— is felt to be an uncomfortable restraint; like an individual who follows us through every path and winding which we take to avoid his presence. Above all, its doctrine of the cross,—staining, as it does, all human glory, reducing the loftiest to a level with the meanest in the sight of God, and making all heavenly blessedness to depend on Him who was crucified as a felon between two thieves,—outrages that high sense of merit which would exalt itself as the eagle and set its nest among the stars. David Hume, somewhere in his writings, acknowledges, as we have already noticed, that his readings in the New Testament were but scanty. And it is not difficult to conceive how such a mind would sit down to the perusal of some of the discourses of the Redeemer and the letters of his apostles. Other infidels, of whom Rousseau is an example, have paid an involuntary homage to the character of the Savior. They have admired Him going about, like the embodied spirit of benevolence, continually doing good. But they have shrunk back from the doctrine of the cross, and the uncompromising requirements of Christ's laws, just as a person with a diseased eye instinctively retires into the shade when the frail organ is about to be exposed to the light of the sun. Mr. Emerson professes to reverence Jesus Christ as belonging to the true race of prophets, as "the only soul in history who has appreciated the worth of man;" and yet he spurns the idea of receiving religion and law from his lips, and of subordinating his nature to the nature of Christ. Mr. Parker does not conceal his hatred to "the popular Christianity," because it represents man as fallen and depraved, and makes so much of the one mediator between God and man. And when Mr. Newman tells us that he was forced, against all his prepossessions, to renounce everything distinctively Christian, and would have us to believe that the will, in his case, durst "not dictate whereto the inquiries of the understanding should lead,"[1]

[1] Phases of Faith, p. 219.

we appeal to his "Phases," for a refutation of such assertions. We have, in such men, the pride without the greatness of the mighty fallen Intellect in Milton, who said,—

> "In my choice,
> To reign is worth ambition, though in hell:
> Better to reign in hell than serve in heaven!"

Oh! these intolerable evidences! Better far be reconciled to all the strange paradoxes implied in disowning Christianity, than submit ourselves to "church, book, person."[1] Such is the choice of men who are laboring to undermine the historical verity of the sacred writings; and who, baptizing an enlightened attachment to them by the ill-sounding name of "Bibliolatry," would cut the link asunder, and leave us to wander at will after the undefined and undefinable thing called "absolute religion."

It is, in like manner, with that cold insensibility to divine truth,— that practical form of infidelity which frequently prevails among the multitude. There is an unbelief common among many of the would-be giants of the earth, and one that exists among the lowly walks of other men. But as the object of their contempt or disregard is the same, so are the specific causes to be traced to the same great evil principle — an inveterate love of those practices and pursuits which the light of divine truth reproves and condemns. There are immense masses of our population who perhaps never spent five minutes of their lives in considering whether the Bible were a revelation from God, or a cunningly devised fable. The Bible, as a book, may be found beneath their roof; but its grand truths have not been rightly apprehended and duly felt, because the volume has seldom been opened, and, when opened, not read with half the interest with which they read some fairy tale. The light which it affords shineth in

[1] Parker's Discourse, p. 372.

the darkness, but the darkness admitteth it not. These individuals would perhaps count it impiety to wield the weapons of the skeptic against the Gospel, were they able for the task, and would shrink with horror from the thought of any way traducing the Divine Savior; and yet they can pass from day to day as little elevated by all that is magnificent and sublime, as little impressed with all that is marvelous in condescension, as little attracted by all that is beauteous in holiness, as if God's Son, in whom meet preëminently all this grandeur and loveliness, had never manifested Himself to the world. This is formalism, and, as a species of unbelief, this is what the Gospel condemns.

The Bible comes to us as a message from the skies. In it God utters his voice loudly and intelligibly in the ears of men. It is a message of mercy from the throne of the Eternal to us the guilty and rebellious, making known a Divine Savior, and offering, on the ground of his atoning sacrifice, a free and a full salvation. In making such declarations, the Bible deals with men as rational and accountable agents. It has no blessings for those who are not deterred by its threatenings, nor won by its promises. It presents to the mind saving truth, which, in order to prove efficacious, must be believed; and, in order to be believed, must be carefully read and rightly understood. How, then, are we to account for the melancholy fact, that men possessing the sacred volume, and acknowledging it to be a revelation from God, are little, if at all, influenced by the momentous statements which it contains? That volume finds a place in the house, but it has no home in the heart. It is assented to as the law and the testimony, the only infallible directory of faith and morals. But its grand truths are seldom, if ever, made the object of devout contemplation; its precepts are seldom taken as a light unto the feet and a lamp unto the path. Whence originates this insensibility to all that is majestic and merciful, this unwillingness to bring the mind into contact with the purifying and elevating truths of Christianity,—but in a deceitful suspicion that its groveling earthly pursuits would be disturbed, that its moral tendencies would be thwarted, that the searching light of the Gospel would make manifest its unholy thoughts and affections, just as a ray of the sun, let through the chink of an old ruin, reveals the unsightly guests that dwell within? It were well if some of our literary men, and philosophic religionists, who cry out against soulless creeds and dogmatic Christianity, would lay the blame at the right quarter, and not give a false value to human nature, at the expense of depreciating historical truth. He who "saw with open eye the mystery of the soul," accounted for the rejection of feeble influence of his Gospel, by saying, "men loved darkness rather than light, because their deeds were evil." And all history proves, what the Scripture affirms, that the natural man receiveth not the things of the Spirit of God.

---

The river is traced up to its source. But, in order to account fully for its rushing waters, we must notice the tributary streams that it receives in its passage. And, among the specific and subordinate causes of infidelity, we are disposed to enumerate—Speculative Philosophy, Social Disaffection, the Corruptions of Christianity, Religious Intolerance, and the Disunion of the Church. These we shall briefly notice.

# CHAPTER II

## SPECULATIVE PHILOSOPHY.

Speculative philosophy inevitable — Indicates a thinking and reflective age — Influences the religion of an age — Has ever been tampering with Christian truth Gnosticism in the primitive Church — Allegorical method of interpretation— Sacramental theory — Platonism — Scholasticism — Connection between modern speculative philosophy and forms of modern infidelity — The sensational philosophy — Deistical writers — Influence of sensationalism on works of science and common literature —The old Unitarianism —French sensationalism: Condillac — School of Voltaire — Protracted influences of sensationalism — The Ideal philosophy: Germany —The human mind made determinator of religious truth — Contempt for evidences — Seen in Strauss — Influence of idealism in our own country — Carlyle — Emerson — Parker — Newman — Mackay — Morell — Importance of maintaining historical Christianity — Harmony between a true faith and a true philosophy.

THE rise of a speculative philosophy, in any age or country where there are thinkers, seems inevitable. It is the natural consequence of the mind's desire to penetrate into the mysteries of existence and to know all things. Man himself is a mystery, the world around him is a mystery, the great God above him is a mystery, and the relations between each and all of them are profoundly and impressively mysterious. And, while the great majority of men never attempt to lift up the veil, but are content with the knowledge that lies on the surface of things, there are those who must endeavor to get beyond and solve the problems of mysterious existence. Every country that has emerged from barbarism, and attained to any degree of mental cultivation, is more or less characterized by philosophical speculation. This, in itself, is not to be regarded as an evil. It indicates a thinking and reflecting age, and marks the advancement of a community in mental culture. The evil is, when it spurns the investigation of palpable facts and indubitable evidence, treats as empirical the honest method of induction, and incautiously passes the bounds of all fair and legitimate inquiry. Then it becomes intolerant of the world of realities, is vainly puffed up, and, intruding into those things which are not seen, would, instead of proving a handmaid to true religion, assume the air of an imperious mistress, and decide its shape, dress and laws. To this charge, the greater number of the systems of philosophy that have emanated from the schools must plead guilty.

It is very obvious that the philosophy of an age must materially influence the religion of that age. The great subjects with which speculative philosophy is conversant, are those which lie within the domain of natural and revealed truth. It cannot touch upon the finite and the infinite, upon man, the universe, and God, without coming into contact with some of the great essential principles of religion. Its speculations upon man affect his position as a fallen being, the subject of moral government, and an heir of immortality. Its speculations upon the universe bear upon the evidences of creative power, and providential control, and the existence of good and evil. And its speculations upon God, the Absolute, as philosophy terms Him, bear upon his personality, independent existence and agency, and the relations in which He stands to the material universe and the human race. Views on these great subjects, at particular periods, notwithstanding the clear and definite statements regarding them in the sacred volume, have been very much moulded by the reigning intellectual philosophy. And that divine record itself, so firmly established in history, and speaking in the tone of heaven's authority, has been made to give forth its utterances according as philosophy dictated and allowed. The servant, usurping the place of the master, has, as commonly happens, stripped the master of every vestige of authority, put words into his mouth, or given the interpretation, and that not unfrequently a false one, of all that he said.

The history of every age, from the beginning of the Gospel until now, too clearly shows that a speculative philosophy has ever been tampering with "the law and the testimony," corrupting the simplicity, and weakening the power, of Christian truth; and been a subordinate cause in producing, or aiding, the irreligion and skepticism of cultivated minds. The Pauline epistles testify, that before the apostles had left the world, philosophy, in some of its forms, was seeking to exert an evil influence on the church; so that Paul needed to protest against its intrusion, and warn the disciples of its spirit. Christianity, in the primitive age, had obtained a footing in many of those cities where, on account of their proximity to Greece, the Oriental and Grecian philosophies prevailed. These philosophies were rife with bold and unhallowed speculations respecting such things as the mode of the Divine existence, and the nature of the Divine agency. The sublime mysteries of the Gospel were just such subjects into which they wished to intrude. And, from a vain philosophy — vain, because transcending the boundaries of fair and legitimate inquiry — the simplicity of the faith had no less to dread than from the misapprehensions and corruptions of Judaism. Gnosticism did in the church, in primitive times, what rationalism has been doing in modern times. "In all cases," says Neander, "the gnostics were for explaining outward things from within — that is, from their intuitions, which were above all doubt."[1] Gnosticism was the philosophic garb in which infidelity, with great professions of reverence, laid its hands on the Gospels, reduced to its own standard the revealed mysteries, and disturbed the peace and purity of

[1] Church History, vol. ii, p. 71 (Clarke's edition).

the early church. This philosophy was a fruitful source of skepticism and irreligion, and from it seem, in a great measure, to have emanated those deadly errors respecting the person and work of Christ which disfigured and tore in pieces the fair form of primitive Christianity.

The corruptions of Christianity pave the way for the denial of Christianity itself. And it has often been remarked, that there is scarcely a corruption of religious truth which might not be shown to have existed during the first three centuries of the Christian age. These corruptions are, in a great measure, to be traced to the prevailing speculative philosophies, abetted and being abetted by the depraved tendency in man to mutilate or add to, deform and weaken, the revelations of heaven. It is to a philosophical influence, for the most part, that we ascribe those unsound methods of interpretation, which, in the shape of allegory and mysticism, were carried so far by Origen and others, and which found hidden meanings in statements that were perfectly plain, and saw nothing incomprehensible in doctrines the most mysterious. The Alexandrian school of divinity, headed by Origen, became famous for its union of a spurious philosophy with Christianity. Some of the Christian fathers employed the same allegorical method in interpreting the inspired record that the Pagan Platonists employed in commenting on popular mythology and the Iliad of Homer. And this tended, very much, to change Christianity from the pure state in which it had been given to the world by the Lord and his apostles.

It is to a philosophical influence, in a great degree, also, that must be traced the sacramental theory. Baptismal regeneration does not date its birth in modern times. It was held by many of the primitive fathers. We find it, where we find almost all the corruptions of Christianity, in the first three centuries; and as a fruit of a vain philosophy tampering with the spirituality and simplicity of the church. It was common to impute a mystic efficacy to the use of certain terms, such as the repetition of the name of Jesus, and to the practice of certain forms. This flowed from the philosophical notions about matter. Matter was alleged to have certain evil tendencies, while, coëxisting with these, were some inherent powers which, being controlled by the divine will, counteracted the evil. This control was believed to be associated with the utterance of certain words and the performance of certain rites. Hence the mystical and superstitious efficacy of the sacraments.[1] But for the physical philosophy of the schools, and the general belief in magic in the early ages of the church, it may be questioned if the sacramental theory would have met with such a ready reception. These invested the ministers of religion with tremendous spiritual power, made them, by virtue of their office, dispensers of the grace of God, and originated that system of sacramental efficiency which, overshadowing the pure Gospel, has corrupted God's religion into man's religion, and, in thousands of cases, has induced thinking men to reject both.

Plato and Aristotle were the chiefs of the ancient schools. In them may be said to have centered all the speculative philosophy of Greece. And the influence of the one in the Eastern churches, for several centuries subsequent to the apostles, was manifested in debasing and changing the very substance of revealed truth; while the influence of the other in the West, during the middle ages, was exerted in defending and strengthening the corruptions. It is not a question with us, what use these philosophies were in whetting the human intellect, or how far they proved to be "the best gymnastic of the mind," but what bearings had they upon that truth which, coming from above, is the

[1] See Vaughan's Corruptions of Christianity, p. 293, etc.

divinest and truest philosophy. And history warrants the assertion that they spoiled it, corrupted its purity, innovated into its very essence, and were fruitful sources of formalism and infidelity.

It has been well remarked, by Dr. Hampden, that of the two philosophies, in their bearing on religious opinion, "Platonism has been more arrogant in its pretensions: it has aspired, not to modify, but to supersede Christian truth. Christianity had to struggle in its infancy against the theology of the school of Alexandria, which regarded the Christian system as an intrusion on the philosophical ascendancy which it had hitherto enjoyed. The New Platonists disputed the originality of the Christian doctrine, asserting that the sayings of our Lord were all derived from the doctrines of their master.[1] Nor was the mischief from the Alexandrian school neutralized, when, its open hostility being found ineffectual, disciples of that school merged themselves into the Christian name. The accommodation which then took place between the theories of their philosophy and the doctrines of the faith proved a snare to members of the church. Hence, upon the whole, resulted, even in the beginnings of the Gospel, an ambiguity respecting the peculiar rights of the antagonist systems. And this ambiguity affected the question of the self-originated divine character of the Christian truth.[2]

It deserves notice that Neander represents Platonism as having had a double influence in relation to Christianity. He, speaking from his own experience, regards it as having been, in many cases, a transition point to the Gospel. But the question is, What was its influence when carried into Christianity itself? The illustrious church historian himself shall answer: "The New Platonism could not bring

[1] Infidelity performs a cycle. Mr. Emerson says — a thing easier said than proved —" Christianity is in Plato's Phaedo."

[2] Hampden's Bampton Lecture, p. 10.

itself to acquiesce, particularly, in that *humility of knowledge*, and that *renunciation of self*, which Christianity required. It could not be induced to sacrifice its philosophical, aristocratic notions, to a religion which would make the higher life a common possession for all mankind. The religious eclecticism of this direction of the spirit could do no otherwise than resist the exclusive and sole supremacy of the religion that suffered no other at its side, but would subject all to itself."[1] Accordingly, as he shows, it was from this school that the most numerous as well as the most formidable antagonists of Christianity proceeded.

While the Platonism of Alexandria was thus gaining an ascendancy in the early church, recommending itself to the imagination of the contemplative as the revealer of mysteries, and thus transmuting the pure gold of Christianity into an impure mixture, the philosophy of Aristotle was, for the most part, regarded with aversion, as the armor-bearer of heretics and of the assailants of the faith. But, during the middle ages, the scholastic philosophy had its throne in the very heart of the Christian church; and its supremacy is still visible in the Romish system — the most corrupt form of Christianity that has been given to the world. From the seventh century, and onward, the philosophy of the Stagyrite began to be exclusively studied; and was resorted to for weapons, not so much in defense of scriptural truth, as for the purpose of strengthening and perpetuating the corruptions and superstitions with which the church was overrun. "The question of the influence of Aristotle's philosophy is more important on this very account, that it has been more subtile, more silently insinuated into, and spread over, the whole system of Christian doctrine. Being employed as an instrument of disputation, it has not been confined, like

[1] Neander's Church History, vol. i, pp. 46, 218 (Clarke's edition).

Platonism, to certain leading points of Christianity, as, for instance, to the doctrines of the Trinity and the immortality of the soul, but has been applied to the systematic development of the sacred truth in all its parts."

It is the metaphysics of the schools which form the texture of the Roman theology, and by which that system is maintained. In the destitution of Scripture facts for the support of the theological structure, the method of subtile distinctions and reasonings has been found of admirable efficacy. It eludes the opponent, who, not being trained to this dialectical warfare, is not aware that all such argumentation is a tacit assumption of the point in controversy; or is perplexed and confounded by the elaborate subtilties of the apologist. . . . The resistance which the Roman church has shown against improvements in natural philosophy, is no inconsiderable evidence of the connection of the ecclesiastical system with the ancient logical philosophy of the schools. There has been a constant fear lest, if that philosophy should be exploded, some important doctrines could not be maintained."[1]

This contentious philosophy, existing in the bosom of the church for many centuries, "clothed in the purple of spiritual supremacy, and giving the law of faith to the subject-consciences of men," was a fruitful source of skepticism and infidelity. Not a few distinguished names, including scholars of eminence and several of the popes, have been mentioned as instances in which doubt and disputation, taking the place of the love of truth, engendered a cold or profligate disbelief. Mr. Hallam, speaking of the unbounded admiration which the schoolmen had for the writings of Aristotle, says, "With all their apparent conformity to the received creed, there was, as might be expected from the circumstances, a great deal of real

[1] Hampden's Bampton Lecture, pp. 12, 385.

deviation from orthodoxy, and even of infidelity. The scholastic mode of dispute, admitting of no termination, and producing no conviction, was the sure cause of skepticism; and the system of Aristotle, especially with the commentaries of Averroes, bore an aspect very unfavorable to natural religion. The Aristotelian philosophy, even in the hands of the master, was like a barren tree, that conceals its want of fruit by profusion of leaves. But the scholastic ontology was much worse."[1] Men, in order to display their ingenuity, involved in perplexity the most important truths, fostered a spirit the very reverse of that with which it becomes us to approach the Sacred Oracles, made the worse not unfrequently appear the better reason, and, in some instances, went so far as to take up the false and destructive position that opinions which were philosophically true might be theologically false. What Milton says of the fallen angels and their speculations is strikingly descriptive of the schoolmen and the dialectical abuses in which they passionately indulged: —

> "They found no end, in wandering mazes lost.
> * * * * * *
> Vain wisdom all, and false philosophy."

And just because the philosophy was false, and the wisdom vain, the Christian faith encountered in it a dangerous enemy under the disguise of a professed friend.

It is, however, of the connection subsisting between the modern speculative philosophy and the forms of modern infidelity, that we wish more especially to speak. Two philosophies, distinguished from each other by very broad characteristics, though, in so far as religion is concerned, often tending substantially to the same result, have played very prominent parts in modern times. We allude to what have been aptly designated *sensationalism* and *ideal-*

[1] Hallam's Europe during the Middle Ages, vol. iii, p. 536.

*ism.* The influence of these philosophies, when pushed to their extremes, has been productive of a vast amount of the infidelity which, during the last and the present century, has prevailed in the departments of scriptural exegesis, literature and science.

The sensational philosophy has had a wide-spread influence, in many quarters, in destroying the very fundamental principles of natural and revealed religion. It was, in fact, in one period, the creed of nearly the whole of philosophical Europe. Hobbes is the precursor of modern sensationalism. He, by resolving every operation of the mind into transformed sensations, based his theory upon avowed materialism, struck at the root of all religion, precluded us from having any real conception of a Supreme Being, and shut us out from all other existences but matter and a material world. His Psychology is expressed in the maxim: *nihil est in intellectu quod non prius fuerit in sensu.* Nothing, according to him, is in the intellect, but what was previously in the sense. It is chiefly owing, however, to the circumstance of his name having become so much associated with that of Locke, that the philosopher of Malmesbury has exerted such an influence in the spread of sensationalism. The system of the "Leviathan," and that of the "Essay on the Human Understanding," have been confounded. And a corruption, or an exaggerated development, of Locke's principles, has been imputed to him, as if he were its veritable author. But the difference between them is fundamental. The sensationalism of Locke has no necessary tendency to materialism, whereas materialism is not only the landing-place, but the foundation of the theory of Hobbes. "They differ," says Sir James Mackintosh, "not only in all their premises, and many of their conclusions, but in their manner of philosophizing itself. Locke had no prejudice which could lead him to imbibe doctrines from the enemy of liberty and of religion." The province which Locke assigns to reflection, and his maintaining that the senses do not furnish the intellect with the whole of its ideas, clear him of the charge of a tendency to materialism. How, then, has his name become allied with the pernicious dogmas of the materialist school that flourished in the eighteenth century; and how comes M. Cousin to say that, "Since the metaphysics of Locke crossed the channel, on the light and brilliant wings of Voltaire's imagination, sensualism has reigned in France without contradiction, and with an authority of which there is no parallel in the whole history of philosophy?" The explanation is to be found in what Sir W. Hamilton calls "the two partial principles" of Locke, which the French school, represented by Condillac and Cabanis, much exaggerated. The sensuous origin of our knowledge, though not to the exclusion of reflection, has a very prominent place assigned to it in the "Essay on the Human Understanding;" and it is this part of his system that the sensational school has drawn out, and founded thereon a scheme of materialism destructive of all the principles of morality and religion.

It has been said, "that Locke distinctly enough foresaw the idealistic and skeptical arguments which might be drawn from his principles. He did not draw them, because he thought them frivolous." But others did. In our own country Berkeley derived from them his arguments against the existence of matter and a material world; and David Hume, taking a bold step in advance, involved both mind and matter in doubt and darkness. Berkeley laid hold on Locke's principle, that our knowledge of external things is not immediate but through the intervention of ideas, and maintained that matter is not a reality but an inference; that "all the choir of heaven and furniture of earth — all those bodies which compose the mighty frame of the world — have not any subsistence without a mind." Hume, too acute not to see the inference, and too skeptical not to draw it, showed that the existence of mind as well as matter was a mere inference, and that nothing real was left us but a succession of impressions and ideas. These speculations were, in the last degree, adverse to the interests of religion.

Philosophical skepticism, within certain limits, does not necessarily imply religious skepticism. But in the case of Hume it was universal — involving in inextricable doubt and confusion the whole region of morals and religion. And its effect on multitudes who had neither the inclination, nor ability, to follow the philosopher through all his subtile windings, was seen in a contemptuous disregard of everything lying beyond the senses as wrapped up in the most perplexing doubt and mystery. It is indisputable that the stupid deistical school of writers which flourished during the last century, a school into which Locke never would have entered, fortified themselves with many of the conclusions that were drawn from exaggerating the somewhat partial principles of his philosophy. It was on these conclusions that they endeavored to ground their doctrines of invincible necessity and stern materialism, thereby tending to confound moral distinctions, and to make God and nature synonymous. And it is just as indisputable that through them descended to the educated classes in general, the disposition to look with indifference on everything supernatural, so fearfully characteristic of the period referred to. The Israelites heard conflicting accounts of the land of Canaan, and being disposed to believe the evil report which suited their indolence and carnality, they said, "Let us make a captain, and let us return into Egypt." And multitudes who are more prone to cleave to earth than rise to heaven, seeing in the progress of philosophic speculation the tendency to materialize everything, or to wrap in perplexity the supersensual, are disposed to leave religion to priests, and virtually say, "Let us eat and drink, for to-morrow we die."

In many of our works of science, and in much of our common literature, the evil influence of an extreme sensationalism has been manifested. Secondary causes are rested in, while an intelligent First Cause is seldom or never adverted to. Providence is either denied, thrust away into a general superintendence, or habitually passed over as a worn-out fiction. And nature is brought into control and account for everything, as if, independent of nature, there were no God. Priestley has been instanced as an example of the influence of a sensational philosophy on religious opinions. He was an avowed materialist; and, though he did not carry his materialism so far as to overturn the principles of natural religion, his theology was unstable as water, having little or nothing in it peculiarly Christian, and being powerless for the promotion of spiritual life. This influence has been felt, and acknowledged, on the unitarianism which, since his time, has existed on both sides of the Atlantic; for it is undeniable that it has been losing whatever spiritually it possessed, and been gravitating more and more toward simple deism. There exist an "Old School" and a "New School," as they are called; and while the latter is, in a great measure, the effect of German idealism, the former represents the influence of the old sensationalism. "It is connected," says Mr. Theodore Parker, "with a philosophy poor and sensual, the same in its basis with that which gave birth to the selfish system of Paley, the skepticism of Hume, the materialism of Hobbes, the denial of the French deists."[1] This,

[1] Parker's Discourse, p. 355.

though the testimony of one who has passed over to the "School of Progress," is true. In short, the influence of a developed sensational philosophy, when brought to bear on religion, has ever been to denude it of its mysteries, quench its spirit, reduce it to a system of material formalism if not to deny it both in substance and name. Mr. Morell thus briefly marks the progressive stages: "The first effect is to weaken our perception of the Divine personality; this, in the second place, makes itself apparent by overturning the doctrine of a particular providence; next, in order to remove the divine working further away from the world, secondary causes are adduced to explain, not only all the phenomena of nature, but also the direction of human life; and then, lastly, the process advancing one step farther, it begins to be an object of speculation and of doubt whether there be a distinct personality in the Deity or not; until, at length, the conception of God is entirely blended with that of the order and unity of nature."[1]

It is to the Continent, however, and especially to France, that we must look for the full and broad effects of an extreme sensational philosophy. Condillac was the great apostle of the sensual philosophy of the Continent. He flourished about the same time as Hume, but his influence was much greater. A professed disciple of Locke, whose essay on the "Human Understanding" was warmly received in France, he, in the course of his speculations, departed widely from him. The English philosopher, while laying great stress on the sensuous origin of our knowledge, recognized two sources — sense and reflection. The French metaphysician obliterated the distinction, and resolved reflection and all our mental processes into sensation. As a philosophy of sensationalism, that of Condillac was complete; and it would have roused the indignation

[1] Morell's History of Philosophy, vol. ii, p. 584.

of the illustrious Englishman, could he have heard his name associated with it, as has often been done on the Continent. "In truth," as Mr. Lewes remarks, "when you see Locke's name mentioned by the French writers of the eighteenth century, you may generally read Hobbes; for they had retrograded to Hobbes, imagining they had developed Locke."[1] The results which followed, in reference to religion, were fearful. The amiable philosopher, spending his time noiselessly in his study, was sending forth speculations, involving germs which afterward ripened into absolute atheism and social convulsions. A host of popular writers arose, who pushing his philosophy to the utmost extreme, founded upon it an ethical system of the most undisguised selfishness, and which substituted physical, educational and political improvement for the duties and sanctions of religion. France, at this period, was renowned for her brilliant writers, her literary society, and men of scientific research. But within these circles everything spiritual was paralyzed under the reigning influence of sensationalism; and an infidelity, sensual, flippant, and daringly impious, ran riot and prevailed. Scientific research was sternly restricted to the material objects and mechanical forces of nature; and, if the philosopher looked beyond these, it was up to a vacant heaven in which he complacently said, There is no God. The moralist viewed man as a being wholly material, all whose mental powers and processes were but manifested sensations, whose moral law was self-interest, and to whom the doctrines of responsibility, a future life, and a living Personal God, were the dreams, pleasing or perplexing, of an unphilosophic age. The school of Voltaire, which completed its cycle of impieties by ridding men's minds of the idea of God — uttering as its watchword, in reference to

[1] Lewes' Biographical History of Philosophy, vol. iv, p. 59.

the Savior of the world, "Crush the wretch;" proclaiming death to be an eternal sleep, and the present scene the whole of man — was just an embodiment of the irreligious influences of the reigning philosophy. Diderot and others of the Encyclopædists were pupils and admirers of Condillac. And the famous atheistical book, "Système de la Nature," a work of which Lord Brougham says, "That words skillfully substituted for ideas, and assumptions for proofs, are made to pass current, not only for arguments against existing beliefs, but for a new system planted in their stead;"[1] was the matured fruit of the French sensational philosophy. And what was the influence of that philosophy on the people at large? They might never have sat at the feet of Condillac, or of any of the chiefs of the metaphysical schools, but, as has been remarked, "They had no difficulty in laying hold of what we may term the formulas of that philosophy — formulas which came before them in very intelligible propositions, declarative of complete materialism, together with an implied denial both of the doctrine of man's immortality, and the existence of a God."[2] The inmost spirit of that philosophy was atheistical, and it was expressed in that bold course of anarchy and impiety which has been too well designated the Reign of Terror.

The extreme skepticism of Hume, and the old French atheistical philosophy, may receive little or no countenance in this age of reviving earnestness, but we have inherited something of their spirit. Reid in Scotland, and Kant on the Continent, may have been instrumental in rolling back the tide, but the destructive effects of it are yet visible on the land. That positive hostility to a pure spiritual religion, or that contemptuous disregard of it, so wofully char-

[1] Brougham's Introductory Discourse, p. 172.
[2] Morell's History of Philosophy, vol. i, p. 22.

acteristic of some modern works of science; that strict care to guard metaphysical speculations and physical researches from the idea of a superintending providence; that exclusive attention to mere secondary causes, to the extrusion of the Great First Cause; that cold, formal air of respect shown by much of our literature to religious truth and the manifest tendency to look with indifference on all religions as very much alike;—the materialism, indifferentism and formalism of the age, are the protracted influences of a waning sensationalism acting on the minds of men that are prone to live without God in the world.

The influence of an extreme *Ideal Philosophy*, in producing religious skepticism, has been not less powerful than an extreme sensationalism; the former having a tendency to run into pantheism, as the latter to run into materialism and atheism. We look to France, at the end of the last century, for the full development of the one; and to Germany, in more recent times, for the full development of the other. The speculative philosophy of Germany differs widely from that of our own country; and, as the mind of a nation is very much reflected in its philosophy, this difference arises out of the different mental habitudes of the two peoples. The English mind is eminently practical, and deals with palpable facts; it respects moral evidence, experience and testimony; and from these makes its way to the higher regions of abstract truth. Hence the clear common sense of our philosophy, and the absence of a vague transcendentalism in our theology. The German mind, on the other hand, is imaginative and fond of speculation, intolerant of the evidence of palpable realities, and, from abstract conceptions, argues its way to a system of science. Hence the extreme idealism of its philosophy, and the vague subtile speculations which, with much that is precious, float in its theology. Our philosophy aims chiefly at analyzing the powers and faculties of the human mind, and thus reaches man's moral and intellectual nature; and there finds, as in the phenomena of the material universe, evidences of the existence, providence and character of God. The German philosophy, on the contrary, busies itself with those great problems of existence which were discussed again and again in the ancient schools, and attempts to solve the questions relating to the being and nature of God, the universe and the moral agency of man. Philosophy, in our country, is not such an engrossing and exclusive object of pursuit, and consequently does not exert such an influence on our religious beliefs. There might be a false philosophy in our colleges, and yet a true theology might retain a strong hold on the hearts of our people. But, in Germany, philosophy occupies a large place, and sways powerfully the minds of the learned, and so close in hand does it go with theology, that the two have almost become identified. The idealism which characterizes its metaphysical disquisitions, characterizes also its religious speculations.

The German Ideal Philosophy dates from the time of Leibnitz. He was an opponent of Locke, and an independent, not a slavish, disciple of Descartes. "The comprehensive and original genius of Leibnitz," remarks Sir W. Hamilton, "itself the ideal abstract of the Teutonic character, had reacted powerfully on the minds of his countrymen; and *Rationalism*, (more properly *Intellectualism*), has from his time, always remained the favorite philosophy of the Germans. On the principle of this doctrine, it is in Reason alone that truth and reality are to be found."[1] Leibnitz placed himself in antagonism to Locke, by maintaining the Platonic dogma that the soul originally

[1] Discussions on Philosophy and Literature, p. 4.

contains the principles of several notions and doctrines which experience affords only the occasions of awakening. And it is in this view of the mind possessing innate ideas, independent of experience, and by its necessary laws arriving at necessary truths, that we have the germs of that philosophical rationalism which, when fully developed, bore such bitter fruits in theology; just as in the sensationalist principle of founding all our knowledge on experience, we have the seed that ripened into the complete skepticism of Hume, and furnished food to the atheistical school of France. The one, attaching an exclusive importance to everything within man, led the way to the finding of all knowledge and life in the depths of the mind; as the other, attaching itself to what lay without, was the occasion of sinking the spiritual in the material. The philosophic thoughts of Leibnitz floated loosely and beautifully on the stream; Wolf, one of his professed disciples, gathered them up and formed them into a rigid system. With him may be said to have begun the modern method of carrying philosophy into the domain of religion, of applying methods of proof to the Christian doctrines which are applicable only to objects of human science, and of arraigning before a stern logic divine revelation and historical testimony. In the wake of this school of philosophy, arose the great chief, Immanuel Kant, who greatly modified it. He was a man of strong subjective tendencies. It is a primary principle of his philosophy that the element of our knowledge coming from without, is merely phenomenal,—having no reality or shape till it is subjected to the laws of the understanding. The metaphysicians of this school, says Dr. Chalmers, will tell us, "that no evidence for a God is to be found in the experimental argument afforded by external and visible nature, not at least till the glorious spectacle of nature, teeming to common eyes with all the indices of design and order, shall somehow have been transformed and sublimated into their own speculations." Kant led his followers to a dizzy height far up in the regions of air, but there they did not stop. The climax was reached by Hegel, in whom idealism has become absolute, and from him have been obtained those weapons which, in the department of theology, have been wielded on the side of a complete rationalism.

Now, one thing is especially observable, amid all the bewildering and shifting speculations of the modern German school — namely, that the human mind is made the determinator of religious truth, and that no weight is given to the external facts and evidences of revelation except in so far as they harmonize with the inward sentiments and conceptions. The religious creed of our idealists is not historical, a matter derived from the past, a light coming from without; but it is metaphysical and personal, wrought out of the human consciousness, and altogether independent of outward testimony. It is a peculiarity of the extreme transcendental philosophy, to begin with the general and abstract notion of being; and, by a dialectic process, to construct a universe, a God, and a religion. Accordingly, the transcendentalist treats alike contemptuously our writers on the evidences of natural and revealed religion, and our experimental philosophers — a Bacon, a Newton and a Herschel. The whole objective element of Christianity, as a religion of historical facts, has no place in Hegelianism. Its place is usurped by the *à priori* conceptions of the human mind. Hegel, as we have seen, has a Christology, but it is the creation of his own philosophy. He deduces, by a process of logical argumentation, a God and the essential doctrines of evangelism; but, with him, God has no personality, except in the human consciousness; and the evangelic doctrines are not historical, inspired facts, but are included in the sweep of a philosophical rationalism.

The matured influence of this philosophy, in the department of theology, is seen in the writings of Strauss. He is an avowed representative of the extreme Hegelian party, and the "Leben Jesu" is the fruit of absolute idealism. His attack on the genuineness of the Gospels, his denial of an historical truth to the New Testament, and his attempt to resolve all its wondrous and well-authenticated facts into mythological representations of great spiritual ideas, have proceeded from his philosophical principles. The fundamental idea of the school is, that religious truth is the development of men's thoughts and intuitions, and not a revelation from without, having a firm footing in well-attested history. Accordingly, the doctrines of the fall, the Trinity, the incarnation, and the atonement, are held not to be historically true, but to have been framed by a developing process of the mind. The Christ of the Gospels, Strauss declares, is not an individual, but an idea. It is in vain that you point such a man to that vast and clear amount of evidence for Christianity as a religion of facts and a revelation from heaven, derived from unquestionable historic testimony, from a keen, searching criticism, from a wide experience, and from the character of Christ,— a character unrivaled in the annals of the world for the perfect harmony of its intellectual and moral elements. He tells you that the question, with him and his school, is one, not of Biblical interpretation or historical testimony, but of philosophical possibility. "First principles," he says, "must be settled on philosophical and dogmatic grounds, before the interpretation of the Scriptures can take effect." A first principle, with him, is the impossibility of miracles; and that arises naturally out of his philosophical creed.

[1] See Strauss, Hegel, and their Opinions. By Dr. Beard.

His philosophy allows not the interposal of a living personal God in the government of the world, or in effecting the redemption of men. The chain of endless causation, it says, can never be broken. All things, both in the physical and moral worlds, fall under the same law of necessary development; and, in harmony with this principle, Christianity must be explained.

Isaac Taylor has somewhere said that every particle of the German infidelity disappears, when once it is proved that Jesus rose from the dead. But the idealist, entrenched behind his speculative philosophy, is proof against this evidence. He does what the French infidels did in another way, supersedes the question of historical testimony, by raising abstract questions. We may speak of the folly of this principle, and show how, if applied to history in general, it would nullify its facts, and reduce its marvels to mere mental conceptions. But the rationalist, armed with his Hegelian weapons, replies, Such is my philosophy, and my philosophy is my theology. And that theology, as Germany too plainly testifies, has left the world without a personal God, and man without moral freedom and immortality. "A life beyond the grave," says Strauss, "is the last enemy which speculative criticism has to oppose, and, if possible, to vanquish." "Ask the extreme idealists of the present day," remarks Mr. Morell, "and they will tell you that God is one with the universe itself. The glorious conception of the great Jehovah, which we derive from the display of his wisdom, power and love in the creation without, the constitution of our minds within, and the intuition of our rational and moral nature, soon sinks down into a vague personification of the human consciousness. The final result of such a theology is, that the divine is dragged down to a level with the human, instead of the human being raised up (as it is by Christianity) to the divine. Thus, then, the extremes of sensationalism and idealism at length meet. The one says that God is the universe, the other that the universe is God. Diderot and Strauss can here shake hands, and alike rejoice in the impious purpose of sinking the personality of the Deity into an abstraction, which the holy cannot love, and which the wicked need not fear. Such is the extreme of idealism in its influence upon Christian theology—an extreme which contravenes and destroys all the good which at first it promised to effect."[1]

The influence of these idealistic speculations is telling, in some quarters, on the religious literature of our own country. Amid much really valuable in the department of theology, which we have imported from Germany, has come the evil genius of its philosophic spirit. The writings of Coleridge, Carlyle, and others, who have drunk deep at the German originals, have done much to diffuse among us the German philosophy. And though idealism in its extreme manifestations has made but little impression on the sturdy and sound English intellect, yet we have not wholly escaped the infection; and, judging from some recent productions of the press, are not likely to get rid of it very soon. A want of real vitality and earnestness in our religious community (to the ungrateful overlooking, we think, of the vast amount of living godliness among us) has been felt, and proclaimed to be the great want of the age. This has been ascribed, in a great degree, by some, to the want of a spiritual philosophy in our schools. And, in order to supply this want, and infuse new life into our cold orthodoxy, certain of our writers would bring a portion of German idealism to breathe upon our prostrate lifeless creeds, shake them, make them stand up and live. Accordingly, a religious philosophy, or a philosophical religion, has, for some time back, been quietly making its way among us; and we

[1] Morell's History of Philosophy, vol. ii, p. 611.

are only now becoming awake to the mischievous influence it is likely to have on an historical Christianity.

Carlyle and the men of his school seem to have a greater love for earnestness than for plain Gospel truths. They are disposed to follow the philosophers of Germany in making religion a creation from within,—not a matter received from without; and to be in danger of including among the shams they cry out against, the experimental and historical evidences of Christianity. Emerson, after the German fashion, and doubtless owing to German influence, finds everything within man, and makes religion merely an effect of mental action. "We run," says he, "all our vessels into one mould. Our colossal theologies of Judaism, Christism, Buddhism, Mahometism, are the necessary and structural action of the human mind."[1] Of course, as man has the fountain of all good in himself, his mind is the determinator of what is true in everything that comes to him from without. Theodore Parker, who has been so well taught by Strauss and De Wette, would have men to use the Bible as they use a well-filled table,—take what suits their palate. Francis William Newman, who has sat at the feet of the same teachers, has come to look upon the study of the Bible and its evidences "as the greatest religious evil of England;"[2] and he "deliberately, before God and man, protests against the attempt to make it a law to men's understanding, conscience, or soul."[3] Mr. Mackay, in his recent contribution to our rationalistic theology,—"The Progress of the Intellect,"—has taken, from the German metaphysical speculations, the development theory; and, with little regard to scriptural statements, and with an unfair use of historical testimony, has applied it so as to account for the religion of the Bible, without leaving

[1] Emerson's Representative Men, p. 2. [2] Phases of Faith, p. 205.
[3] The Soul; her Sorrows and Aspirations, p. 199.

any authority to the Bible itself. It is with much reluctance, we add, that Mr. Morell, who, in his first valuable work, pointed out and denounced the influences of an extreme idealism, has, notwithstanding the friendly warning of Dr. Chalmers, since shown a strong tendency to construct, somewhat after the German mode, a religion from within, and to attach comparatively little importance to that which comes independently from without. It is but justice to say, as we have formerly said, that there is a wide difference between the spirit of Mr. Morell and some of the rationalistic writers adverted to. He is by no means eager, we are persuaded, however his principles may tend in that direction, to subvert the great Christian truths. Nevertheless, his "Philosophy of Religion" is the product of the German religious philosophy. And, in contending "most earnestly for this position — that the simplicity of the gospel of Christ is to be looked for, not in our *logical systems* of doctrine, but in the clear elimination from all systems, or rather from the religious intuitions of *all good men*, of the vital and essential elements of Christian faith and love, hope and joy,"[1] — he shows his strong subjectivity, and a tendency to number among logical forms what the Christian world has ever regarded as the essence of Christian doctrine.

Christianity, as we simple folks have imagined, is a fixed and not a floating thing — having an objective and authoritative standard in the Scriptures, being supported by a powerful force of external and internal evidence; the truths of which enter into the understanding and descend into the heart, quicken and purify all its sensibilities, and manifest their lovely fruits in the conversation and life. But, according to our idealist writers, revelation is spontaneous and intuitional, a process of the mind gazing intui-

[1] Morell's Philosophy of Religion, Preface, p. xxii.

tively upon eternal verities, a thing altogether subjective; and no other authority is left to the Scriptures than in so far as they harmonize with the mind's intuitions. "No one," says an able reviewer, "can have read books of this class — from those of Mr. Carlyle downwards — without marking the special aversion of this whole school of authors to what are called the 'Evidences.' By this term they mean the external and critical evidence which determines the historical truthfulness and the just interpretation of the sacred writings. There is no end to the repugnance evinced by them toward this department of investigation."[1]

In all this, we see the influence of the modern transcendental philosophy, a philosophy subtile, daring, proud, — intolerant of the world of realities lying without, and which assumes to weave, by its own dialectics, all truth from the mind within. Let us hail, from whatever quarter it may come, any goodly element of vitality that would quicken the good things which remain and are ready to die. But let us be jealous of every system, whatever be its pretensions, that would transmute a Christianity founded in facts, into a matter of the mind's own fashioning; and that would dismantle the towers and bulwarks of an historical faith as if they were only fit for a bygone age. "Christianity comes to our times as the survivor of all systems; and after confronting, in turn, every imaginable form of error, each of which has gone to its almost forgotten place in history — itself alone lives,"[2] — lives, not as a creature of the mind's development, — a thing of mere sentiment or intuition, but lives with its firm footing in history, and its powerful hold of men's hearts.

Faith and philosophy are not enemies by nature. They are both children of the light and of the day, and were designed to walk hand in hand through the world. But, "in

[1] British Quarterly, No. XIX, p. 167. [2] Taylor's Spiritual Christianity, p. 6.

pride, in reasoning pride, our error lies." Men have often put asunder what God hath joined together. Speculation has been arrayed against the power of fact. Man's mind, vainly puffed up, has risen against God's mind. Philosophy, having either become sensual or vaguely transcendental, has been changed into that which is devilish and spurious, and has then fought against the truth of God. But "truth is strong next to the Almighty," and will prevail. Meanwhile, we note that speculative philosophy, whether in the form of an extreme sensationalism, or of an extreme idealism, has, as a subordinate cause, been productive of no small amount of infidelity. Paul's exhortation is still needed,—"Beware lest any man make plunder of you, through philosophy and vain deceit." "Which words," says Thomas Fuller, "seriously considered, neither express nor imply any prohibition of true philosophy, but rather tacitly commend it. Thus, when our Savior saith, 'Beware of false prophets,' by way of opposition, he inviteth them to believe and respect such as are true ones."[1]

[1] Fuller's History of the University of Cambridge.

# CHAPTER III.

## SOCIAL DISAFFECTION.

Social agitation not always to be deprecated — It is often a mark of right progress — Deep social discontent has, nevertheless, often proved favorable to infidelity — Great French Revolution — Social disabilities of the working classes — Existing social discontent the stronghold of infidel socialism — Desirableness of severing the socialist question from irreligious elements — Injurious influence of the prevalent theories: they make a religion of political liberty — Attempt to identify them with Christianity itself — Their pantheistic tendency — Admiration of political principles of infidels seductive in times of social agitation — Infidelity employed as an organ of political convulsion.

SOCIAL agitation is inevitable in a community that is suffered to develop its energies, and is, to some extent, salutary and beneficial. It often marks the progress of a state from barbarism to civilization, from despotism to civil and religious liberty. The grumbling and the upheaving are not unfrequently symptoms of advancement from a wrong to a right position. There are many things we like not the less because they are subject now and then to a shaking, and give forth a growl. Protestantism, with its conflicting sects and healthy rivalries, is infinitely preferable to Romanism with its leaden uniformity. Britain, with its free constitution, its limited monarchy, and right of public discussion, is a happier and safer government than Russia, under the iron hand of absolutism. The storm that rends the heavens and shakes the foundations of the earth, may be attended with many disasters; but if it be instrumental in purging the atmosphere, and rendering it salubrious, it is much more desirable than the dead noxious calm in which animal and vegetable life become oppressed. Our sympathies are more with the principles of a Sidney and a Hampden, than with those of a Filmer and his modern disciple, who declared that the people have nothing to do with the laws but to obey them. We would not, then, that the political world were lulled asleep, and that peoples' minds were drawn off from discussing the affairs of government. For, whatever injurious influence may affect religion amid the social heavings, it is assuredly not under the pall of despotism that it flourishes in its loveliness and vigor. Political science and religious truths are not points of repulsion, and a moderate attachment to the former is not necessarily counteractive of the influence of the latter. There is no necessary connection between the principles of political freedom and infidel opinions. It has often been remarked that the chief advocates of civil liberty in the reigns of the Charleses were the Puritans — men of whom the world was not worthy, some of whom were republicans, and others of them the firm adherents of a limited monarchy. Amid the storms of that period the cradle of British freedom was rocked, and rocked too by the saints, the excellent ones of the earth.

It may, however, be safely maintained, that political agitation, when running very high, has often for a time proved detrimental to spiritual Christianity, and advantageous to infidelity. It is not for us to balance the good and bad effects of the great French Revolution, which, in its results, marked a new era in the nations of Europe. But there can be no doubt, that the deep discontent engendered at the heart of French society, by social wrongs and abuses, rendered the soil receptive of the infidel principles of the philosophers, and that, in the terrible upheavings that followed, these principles were carried forth triumphantly like a flood. They were at once partly the cause and partly the effect of the social disorder. They set fire to the materials that had long lain ready to be kindled, and in the blaze they yelled, sported and exulted like fiends. The enormous abuses both in the civil and ecclesiastical institutions of the country — the church richly endowed, and yet leaving the mass of ignorance and vice around her to grow and strengthen; the venality and corruption which characterized the administration of justice, the unequal and oppressive taxation imposed upon the lower and middling classes, the mental degradation to which they were subjected in consequence of long-standing feudal distinctions, the luxury and frivolity of the court and many of the nobles,— these and such like abuses, which had separated one part of French society by a great gulf from the other, were the elements which infidelity quickened into a convulsion and in whose excesses it reigned.[1] An ill-taught and oppressed populace, overborne by a corrupt church and a despotic government, lies open to infidel teaching when allied with liberal politics, and in the agitation or revolt thereby produced, infidelity finds its element. Political and social harangues strongly interest the prejudices and passions of mankind, and tend, even when containing no infidel mixture, to draw the mind off from religious objects, unless they meet with a strong faith in eternal verities to counteract the evil. But when such discussions are associated with irreligious principles, and are brought to bear on minds socially disaffected and at the same time indifferent or hostile to vital Christianity, the influence on behalf of infidelity becomes powerful indeed. The poison, mingled with the water, flows on as fast as the water itself, and infects all who drink it. "The Rights of Man" renders palatable to many minds "The Age of Reason."

This is very much the case with many of the political and social theories afloat in our day, more especially on the Continent. The great problem in modern politics, is the elevation of the industrial mind so as to secure the great-

[1] See Brougham on French Revolution ("Statesmen of the time of George III").

est good to society in general. Comparatively few persons will maintain that the arrangements of society are as they should and might be. The spread of intelligence among the working classes has made them sensible of the social disabilities under which, in many parts of Europe, they have been long lying. The rebound is fully proportionate to the pressure. And the industrial interests rising up from the one extreme of depression, would ascend to the other extreme of elevation. The servant brooding over years of neglect and harsh treatment, would now avenge himself by becoming lord. The truth is, governments, by foolishly continuing those restraints on the popular mind in an enlightened age, which were suited to a past and different state of society, not unfrequently suffer a penalty somewhat similar to that which a landed proprietor suffers in damming up a stream. Arbitrarily checked in its course, it swells and chafes against the barrier; at length it sweeps all before it, and carries wasting and desolation, where it otherwise would have contributed to the fertility and picturesqueness of the country. Even in our own England, which is the home of freedom in Europe, and which, in the language of one of our old poets,

——"was sure designed
To be the sacred refuge of mankind,"—

the consequences of past neglect are too manifest. There are large classes among us who, from regarding almost everything established with blind reverence, have come to look upon almost everything really sacred with growing aversion. "In many cases," says Dr. Arnold, "the real origin of a man's irreligion is, I believe, political. He dislikes the actual state of society, hates the church as connected with it, and, in his notions, supporting its abuses, and then hates Christianity because it is taught by the church."

The problem to which we have adverted is that which the several socialist schools, with their widely-conflicting theories, propose to solve. The possibility of a great and sudden amelioration in the condition of the working classes, is the common faith of them all. Politically and socially they vary, and frown upon each other, from St. Simonianism, with its somewhat hierarchical arrangement of classes, to the humanist theory, the latest form of socialism, with its intolerance of any vestige of inequality. But tested by a religious standard, they all bear the mark of Cain, are vagabonds on the earth, and the last of them is worse than the first. Owenism, though it never had a strong hold on any large portion of the English people, and for some years has been losing the hold that it had, is steeped in atheism. It sees omnipotence nowhere but in external circumstances. And through this wretched system appealing to existing social disaffection, not a few are to be found here and there in our workshops and factories, who have been led over to the ranks of infidelity. In France, Germany, and other parts of the Continent, socialism has leavened the masses, and is still rapidly diffusing itself; and — what we wish especially to mark — the poison of infidelity is almost everywhere mixed up with it. It would seem that the socialist theories of the Continent can no more keep neutral in reference to religion, than the continental speculative philosophies. Indeed, these theories have, in some measure, been the fruit, or formed a parcel, of the philosophies. Fuerbach and Grün, who are of the extreme left Hegelian party, are the great teachers of humanism — a system which finds everything in man, which ignores all motive power but the human will, and which is as intolerant of the existence of religion as of private property.

There are good men, in our own country and elsewhere, who, being persuaded that socialism is no temporary ebullition of social discontent, but, as Mr. John Stuart Mill remarks, "Has now become irrevocably one of the leading elements in European politics," would seek to deal with the questions involved in it in a Christian manner. This we deem praiseworthy. The working classes have been left too much to the will of infidel socialist teachers, who exaggerate their grievances, lay upon evangelical religion the blame that belongs only to its corruptions, and hold out to them false hopes of amelioration. They have grievances which must be dealt with. And, convinced as we are that existing social arrangements admit of much improvement, that the relation between the capitalist and the workman, the governors and the governed, might be more satisfactory, we would have Christian men both in the Church and in the State to step in and deal fairly with the socialist question. We see no necessary connection between it and infidelity. And, without giving any opinion here as to the truth or justice involved in its essential principles, we would have it dissociated from the irreligious elements which have been hitherto so much mixed up with it, and let it stand forth simply as a question of political economy. But, be it the system of Owen or Fourier, of Louis Blanc or Fuerbach, all, notwithstanding the religious sentimentalism that may be found in some of them, have been of an irreligious tendency, and influential in making democracies at once fierce and ungodly.

The first thing, in the way of injurious influence that presents itself, on examining these theories, is the hope of happiness which they hold out, from entirely remodeling the framework of society. Differing as they do on important points of polity, the prophet of this school ridiculing the prophets of all other schools as fanatics and impostors, they agree in making a religion of political liberty, and looking for Paradise restored to a new arrangement of property and industrial interests. The real devil of the world, in their estimation, is private property. The depravity and wretchedness existing among men are ascribed to the factitious arrangements of society, and the regeneration of the race is to be expected from thorough-going social changes. It is in vain that history tells of speculations and schemes of a similar character having been tried in the past, having aggravated instead of having mitigated the miseries which they proposed to cure, and having been numbered long ago among the follies whereby visionary projectors thought to make a new world. So long as these speculations were not theirs, there is room, they imagine, for the trial of their own. The world must have its golden age, and these prophets of a social regeneration are to be instrumental in exalting every valley, making low every mountain and hill, making the crooked straight and the rough places plain. It were really amusing to sit, as in a panorama, and see how one plan of the world's reformation has absorbed men's attention for awhile, passed away as a vain show, and then given place to another destined to share the same fate, were the thought not to arise that these visionary projects have not only left society a prey to numerous vices and miseries, but have in a great measure diverted men's minds from "heaven's easy unencumbered plan,"—a plan which has survived all others, and which experience, as well as the voice of God, assures us is the only one fitted to make all things new. It is with this evil influence that all the socialist theories which have lately played such a prominent part are fraught. It were well enough did their abettors insist on social reforms as necessary to the physical and moral well-being of man. But to bid men look to these reforms as the panacea of all ills, the means of regenerating the race, and bringing about a heaven on earth, is as ungodly as it is visionary, as antagonistic to the gospel of Christ as it is deluding and destructive to men. Once persuade an individual or any body of individuals that all their miseries originate in political and social causes — that the source of the evil lies chiefly or exclusively without, and is to be removed by the prevalence of certain modes of education and civil government, and you leave no room whatever for the influence of that truth which coming from above is above all. And yet this is the teaching to which myriads of men in our own country, and more especially on the Continent, have eagerly listened at the feet of the apostles of social regeneration.

It has been well said by a respectable London journal,[1] that "the socialist principles are inevitable in any thinking country which has shaken off religious belief. If the Christian dispensation does not rise as the great and all-explaining truth before man's eyes, the philosopher cannot be contented with the inequality of human conditions, or avoid devising material plans for its removal. The more unformed intellect of the poor will eagerly follow in this path. And happiness being considered a compound of comforts, he will infallibly ask by what right he is excluded from his share of what the earth and industry produce, when his creed cannot enjoin the duty of patience or point to any present or future compensation." The truth is, that in all the socialist theories, as in the great expectations cherished from philosophical illumination in a preceding age, three very palpable facts are forgotten or denied. The first is, that a personal change of heart, and not a mere social or political amelioration, is the indispensable condition of all real and lasting improvement. National can

[1] The "Daily News."

only be the effect of individual regeneration. It is out of the heart, as the Great Teacher taught, that proceed the things which defile a man. And were the external arrangements of society ever so perfect, yet, without a radical change in men individually, these arrangements would be ever liable to corruption and attended with much misery. The second is, that inequalities and sufferings, in some form or another, are inseparable from man's lot upon earth. It is a principle in God's moral government that where there is no sin there is no suffering. Sin, however mysterious the fact, has entered this world, and suffering as a penal consequence has followed it. And that suffering is disciplinary as well as penal. The prophets of social regeneration, however, lay out their perfected world in the present state, and by the overthrow of the existing arrangements of society, would at once usher in the new heavens and new earth. The third thing of which they are oblivious or disbelieving is, that the gospel of Jesus Christ, not a mere political gospel whose favorite theme is equality and fraternity, but a gospel bringing glad tidings of a free and full salvation, containing ample provision for expiating human guilt and subduing human depravity, and giving the hope of life and immortality beyond the grave, is alone capable of realizing all the good for which pants the soul of humanity. These are facts confirmed by experience, and by none more than what is learned from the recent shakings among several of the European nations. The rise of a new and better order of things among mankind is no mere dream of projectors. The revelations of heaven warrant us to anticipate it. But we must look for its realization chiefly to the influence of nobler principles than political and social theories. Grapes are not to be gathered from thorns, nor figs from thistles. And to hold out, as all socialist projects that have been recently in agitation do, the hope of happiness from new social arrangements, is to delude men and abet the cause of infidelity. A religion of political liberty is thus substituted for the gospel of the grace of God.

The second thing in the way of injurious influence, noticeable in many of these theories, is the endeavor to identify them with Christianity itself. The existence of Christianity is an influential fact, the sanction of which other systems, however visionary and destructive of its spirit, are anxious to obtain. This they can do only by misrepresenting and virtually falsifying it. In the first great French revolution, there was no compromise. It was a war of open extermination against everything that bore the Christian name. The infidel leaders proclaimed the Christian system and the institutions connected with it to be the great hindrances in the progress of humanity, and they avowed their purpose to crush and extirpate the whole. But infidels now-a-days are covetous of the Christian name, and each one would have his respective system accounted the gospel which is designed to regenerate mankind. Many of the leaders of socialism have claimed to be regarded as the faithful expositors of Christianity. The reformation preached by Christ and his apostles is declared to have been a social regeneration. The Savior of the world is hailed as the prince of the communists. The substance of the Gospel is to be found in those texts which inculcate mutual love and affection; and the kingdom of God on earth, is the reign of equality and fraternity. Hegel, as we have seen, recognized Christianity, and the leading doctrines of the Trinity, incarnation and atonement; but it was only to bring them within the sweep of his law of necessary development, and to destroy them as facts on which men rest their faith and hope. In like manner, Fourier and his disciples, and even Pierre Leroux the pantheist, who has been acknowledged by the French to be the metaphysician of socialism, have sought to graft their speculations into Christianity, and have represented the one as naturally rising out of the other. In short, socialism lays hold of a peculiar characteristic of Christianity, which it severs from other and yet more prominent characteristics, and then preaching it up, as if it were the whole, does all the mischief which infidelity could wish. The religion of paganism and of a corrupt Christianity have had much of the arrogance and assumptions of caste about them. They have endavored to distribute men into classes, and have had their esoteric and exoteric doctrines. But the characteristic of Christianity to which we refer is, that it spreads a feast before all people, that it makes little account of natural or artificial distinctions, that it propounds and offers truth without reserve to the mass of mankind. This want of monopoly in Christianity, which, after all, is but its external aspect — the big-hearted and benignant attitude which it assumes toward the nations — is held up as if it were its essence. Socialism loves the generous and compassionate look of the Gospel, but it hates its holy humbling requirements. It would substitute Christianity as a mere liberal social economy, for Christianity as a system of pure spiritual truth. However visionary and absurd this may appear, yet its influence in promoting infidelity among the masses must have been great. It would be congenial, in the highest degree, to the social disaffection that existed; and, though utterly destructive of spiritual Christianity, would in multitudes of cases be the more welcome that it came under the pretended sanction of Him whose "name is ploughed into the history of the world." The faith of the French people, in the nineteenth century, is a political faith. It has no reference to man as guilty before God and radically depraved; it does not lay hold of the Gospel as in the highest sense a restorative economy, and seeking to make men free by delivering them from the state of the condemned, and forming them to a high and holy character. It is not a new thing in the world's history for infidelity to have propagated itself under the Christian name, and with a show of respect to Christianity's Great Founder.

We are led to remark, thirdly, the strong tendency of many of the recent socialist theories toward pantheism. Humanity is everything with them. The highest being is man. The perfectibility of the race is asserted. And in a paradise of social interests here, the idea of a happy world beyond is excluded. This is more especially the case with the humanists, who, in their rejection of an historical and spiritual Christianity, are in advance of other schools of socialism. In fact, pantheism has become the orthodox creed of the system. The extremes of idealism and socialism meet in declaring that religion comes not from without but from within, that it has no objective reality, but is purely a matter of the mind's own creation. We say that the sum and substance of religion is to be found in the Bible, a well-attested revelation from heaven, and that it only becomes the religion of man individually when it is received by faith, and thus incorporated with all his springs of thought and feeling. But the humanist says, Not so. In man himself, or in humanity, is to be found all that constitutes religious truth. It is not a thing without, lying in the world of facts, as the fortress on the hill and the river that runs at its base, but it is part of man himself, having neither origin nor objective reality independent of himself. Ask the apostles of this system, Where is your God? They at once reply, God is man. He is incarnate in humanity, and dwells in every member of the human race. Man as an individual dies, but humanity is indestructible, in the continual reproduction of the race he lives; and this is the life and immortality brought to light by the gospel of socialism. This system is just as intolerant of religion as an historical fact, as it is of private property as a thing existing in law, and it would proclaim the jubilee of humanity by abolishing both. Socialism, in its advanced form, has thus been influenced by the extreme ideal philosophy; and, in return, lends its helping hand to annihilate an historical Christianity. If it passed from France to Germany, and was originated by Rousseau and the infidel philosophy of the last century, it has been thrown into the German mould, and has come out in the shape of undisguised pantheism. And vast multitudes who have neither the capacity nor the inclination to follow the transcendentalist philosopher in his lofty and bewildering flight, sit at the feet of the socialist teacher, and through him imbibe all the infidelity with which that philosophy is pregnant. Masses of men who are socially disaffected, and in whom exists little or nothing of vital religion, and whose disaffection, it may be, is turned toward some corrupt form of Christianity among them, are readily carried captive by a pantheistic socialism.

Our last remark here is, that admiration for the political principles of infidels often leads men to think lightly of religion, and ultimately to cast it off. This is especially the case in times of social agitation. There is no necessary connection between politics, be they conservative or liberal, and infidel opinions. Pious as well as irreligious men are to be found in the ranks of all political parties. Principles of civil polity are nothing the worse because infidels have held and advocated them. The famous Declaration of American Independence was not the less illustrious because Thomas Jefferson, who prepared it, unhappily did not believe in the great truths of the Gospel. It is true, however, that those who think favorably of the political principles of infidels, are apt to be drawn away, so as to look with no unfriendly eye on the infidel principles themselves. This, owing to the original depraved bias of the mind, is likely to be much more frequently the case, than that love for the political principles of a Christian should lead men to embrace his Christianity. It has been not unreasonably supposed that admiration of Hume as a metaphysician and frequent intercourse with him, had no small influence with Smith in inducing him to expunge from his "Theory of Moral Sentiments," the well-known and remarkable passage in which he recognizes the doctrines of the Christian revelation as harmonizing with the original anticipations of nature. And it is not unreasonable to believe that multitudes have been prejudiced against Christianity, being kept from embracing it, or being induced gradually to renounce it, from a regard to the political principles of the men at whose feet they have sat. This will have been the case especially when the waters at the base of the social edifice have been running high, and men's minds have been agitated under real or imaginary social wrongs. If it has been so with political and social theories, containing no irreligious elements in themselves, but dangerous only when advocated by influential infidels, much more must it have been the case with many of the recent speculations of socialism, in which the liberal political creed and the infidel sentiments have been so blended together that, in imbibing the one, men could scarcely avoid imbibing the other.

Infidelity has come before the industrial classes in our day in an alluring shape. It does not stand forth in its own proper character. It has appeared in the garb of a liberal system of politics, professing to redress their grievances, and holding out to them the hopes of social elevation. The liberal polity, from its very connection, has recommended the infidel opinions, and, as the former has progressed, so have the latter. Robert Hall remarks, "The efforts of infidels to diffuse their principles among the common people is peculiar to the present time. Hume, Bolingbroke, and Gibbon, addressed themselves to the more polished classes. While infidelity was rare, it was employed as the instrument of literary vanity. Its wide diffusion having disqualified it for answering that purpose, it is now adopted as the organ of political convulsion." He is speaking of the time of the great French Revolution, but the remark is no less applicable to our own age. Since the close of last century political knowledge has made great progress among the people. It was no longer with fiercely ignorant democracies that many European Governments have to deal. The schoolmaster, in many shapes, has been abroad. The knowledge imparted by him has often served to awaken men to a sense of the social evils by which they are surrounded, without any salutary counteractives following the discovery. Social disaffection, the inevitable consequence of letting light in upon darkness, has been engendered. Hot-beds of infidel socialism have thus been prepared. While governments have been making too much ado about the people's duties and too little about their rights, the socialist teachers, with no small measure of success, have been incessantly calling the attention of the masses to their rights, and saying nothing or next to nothing about their duties. Out of the social discontent, occasioned by oppression or neglect, has come forth an evil spirit, uttering at once threatenings against the kings of the earth, and blasphemies against the God of heaven.

# CHAPTER IV.

## THE CORRUPTIONS OF CHRISTIANITY.

Not wonderful that Christianity has been corrupted — It has been so with truths of science — No promise that Christianity should be exempted — Corruptions in apostolic churches — Paul foretold them — Christianity not to be confounded with them or made responsible for them — Evil in judging of one by the other — Two evils flourish in the bosom of corrupted Christianity: superstition and unbelief — Reciprocal influence of these — Remark of Plutarch — A corrupted Christianity, and Romanism in particular, ministers to infidelity in three ways: It often produces aversion in cultivated minds to Christianity itself — The middle ages — France and other Catholic countries in last century — Remark of Macaulay — Italy, Spain, France, at present time — Tendency of Oxford Tractism — Remarks of Rogers and Whately — It leaves the mass of the people, in times of excitement, to be captured by infidel leaders — Instanced in France — It furnishes weapons for attacking Christianity itself — Parallel between corruptions of Christianity and the base citizens of a great nation.

THE best of things in this world are liable to be perverted and abused. Good is often made to assume the shape of evil, and then to be evil spoken of. Christianity is the very last system that could be anticipated to escape corruptions. Its doctrinal truths are so elevating in their character, and humbling to the pride of the human intellect, that men would be sure to distort their simple grandeur, and bring them down to the level of their own enfeebled perceptions. Its morality is so strict and pure,— being a discerner of the thoughts and intents of the heart, and admitting of no compromise with aught that is unholy,— as to induce those who are unwilling to follow its dictates, and yet anxious to have its sanction, to bend it to their own prevailing inclinations. Its rites are so few, simple, and destitute of attractions to the carnal mind, as to make it no matter of surprise that men who seek righteousness in mere outward observances, should add to their number, and render them meet for the lust of the eye. Christianity has been frequently so much corrupted in its doctrines, morals, and institutions, as to have rendered it somewhat difficult to trace any resemblance between the blotched copy and the fair original.

Every system of truth has been more or less corrupted under human influence. The sublime science of astronomy has appeared in the somewhat ridiculous shape of astrology. The simple science of chemistry, in the hands of the alchemists, was a science of sheer extravagancies. Natural philosophy was once represented by magic. Jurisprudence, rightly understood and applied, protects the helpless, shields the innocent, and promotes the liberty and prosperity of a state; but it has often been systematized into an engine of lawless oppression. If these earthly things, which are by no means uncongenial to human nature, or at variance with its predominating tendencies, have been corrupted in the hands of men, it is not wonderful that heavenly things, in coming down to the earth, should have been subjected to a similar influence. It might rather have been anticipated, that, in proportion as the revelation from above was purer and loftier than the principles of human conduct, would men endeavor to distort and corrupt it.

It is divinely promised that Christianity shall never be destroyed, but there is no promise that it shall, in every case, be kept free from corruptions. So far from this, that, even under the watchful presidency of inspired men, there were false teachers who crept into the church and endeavored to pervert the gospel of Christ. Yea, Paul, in his farewell address to the elders at Miletus, not only spake of the "grievous wolves" that should enter into the church after his departure, but he warned them that, even from the midst of their own selves, should men arise, teaching a corrupted gospel, to draw away the disciples after them. And the most influential and extensively spread form of a corrupt Christianity that ever existed was clearly foretold in the apostolical writings. They speak of damnable heresies, of a falling away, of the man of sin being revealed, and of the working of the mystery of iniquity.

Christianity is not, however, to be confounded with its corruptions, or made responsible for them. The solar light is pure and resplendent in itself, though often much bedimmed in the dense medium through which it passes. The fountain may be clear as crystal, and cast up no mire and dirt, while the streams are much polluted. The sacred text is to be distinguished from the false interpretations that have been given of it. The doctrines, precepts, and rights of Christianity, are to be judged of, not as they appear in the pages of the fathers, or as they are exhibited in Romanism, but as they are made known in the pages of the apostles, and were originally held forth in the churches which they planted. Astronomy, chemistry, and jurisprudence, are true sciences; but we would form very unfavorable opinions of them, did we estimate them by the frauds of the astrologer, the dreaming extravagancies of the alchemist, and the pleadings and practices of the corrupt lawyer. "In the view of an intelligent and honest mind, the religion of Christ stands as clear of all connection with the corruption of men, and churches, and ages, as when it was first revealed. It retains its purity like Moses in Egypt, or Daniel in Babylon, or the Savior of the world Himself while He mingled with scribes and pharisees, or publicans and sinners." [1]

The evil is, that multitudes persist in judging of the grand original from the gross caricature; which is just as if we were to form our estimate of the Savior's character

[1] Foster's Essays, p. 195.

from the representations given by the chief priests and rulers, instead of beholding Him, who, in the midst of his enemies, could challenge the most fierce and watchful of them to convince him of sin. And it is a still greater evil, that, in consequence of taking away the key of knowledge, suppressing religious inquiry, and prohibiting the perusal of the Scriptures, men have had often no other standard by which to estimate Christianity as a revelation from heaven than the corrupt form. It might indeed be said, that the very corruption of the doctrines, precepts and rites of Christianity, originating as it does in a tendency to assimilate the divine to the human, would have made it more accordant with the tastes of depraved human nature, and thereby secured it a wider and firmer reception. Such has been the case. Christianity in its debased forms has had a much more extensive sway, and numbered vastly more adherents, than Christianity as it came from God, holy, benignant and undefiled. But this has only been detrimental to the truth as it is in Jesus. Christianity in its undefiled form is the great antagonistic influence to the power of Satan on earth. He, the father of lies and the seducer from the beginning, has polluted the streams in order to divert men from the fountain. And the Divine Author of Christianity, whose prerogative it is to bring good out of evil, has permitted the adversary, in a considerable extent, to succeed.

It deserves notice that in the bosom of a corrupted Christianity two evils flourish — superstition and unbelief — and that the former is, in some measure, the cause of the latter. It was so with the religions of the old Pagan world, all of which were gross corruptions of the religion of nature; as Romanism and some other Christianized forms are gross corruptions of the religion of revelation. The ignorant and debased, in the presence of the corrupt system, generally sink into the arms of an unbounded superstition; while men of cultivated and philosophic minds, conforming, it may be, from policy, to the outward ceremonies, run off to a cold and hardened unbelief. It is an historical fact that, in the Augustan age, when the larger proportion of the Roman people were swelling the number of false gods, and yielding themselves up to the most degrading superstitions (in which they were countenanced by the emperor and the nobles), the Epicureans were outstripping all other philosophic sects in the propagation of their infidel principles. The priest laughed in his sleeves at the delusions of the people whom he himself was deluding; the orator, in the senate, avowed his disbelief of a future life, and repudiated the fabulous legends respecting the gods and the infernal world; and the historian, in quoting the popular religious traditions, intimated that he did not believe them. The infection spread from the higher and more intelligent classes to the illiterate multitude, and many, in renouncing the gross fables of Paganism, shook off all belief in invisible power and immortality.

Plutarch, whom Tholuck has characterized as the individual among the ancients who has spoken of belief, unbelief and superstition with the greatest wisdom and the deepest knowledge of mankind, has said, "Unbelief never gives occasion for superstition, while the latter does not unfrequently occasion the former; for when we teach perverted views in reference to divine things, we hold out occasion for total skepticism." The first of these statements is by no means to be assented to. The extreme of unbelief has often led to the extreme of superstition. Men from believing almost nothing, have come to believe almost everything. Into the void created by infidelity, superstitions have rushed and been eagerly received; just as the prodigal son, in the parable, would have welcomed the husks, when he began to be in want.[1] But what Plutarch says of superstition as the cause of unbelief is accurate and profound. And not less worthy of his wisdom is his admonition, in respect to the prevailing tendency of his age, "Let every man be well on his guard that, in order to escape robbers, he do not plunge into an impassable chasm; that while escaping from superstition, he do not fall into the power of unbelief by leaping over that which lies between them — viz., true piety."[2]

Superstition and unbelief, in the ancient world, generally increased as the corruptions of religion developed themselves. And multitudes, knowing no other alternative than the robbers or the chasm, escaped from the former and plunged into the latter. So has it been in the presence of a corrupted Christianity. The religion of nature was in nowise responsible for the corruptions in which heathenism enveloped it. The heavens declared the glory of God and the firmament showed forth his handiwork, notwithstanding the unbounded superstition and unbelief that prevailed. The religion of revelation stands clear of all the distortions into which men have wrought it, and of all the abominations with which they have associated it. It brings glory to God in the highest, peace on earth, and good will toward men. But the fine gold has been changed; and in tossing away the

[1] Neander states very truly the mutual connection between superstition and unbelief: "These two distempered conditions of the spiritual life are but opposite symptoms of the same fundamental evil, of which the one passes easily into the other. When once the inner life is become thoroughly worldly, it either suppresses all religious feeling and abandons itself to infidelity, or, blending itself with that feeling, gives to it an interpretation of its own. and thus turns it to superstition. The desperation of unbelief surrenders the troubled conscience a prey to superstition; and the irrationality of superstition makes religion suspected by the thoughtful mind."—Church Hist. vol. i, p. 18. (Bohn's edition.)

[2] Tholuck on the Moral Influence of Heathenism, p. 74.

counterfeit, men have often lost sight of the heavenly reality. The counterfeit, however, must bear a portion of the guilt in the dishonor done to the pure original; and to a corrupted Christianity, as a subordinate cause, must be assigned no small amount of influence in occasioning the rejection of Christianity itself. Dr. Arnold believed the great cause of hindrance to the triumph of Christianity to lie in the corruption, not of the religion of Christ, but of the Church of Christ. The distinction serves only to mark off more broadly the divine revelation from the human corruptions, while it leaves the latter to bear much of the blame of the rejection of the former. "Christianity," says he, "being intended to remedy the intensity of the fall by its religion, and the universality of the evil by its church, has succeeded in the first, because its religion has been retained as God gave it; but has failed in the second, because its church has been greatly corrupted."

Romanism is not the only form of a corrupted Christianity. There is the Greek church, in which are to be found many of the same corruptions as are found in the Romish. There, in the very bosom of Protestantism, are the Tractarians; "those factors for Rome," as Archbishop Whately calls them, who "remind one of Charon, in the old mythology, that 'grim ferryman whom poets write of,' continually ferrying over multitudes across the 'melancholy flood,' to a gloomy shore, from which he regularly returned himself alone, to take in a fresh cargo."[1] And, under the same category of a corrupted Christianity, must come much of the nominal Protestantism of the Continent, out of which has arisen a cold, deadening rationalism. But Romanism occupies the bad pre-eminence. Most of the other distorted shapes have been but mole-hills; this is the great

[1] Cautions for the Times, p. 302.

and hideous mountain. That salvation is attainable in the Romish church, we no more doubt than we question the exalted piety of such men as Borromeo, Fenelon and Pascal. But, consistent with this admission, history bears us out in affirming, that it is the most corrupt form of Christianity that has prevailed to any considerable extent; and that, in proportion as it gains ground, the pure spiritual Christianity of the New Testament is supplanted or impeded, and superstition and unbelief appear. It has no more been able wholly to extinguish the flame of vital piety, than the Egyptian bondage was to crush the Israelitish spirit. Even when a thick darkness that might be felt has overspread the land, the children of Israel have had light in their dwellings. But how large a space does it occupy in the history of the church and the world; how very numerous are the points of contrast which it presents to the simple truth as it is in Jesus; and, itself the offspring of darkness, how great the darkness in which it has shrouded, for ages, a large portion of humanity!

It is of the system as a whole that we speak. We know that within its pale exist men of every grade, from the spiritually-minded down to the grossly superstitious and idolatrous. And, as a system, it is doubtless the most corrupt that ever bore the Christian name, and has proved more prejudicial to the pure gospel of Christ than any or all of the corrupt systems which have not professedly waged war against it. It may claim a venerable antiquity, but Christianity, as it came down from heaven, clothed in fine linen clean and white, dates beyond it. And the centuries that it reckons up in its age, only remind us how very soon the mystery of iniquity began to work, and the fine gold became dim. If that be not the most corrupt form of Christianity, which, under the penalty of anathemas, forbids the common people to read the Scriptures, denies that they are a complete rule of faith and practice, and exalts vain traditions as of equal authority; if that be not the most corrupt which enjoins the worship of saints, images and relics, virtually denies the perfection of the Christian atonement by offering up the sacrifice of the mass, multiplies the number of the sacraments, and loads the simple divine institutes with a gorgeous host of ceremonies; if that be not the most corrupt which enslaves the mind and keeps it in ignorance, and which, in making darkness its pavilion, is ever jealous of the light; we know not where a corrupted Christianity is to be found. It preserves the name of Christianity, and, nominally, at least, retains its doctrines; but, under an enormous mass of corruptions, entombs its spirit.

It is not as now existing in Protestant countries, surrounded and in a great measure influenced by the light of the Reformation, that we are to form our estimate of it, but as it appears in Italy and Spain, where it develops itself according to the authorized canons of the church; and even there it is somewhat under the check of the advancing mind of the nineteenth century. It had its origin in the attempt to reconcile the adherents of the worn-out pagan worship, who were scattered in considerable numbers throughout the empire, to the Christian faith which had silenced the oracles and overthrown the altars of polytheism. It was a kind of compromise between the old worship and the new. The church hierarchy, so early as the days of Constantine, evinced a tendency (so often shown since by Romish missionaries) to give Christian baptism to individuals while yet in the bosom of heathenism, and to make old superstitious practices fit into the Christian worship. The striking resemblance between the superstitions of Papal Rome and Pagan Rome has often been pointed out. Romanism, by its perversions of great Christian doctrines, and by the meretricious ornaments with which it has loaded simple Christian rites, has earned the title of a baptized paganism. No enlightened mind, looking at Christianity as it is taught in the New Testament, and exemplified by the apostles and early churches, and comparing it with the Papal system as enunciated in the decrees of councils, embodied in its existing institutions, and manifested in the moral condition of those lands where it predominates, can help concluding that Popery is the most decrepit and corrupt form of Christianity.

"In the stagnant marshes of corrupted Christianity," remarks Robert Hall, "infidelity has been bred." Romanism has nourished the grossest superstitions, and given rise to the most dissolute skepticism. By locking up the treasures of divine knowledge, and substituting penances, indulgences, and pompous ceremonies, for an enlightened and operative faith, she has kept the great mass of her people as ignorant and slavishly superstitious as Hindoos; while she has disgusted the more intelligent, and driven them into secret or open infidelity.

It will be found, then, that there are three ways in which a corrupted Christianity, and more especially the Papacy, the masterpiece of corruptions, ministers to infidelity.

1. In the first place, it often produces *aversion in cultivated and reflecting minds to Christianity itself*. Men have often known Christianity only by Popery—its most corrupt form. The Romish Church and the Christian Church, the Catholic doctrines and the Gospel doctrines, they have been taught to consider as identical. All the good effected by Christianity in the world, is claimed for the Papacy. M. de Falloux, one of the most staunch Romanists among the French statesmen, strikingly confounded Christianity with Romanism, when, in a recent speech in the French Assembly, he went on to say the Papacy has done this good

and that good. All the corruptions of Popery, on the other hand, are laid by multitudes at the door of Christianity. If they read history, so large a space does Romanism occupy, that (overlooking the little uncorrupted church of Christ which has ever been as a green islet in a troubled sea or as a light shining in a dark place), the history of the Papacy is with them the history of Christianity. And that history is dark, foul and loathsome. It is a series of dire oppressions and hideous corruptions; the record of a system which, professing to free and elevate man, has debased and enslaved him; a system loving the darkness and hating the light, full of pious frauds and outrageous crimes. They look around the land in which they dwell, and Romanism, unchangeable in its mummeries and corruptions, in its enslaving and benighting influences, rises up before them as the all-explaining fact of the Christian Dispensation. Such men, on becoming enlightened, and emerging out of the superstition in which the masses are sunk, inwardly, if not avowedly, loathe the gross doctrines, cumbersome rites and absurd practices of the church. And if they know not a purer faith, or, by the very loathing which they have contracted, are averse to inquire after it, the consequence will be either that, retaining, from policy, an outward connection with Rome, they secretly cherish infidelity; or, adopting an honester though still a fatal course, they pass openly over to the ranks of those who denounce Christianity as a cunningly-devised fable.

This is no mere supposition. The history of the past and the experience of the present corroborate it. During the dark ages, Christianity, in the hands of Romanism, sunk into the grossest superstition; and that superstition was the occasion of a vast amount of the then existing infidelity. A pure gospel was then, as always, in the world, but it was wandering in deserts, and in mountains and in dens and caves of the earth, being destitute, afflicted, tormented. It was a sadly depraved Christianity, more like a demon of darkness than an angel of light, that stood before men; and no wonder that multitudes mistook the demon for the angel, and in rejecting the one, rejected the other also. In the fifteenth century, when monkish superstition overspread the world — a thick darkness that preceded the break of day — men of learning and classical attainments in the church, such as Leo the Tenth, Bembo, and many others, were infidels; and their infidelity, even amid the abounding degeneracy, they could scarcely conceal. Under the shadow of the church were at once nourished a gross superstition and a profligate skepticism.

It was even so in the latter half of last century. Protestantism had, in many quarters, sunk into a deep apathy. A dry and sapless orthodoxy, followed by a carnal life, had supplanted the life-giving gospel in the churches. Romanism, on the other hand, had increased greatly in insolence and corruptions. The pure form of Christianity, except in a few places, had lost its vigor; and the corrupt form had become proportionably more corrupt. The consequence was an inexpressible disgust in the minds of enlightened men at the doctrines and practices of the Romish Church, followed afterward by an outburst of infidelity and impiety. The church of France, before the Revolution of 1789, had left the great mass of the people in the most extreme ignorance, and had disguised religion in a tissue of frauds and impostures. Its intestine quarrels, its grievous oppressions, its benighting influences, its absurd pagan mummeries, had rendered it an object of disgust and contempt to the more intelligent portion of the nation. The spirit of infidelity waxed mightily. Romanism, being the only form of Christianity that came prominently under men's notice, was confounded or identified with Christianity itself. And men, in making a rebound from a gross and oppressive superstition, overlooked the little true piety that lay between, and fell into the abyss of unbelief. The growing corruptions of the system opened men's eyes, and convinced them of its falsehood; and some being unwilling, and others unable, to make a distinction between Christianity as a revelation from heaven, and Christianity as distorted and deformed by Popery, the former had to bear the crimes of the latter, and, in the fierce onset, the destruction of Romanism was hailed as the abolition of Christianity itself. The Archbishop of Paris and others, in publicly renouncing Popery, proclaimed their disbelief in Christianity.

Such was the case, to a considerable extent, in all the other Catholic countries of Europe, during last century. The Church of Rome was fast losing its hold on men's minds. Infidelity, in many places, gained the ascendant. Multitudes, in escaping from superstition, rushed into unbelief. Mr. Macaulay remarks, that "at the time of the Reformation, whole nations renounced Popery without ceasing to believe in a First Cause, in a future life, or in the divine mission of Jesus. In the last century, on the other hand, when a Catholic renounced his belief in the real presence, it was a thousand to one, that he renounced his belief in the Gospel too."[1] The reason of the difference is obvious. The Reformation was a voice calling aloud, like a trumpet, on the slumbering nations to awake. It was liberty, in all the vigor of youth, undoing the heavy burdens, breaking every yoke, and bidding the oppressed go free. It was the gospel of the grace of God, as fresh and mighty as when preached by Paul, proclaiming the acceptable year of the Lord, and bringing the good news of a free and full salvation to distressed and wearied souls. The men who called upon others to escape from the rob-

[1] Review of Ranke's History of the Popes.

bers, pointed them to the city of refuge, and thus the nations escaped the chasm. But the Protestantism of the Continent, during the eighteenth century, had, to a fearful extent, lost the life which the Reformation originally breathed into it. It was slumbering on the lap of rationalism. The trumpet had fallen from its lips. It had substituted mere abstractions, or negations, for the life-giving word. And when multitudes were rushing, like prisoners let loose, from an oppressive superstition, Protestantism, shorn of its locks, wanted the power to arrest them at an intermediate point, and prevent them from falling into the abyss of infidelity.

Again, if we look to those parts of the Continent where a corrupted Christianity is dominant in our own day, we find abundant illustrations of the position which we are endeavoring to establish. These two excrescences of religious life, as Tholuck calls them, superstition and unbelief, appear very prominently. One portion of the people, generally the more ignorant, are sunk in superstition, and blindly devoted to gross ceremonies. The other, and more enlightened portion (saving those who have embraced the genuine Gospel), having confounded the pure and the corrupt, have lapsed into secret or open unbelief. In the bosom of Romanism men have been taught to regard every species of Protestantism as an upstart faith, and lying without the pale of the true church. And multitudes, in abandoning the one for its corruptions, have not been divested of their prejudices in reference to the other so as to seek in it a religious home. It has been deemed no libel to affirm that many intelligent Romanists on the Continent, who are too clear-sighted to be befooled by the mummeries of the Papacy, and too politic openly to proclaim their hostility, have no faith in the Christian revelation. In Italy, in Spain and France, Romanism, in the eyes of the nation, is

Christianity, and Christianity is Romanism. Men still judge of the pure gold by the base counterfeit, they decide on the merits of the heavenly original by the earthly caricature. Indeed, in many cases, the distorted form is still the only shape in which Christianity comes under observation, so that, in losing their hold of the one, men give up all the Christianity that ever they knew. And in other cases, the rebound from Romanism, in cultivated minds, is proportioned to the former pressure, so that, to repeat Plutarch's saying, "Men in escaping from the robbers, plunge into the chasm."

"Italy," says Dr. Achilli, "pants to shake off Popery. But, with few exceptions, men who have seen Popery and Christianity so intimately connected with one another, have not spiritual discernment to separate the one from the other, and with the falsehoods of Rome they reject the sublimest truths of Christianity. . . . Italy is full of men who, ceasing to believe in the Romish dogmas, have ceased to believe in the gospel of the Lord Jesus Christ. One main cause of this is their ignorance of Holy Scripture. Pantheism and deism are, accordingly, occupying much of the ground in the Italian peninsula which has been prepared, though lost, by Romish superstition. Dr. James Thomson, whose acquaintance with the moral and religious condition of Spain is so extensive, tells us, that "many of the middling classes are free-thinkers or atheists. They could not be easily brought to read the Bible, for being disgusted with priestcraft and its impositions, they believe nothing and will hear of nothing." The corruptions of Christianity in that once proud land are fearfully glaring, and infidelity, as the consequence, is ravaging the country. Romish pretensions in France, since the revolution of 1848, have revived. But France has no faith in them. They may be made to play a part in the shifting scenes of the political drama. But discerning men predict that they will revive the spirit of Voltaire, and extend the dominion of infidelity. "For the great masses of our French population," says M. Roussel, "Christianity is Romanism, and Romanism is the mass, confession, ceremonies, fasts, and a thousand ridiculous superstitions; and here we have a distinct reason why infidelity prevails in France."

And, to come home, what have we in the "Oxford School" but a source of corruption, one stream of which is continually running to Rome, and another going off to skepticism. Mr. Henry Rogers affirmed in 1843, in an article in the "Edinburgh Review," that "the desperate assertion that the 'evidence for Christianity' was no stronger than that for 'church principles,' must, by reaction, lead on to an outbreak of infidelity." And he can now say, "that prophecy has been to the letter accomplished."[1] Newman, Foxton, Froude and others, who are waging war against Christianity, are the result.

The present Archbishop of Dublin devotes several numbers of his "Cautions for the Times," to show that the Tractite party, in deprecating the investigation of Christian evidence, and insisting on an implicit faith in what is taught; in putting the Scripture miracles on a level with the absurd miracles of later times; in covertly and by implication discouraging the study of the Scriptures, and exalting the authority of "traditionary revelation;" in earnestly deprecating the exercise of private judgment in religious matters; and in making Christianity assume the form of a religion of mere outward rites and observances; — are doing "more to shake the authority of Scripture than all the attacks made by infidels directly upon it ever have done, or ever can do. For Scripture is, in itself, invulnerable; and they who attack it, do but dash them-

[1] Reason and Faith.

selves to pieces against a rock. But it may be easily shown that "the fathers of the church" are mere human teachers, who often deliver false, and sometimes even absurd things, as true doctrine. To encumber Christianity, therefore, with the defense of *their* errors and absurdities, and make *that* essential to the safety of our religion — is voluntarily to exchange an impregnable fortress for a position which cannot be maintained against the enemy."[1] Once persuade men, as the Oxford Tractarians endeavor to do, that there is no alternative between their church principles and infidelity, and many, seeing the sorry foundation on which the former rest, will be led to pass over to the latter. "One might almost thank you," said a thoughtful young man, on leaving the Church of St. Mary's, Oxford, where one of the most determined of the Tractarian preachers had been holding forth in this strain, — "one might almost thank you for infidelity as an antagonist to this God-dishonoring and man-debasing system."[2] Thus it is that superstition, baptized with the Christian name, leads on, by reaction, to unbelief.

2. Another way in which a corrupted Christianity, and more especially the Papacy, ministers to infidelity, is — that *it leaves the mass of the people, among whom it prevails, to be captured by infidel leaders in times of national excitement.* The times of the great French revolution furnished abundant and fearful illustrations of the truth of this remark. The only religion which the great body of the French people, at the period referred to, was familiar with, was a bastard Christianity. And that bastard had hoodwinked, pilfered and enslaved them. It had interdicted religious inquiry, it had jealously withheld from them the pure word of life, and, in the room of the glad tidings of great joy, it had presented them with a system of impostures and false-

[1] Cautions for the Times, p. 243. [2] "Christian Times" (Nov. 1850).

hoods. The atheistical philosophers, men who knew of the existence of a purer religion, but who wished to bring every form of religion into the same condemnation, found the people in this condition, and determined to turn it to their own destructive aims. It was easy to point out to the people the trash, which, in the name of religion, had been gathering during ages of darkness and ignorance around them; easy it was to expose and hold up to ridicule the absurd doctrines, puerile ceremonies, extravagant pretensions, and oppressive exactions of the church of which they were children; and easy too it was, amid the darkness, to confound Popery with Christianity, and make ignorant and enslaved men believe that the religion of Christ was opposed to the rights of man, that *it* was the wretch, the oppressor. The lamp of Christian truth, as a light shining in a dark place, was in the land, but it was well-nigh overpowered by the surrounding obscurity. And men, having been trained to regard Romanism as the only true Christianity, were now easily persuaded by their infidel leaders, in abjuring Romanism, to reject Christianity itself.

Had the church of France, previous to the Revolution, instructed the people in the gospel truth, put into their hands the pure word of God, and preached the doctrines of the cross from her pulpits; had she stood forth before the eyes of the nation identified with all that is pure and lovely and of good report in Christianity; then, though a revolution had been necessary, and infidel leaders might not have been wanting, the body of the people would have been kept from those dreadfully impious excesses with which the Revolution was stained. As it was, however, the fair form of religion wore a repulsive disguise, lay upon the neck of the nation like a yoke, had kept it in a worse than Egyptian bondage; and, the people being thus left a prey to pretending philosophers, were taught to avenge themselves by throwing off the heavy burden, and trampling everything bearing the name of Christianity in the dust. A corrupt church left the people to be seduced by an atheistical philosophy; and the protracted effect is seen at the present day, for, amid the illumination of the nineteenth century, the French nation is nominally Roman Catholic, but at heart without faith in the Christian revelation. This, then, is one of the chief ways in which a corrupted Christianity ministers to infidelity. It plunges the people into superstition, and out of that superstition, at the call of the ungodly leaders, rises the demon of unbelief. *That* demon is now stalking abroad in many lands.

3. The corruptions of Christianity form also *an armory out of which infidels take weapons to attack Christianity itself.* Their own infidelity may be accounted for in another way; but their hands are strengthened by the impostures, absurdities, and oppressions, which, bearing the Christian name, have converted that which is a blessing into a curse. A good cause when depraved and made hideous by professed friends, becomes auxiliary to its avowed enemies. It is rarely that such men attack Christianity as it is developed in the sacred volume, and exemplified in the lives of real Christians, but as it has been misrepresented by themselves, or as it exists imbedded in a mass of corruptions. They are wont to appeal to the ignorance and superstition, the priestcraft and crime, existing under a grossly perverted Christianity — of which unhappily the greater part of church history is too full, and nations nominally Christian present too abundant illustrations — and, with a dishonesty wofully glaring but often effectual, represents the evils as if they were the fruits of Christianity itself. These were the weapons which were brandished by Paine and his school; Holywell Street bristled with them; and they are

not unfrequently taken up by a class of adversaries who would repudiate all sympathy with Paine in his coarse blasphemy and vulgar impudence. The grossest darkness and superstition have existed and been retained under the shadow of the church, the direst oppressions and the most outrageous crimes have been perpetrated in the Christian name; and these, the effects of a sadly distorted Christianity, are, with little ingenuity and less modesty, thrown in the face of undefiled Christianity itself. Men can distinguish between astrology and astronomy, between chemistry and alchemy, between natural philosophy and magic, and they never think of employing the one to fight against the other. But they have other interests than those of truth to serve, in being unwilling to distinguish the heavenly from the earthly — the religion of God from the religion of man.

Upon the whole, then, we may say, that it has often fared with Christianity, on account of its corruptions, as it has sometimes done with the character of a great nation, because of the degeneracy of those who were considered to represent it. The inhabitants of a distant land, who never saw any better specimens of the English character than the drunken ship's crew that time after time visited their shores, and perpetrated fraud, robbery and oppression, have no faith in the virtue of the English nation. They identify it with intemperance, deceit and cruelty; and look with jealousy and detestation on every white man that sets his foot on their soil, even though he comes to bless them. The English in India, during the seventeenth and eighteenth centuries, by their rapine, impiety and licentiousness, led the natives to regard them as little better than fiends let loose from hell to ravage their coasts. Other peoples again, who know full well that the depraved class, which now and then come under their observation, are but spurious specimens of the true Britons, choose, out of ill-will or some unworthy motive, to hold them up as types of England's character. There is a true national character which gives the lie to the libel, and there is a pure benignant Christianity which disowns the corrupt as its representative. Nevertheless, the base citizens, in the eyes of foreigners, produce and strengthen skepticism in regard to the national honor; and, in like manner, the corrupt form of Christianity gives occasion for rejecting the true.

# CHAPTER V.

## RELIGIOUS INTOLERANCE.

Much intolerance without the Church — Christianity itself stands clear of all within it — Its Founder the most tolerant of beings — Precepts and doctrines of the New Testament, and the lives of the best Christians, acquit the Gospel of the charge — Accidental association of intolerance with the religion of Christ has often been injurious to it — Three manifestations of intolerance noticed: 1st. Jealousy in reference to science — Nature and revelation in harmony — Astronomy and the Bible once set at variance — Galileo — A right principle of Scriptural interpretation harmonizes Bible language with the true system of the universe — Geology — Great antiquity of the globe a result, not an assumption — Perfect harmony between this and the Mosaic record — Injurious influence of refusing the harmonizing principle — 2nd. Jealousy in reference to any departure from the common mode of pulpit teaching — Want of Paul's principle of accommodation in consistency with great prominence to doctrines of the cross — Necessity of a wider and more diversified range — Chalmers' Astronomical Discourses — 3rd. Intolerance of different forms and observances — Much handled by infidels — Causes disaffection to Christianity in many intelligent and liberal minds — Such a spirit rebuked by Christ.

IT should never be forgotten that a great deal of the intolerance in the world lies without the pale of the church, and that from all the intolerance found within it, Christianity itself is entirely free. One would imagine, to hear some objectors, that the thing had no existence except among the adherents of the Christian system, and that it was the native fruit of the system itself. Some men see corruptions, divisions and intolerances nowhere except within the province of revealed religion; and they cannot, or will not, distinguish between that religion and the abuses that have crept around it, or the evils done in its name. It is necessary, accordingly, to remind such individuals that intolerance has had a place in the schools, and in the senate, as well as in the church; that philosophy, literature, and politics, have keenly manifested it, as well as systems of religion; and that while the evil could often be shown to have been the natural effects of the human system, it could as easily be shown to be foreign to the divine.

The character of Christianity is to be judged of by the spirit of its Founder, by its precepts and doctrines as contained in the New Testament, and by the conduct of those who have been acknowledged to be most under its influence. The man Christ Jesus — the holy, harmless, and undefiled One — was the most tolerant of beings. In him were harmoniously blended two great principles: an uncompromising attachment to the truth, and great forbearance toward those who were weak in faith, or as yet strangers to its power. He declared before Pilate, "To this end was I born, and for this cause came I into the world, that I should bear witness unto the truth." And so ardent was his zeal for the truth, and so faithful his attachment to it, that men who take a one-sided view of things, and confound an enlightened regard to truth with intolerance, might indeed bring the charge against the Savior Himself. Had some persons, who are ever raising this cry against Christianity, seen Him, in holy indignation, expelling the buyers and sellers from the temple; or heard Him utter such uncompromising language as this, — "He that is not with me is against me — If any man will be my disciple, let him deny himself, and take up his cross and follow me," — they would, in all probability, have ascribed it to an intolerant spirit. How libelous would have been the charge! For we have only to behold the faithful and true witness, while firmly grasping the truth, exemplifying its kindly spirit, and discountenancing in his followers any manifestations of temper inconsistent with it. He rebuked the various kinds of intolerance that were manifested in his day. There was the intolerance of the synagogue, or of church exclusiveness, which expresses itself in the cry,

"The temple of the Lord, the temple of the Lord, are we." And He said to it, "I tell you of a truth, many widows were in Israel in the days of Elias, when the heaven was shut up three years and six months, when great famine was throughout all the land; but unto none of them was Elias sent, save unto Sarepta, a city of Sidon, unto a woman that was a widow. And many lepers were in Israel in the time of Eliseus the prophet: and none of them was cleansed, saving Naaman the Syrian." There was the intolerance of a monopolizing caste, the germs of which appeared in his own partially enlightened disciples, who would forbid the man casting out demons, because he did not form one of their company. And Jesus said, "Forbid him not: for he that is not against us is for us." There was the intolerance of misplaced zeal, as manifested by James and John, who, in the times of their ignorance, would have commanded fire to come down from heaven and consume the Samaritans, because they did not receive the Master. But he turned, and said unto them, "Ye know not what manner of spirit ye are of." Intolerance in Him was reserved for a base and sanctimonious hypocrisy, and then it became a virtue to manifest it. But the bruised reed he did not break, and the smoking flax he did not quench. And, with an enlarged heart, he recognized in every one who did the will of God, his mother, his brother, and his sister. Let the charge of intolerance be made against whatever religious systems and teachers men will; but let the life and doctrine of Him who taught his followers to love their enemies, and who on the cross prayed for his murderers, stand clear of it.

The same two great principles to which we have adverted, are exemplified also in the character and writings of the apostles. It is not to the time when they were beset with Jewish prejudices that we refer, but when they were in the very height of their noble career as Christians and ambassadors, and most of all under the influence of the truth. Look at John,—Boanerges, the son of thunder, —him who would have brought down fire on the Samaritans. He has lost none of his zeal for the truth. "If there come any unto you, and bring not this doctrine, receive him not into your house, neither bid him God speed." But how deeply is he imbued with the kindly and tolerant spirit of that truth. "We know that we have passed from death to life, because we love the brethren." Look at Paul, once a persecutor and injurious. In him were combined uncompromising attachment to great truth, and forbearance to all who held it, though differing on other matters. He who withstood Peter to the face, because the truth was likely to suffer through his dissimulation, became all things to all men in order that he might win some. It would be a difficult task for any man to find a single precept or doctrine in the apostolical epistles, or anything in the conduct of the apostles themselves after they had been enlightened, on which to fasten the charge of intolerance, unl.ss he confound with it an enlightened attachment to the truth itself. And there are thousands of Christians, in every age, whose temper and conduct, being under the influence of the truth as it is in Jesus, give the lie to the insinuation that Christianity fosters narrow-mindedness and intolerance. It is a petty, unmanly, dishonest way of attacking the Gospel, to father upon it all the weaknesses and vices of its professors; when in the character of its Author, and both in its letter and spirit, it rebukes intolerance of every shape. Happy is it that, amid the false imputations thrown on Christianity by its enemies, and the unfavorable representation often given of it by being associated with the imperfections and errors of its professed friends, we can contemplate its native undiminished grandeur in the sacred page, and see its holy benignant influence manifested in so many of its true disciples, as warrant us to say that the Gospel has as much communion with intolerance as light has with darkness.

But, although the religion of Christ disowns all connection with the narrowness and bigotry of its avowed disciples, it cannot be doubted that, in consequence of such associations, it has presented a repulsive aspect to many minds. We mean, therefore, to notice some of the forms of religious intolerance, which have thrown a stumbling-block in the way of a pure and benignant Christianity.

1. The first to which we advert is,—*the jealousy with which some religious men regard the advancement of science.* The Book of Nature and the Book of Revelation have the same Author, and, when rightly interpreted, both declare the glory of God, and show forth his handiwork. There may be apparent discrepancies between them, but there can be no real contradictions; and, in proportion as scientific research is prosecuted in the right spirit, and true principles of interpretation are applied to the scriptural page, will the harmony be manifested. The one, however, has often been arrayed against the other, to the injury of the truth of God. We refer not so much to the vaunts of infidels that the age of philosophical illumination and scientific discovery would eclipse and falsify the scriptural revelation, or to the fact that some philosophers have, unhappily, been unbelievers in the sacred record — circumstances which have had considerable influence in prejudicing some good, though not great men, against such pursuits — as to the fact that Christians themselves, in many cases, have countenanced the notion that there is real enmity between them.

It was once a dogma both of philosophy and of the church, that the earth is the greatest body in the universe, placed immovable in its center, and that all the heavenly bodies were created solely for its use. The influence of Aristotle riveted the notion of the earth's immobility on men's minds for ages, and the whole body of the faithful received it as the very doctrine of the Bible. At length when the Aristotelian dogmas respecting motion were overturned by the discoveries of Copernicus, Kepler, and Galileo,—and the motion of the earth round the sun, as the center of the planetary system, was, on demonstrable evidence, asserted,—science and religion were set against each other, and what is now universally regarded as a true astronomy was denounced as inconsistent with the Christian faith. It is well known that the Vatican thundered its anathemas against those who held the Copernican doctrine, and that the famous Galileo was sent to the dungeons of the Inquisition for thinking, as Milton says, in astronomy otherwise than the Franciscan and Dominican licensers thought. And even men of learning and piety were to be found some time afterward in the Reformed Church, who maintained it to be antiscriptural to believe otherwise than that earth is at rest, and that the sun performs a daily revolution around it. David, the man inspired of God, was boldly set against the philosopher Galileo; and because the former sung, "God hath established the earth upon its foundations; it shall not be moved for ever and ever. The going forth of the sun is from the end of the heaven and his circuit unto the ends of it," and the latter could not but maintain, on the ground of sure evidence, that the earth moved,—philosophy was placed under the ban, and stigmatized as heretical and infidel.

The famous rule of interpretation, so fully adopted by expositors in modern times, that the sacred writers speak of natural objects according to the popular mode of comprehending them, "ex veritate *optica* non *physica*," as Rosenmüller says,— a rule which Galileo himself, who held both by the truth of the Scriptures and the truth of the new philosophy, seems clearly to have understood — was little thought of, or generally repudiated by divines as an example of wresting the Scriptures from their plain and obvious meaning. The persecuted philosopher could have told them that, as the sacred writers, in accommodating their language to the wants and capacities of men, speak of God Himself under the semblance of human properties; so do they, in speaking of his works, adopt those popular forms of speech which could readily be comprehended.[1] But the church, intellectually, as well as in other respects, was intolerant. The philosophy of nature, however clearly established on fact, must bend to men's narrow interpretation of Scripture. It refused to do so. The philosopher, after his humiliating recantation, rose from his knees, stamped his foot on the ground, and exclaimed, "It moves after all!" A perpetual imprisonment was the penalty; and that very astronomy which gives us such enlarged conceptions of the God of nature and of grace, and which we regard as in perfect harmony with scriptural truth, had, for years after the time of Galileo, to bear the brand of heresy. That many of the philosophical minds of that age were strengthened in their secret opposition to Christianity, by such a course of intolerance, we may well believe, when we consider how much it is appealed to by the enemies of revelation, and how a similar, though less fierce, mode of intolerance affects some minds in our own day.

The once apparent inconsistency between astronomy and revelation has vanished; the globularity and mobility of the earth are no longer viewed by the enlightened friends of Scripture as in conflict with its statements; and they can view the march of that sublime science, not only with-

[1] Dr. Smith's Scripture and Geology, p. 192 (4th edition).

out jealousy of any injury accruing thereby to Christianity, but with the satisfaction of seeing it contribute to enlarge our conceptions of Him who is the Savior of the world and the Upholder of all things. The application of a right principle of scriptural interpretation harmonizes the language of the Bible with the true system of the universe; just as the discoveries of the microscope, evincing as they do the care of the Almighty for the little as well as the great, ward off the objections which infidelity has drawn from the discoveries of the telescope, on the ground that the magnitude of the creation is opposed to the belief that our little earth has had concentrated upon it so much of the divine regards as is implied in the scheme of redemption. But if the elder science of astronomy has been cleared of the stigma of being opposed to religion, the younger science of geology has incurred the reproach, and still labors, in some measure, under it.

Geology has secured its place among the inductive sciences; and, "in the magnitude and sublimity of the objects of which it treats, undoubtedly ranks, in the scale of the sciences, next to astronomy."[2] It is a fixed principle of this science — which extended observations are constantly strengthening, and in reference to which great unanimity prevails among geologists — that the materials of which this globe is composed are of a very high antiquity, and date far beyond the six thousand years which are the commonly assigned age of the earth. This is no mere hypothesis. Physical phenomena, which lie patent to the eye of every observer, prove that our planet has passed through several different states, separated from each other by immense intervals of time, long before man, or any of the other creatures now existing, had been created. Several miles of strata upon strata have been carefully exam-

[2] Herschel's Discourse on Natural Philosophy, p. 287.

ined by scientific men of the first eminence, and they are agreed, upon irresistible evidence, in affirming, that the formation even of those stratified beds which are nearest the surface, must have taken periods of time which carry us immeasurably beyond the commonly received date of the creation. The facts that no remains of the human species have been found in any of the regular geological deposits, that these deposits bear indubitable marks of having occupied vast ages in their formation, and that the temperature of the globe during the processes must have been such as that man could not then have existed, prove the antiquity of the globe to be so great that, in comparison, man's stay upon it dwindles into an insignificant point of time. This is one of the grand conclusions of geology, carefully and legitimately drawn from the records contained in the bosom of the earth, and a conclusion which nothing whatever can falsify. "No geologist worthy of the name," says Mr. Hugh Miller, "*began* with the belief of the antiquity of the earth, and then set himself to square geological phenomena with its requirements. It is a deduction, a result; not the startling assumption, or given sum, in a process of calculation, but its ultimate finding or answer."[1] Men of skeptical principles have arrayed this conclusion against Scripture on the one hand, and some men of piety have arrayed Scripture against it on the other. It is with the latter that we have at present to do.

That there is an *apparent* discrepancy between the teachings of geology and the teachings of the Bible in this case, must be admitted; and that something like alarm should at first have been produced thereby in serious minds, is not to be wondered at. No truth appears all at once full-orbed and complete. Some of the noblest ideas of science and philosophy, that are now as the sun shining

[1] Footprints, p. 265.

in its strength, seemed, at their early dawning, to conflict with Christianity, because opposed to some of the popular but mistaken interpretations of the sacred record. Cowper had something like an excuse in his day, which he would not have had now, in saying—

"Some drill and bore
The solid earth, and from the strata there
Extract a register, by which we learn
That He who made it, and revealed its date
To Moses, was mistaken in its age."

It is unfortunate, however, that such jealousy should exist; for believing, as such men must do, that the records of nature and the records of revelation have the same Author, they might be assured that the true interpretation of the one could never really be at variance with the true interpretation of the other. Had Moses, the man of God, anywhere asserted that the materials of which this globe is composed were called into being a few thousand years ago, had the inspired historian identified the original act of forming the world out of nothing with the six days of the Adamic creation, science and revelation would then have been at open war, and the consequences would have been serious. Geologists can no more renounce their belief in the great antiquity of the earth, than the followers of Copernicus can give up the creed that the earth moves, and that the sun is in the center of the planetary system. The convictions in the one case, as well as in the other, are consequents—not antecedents. Moses nowhere asserts that the chronology is different. The variance between his record and the geological evidence is only apparent, not real; it vanishes before a sound principle of scriptural interpretation. What we complain of, however, is, that some good men disown the harmonizing principle, and, to the injury of Christianity, cling doggedly to their narrow principle of interpretation, and denounce as heretical and infidel one of the most legitimate conclusions of science. Let it once be admitted that the first sentence in the Book of Genesis stands as a distinct and independent proposition, that it refers to an undefined antiquity when the Almighty created the materials of the universe out of nothing, and then, as Dr. Chalmers remarks, "we can allow geology the amplest time for its various revolutions without infringing even on the literalities of the Mosaic record."[1] This principle of interpretation is no novelty, no mere bending of the sense of Scripture so as to meet the claims of a young science. It is to be found in many of the ancient Christian writers, it was supported by some of the most learned and pious men in more modern times, but who lived before geology had obtained a place among the inductive sciences, and it is becoming more and more generally acceptable among judicious and devout expositors of Scripture in our own day. But the outcry has been heard, here and there, from the pulpit and the religious press, that the geological doctrines are antiscriptural. The Mosaical and Mineral geologies have been compared and contrasted, as if they were actually conflicting; and the most sweeping charges of atheism and the like have been made against a science that appeals to palpable evidence in support of its conclusion, that the earth is greatly older than the date commonly assigned to it.[2] It is but lately that a correspondent, in a respectable public journal, said, "I hold by my antiquated tenets, that our world, nay, the whole material universe, was created about six or seven thousand years ago, and that in a state of physical excellence of which we have in our present fallen world only the 'vestiges of creation.'" The holders of such an opinion, we hope, in all charity, are rapidly diminishing.

[1] Daily Scripture Readings, vol. i, p. 1.
[2] See Dr. Smith's Scripture and Geology, p. 130, etc.

But who can estimate the amount of injury thus unintentionally done to the interests of Christianity, and the advantage afforded to the ranks of infidelity. It unfortunately happens that not a few scientific men have, independently altogether of such representations, no favorable prepossessions for the Christian religion, and are criminally strangers to the strength of its evidences and the grandeur of its truths. And surely the intolerance of which we are speaking is calculated to strengthen their indifference or hostility, and to induce them to rest in the conclusion that the Gospel is either a cunningly devised fable, or a system inimical to enlightened and philosophical inquiry. It betrays, indeed, no small degree of intolerance on the part of some philosophers themselves, and evinces a little-mindedness altogether unworthy of them, that they can coolly dismiss Christianity and refuse to examine its claims, because it has occasionally come before them associated with the weaknesses and prejudices of some of its professors. They are guilty of acting the same way toward religion that the Christian professors, of whom they complain, act toward science; and the charge of intolerance, which they bring against others, might justly be retaliated upon themselves. But this does in nowise weaken the fact that the attempt, on the part of some, to limit the Mosaic account of the creation to the date of six thousand years, in opposition to geological conclusions carefully drawn and now firmly established; and the attempt, on the part of others, to put the mark of Cain on the science—have operated injuriously on some minds in fostering a secret or open contempt for Christianity. There is a natural indifference in the human mind to the things which are revealed of God, and it is unfortunate when men can lay hold of some of the repulsive associations of Christianity as a pretext for disregarding Christianity itself. Revelation cannot be made to conflict with reason, Christianity cannot be arrayed against science, without provoking enmity on the other side, and giving an immense advantage to infidelity.

Mr. Babbage says, "It is a fact, not to be disputed, that some of the most enlightened minds of the day have nurtured a secret opposition to the doctrines of Christianity, owing to the intellectual intolerance of its abettors." And while it may be that some men of philosophical pursuits are claiming much more for reason than its due, or than it would be consistent with the paramount claims of Christianity to concede, and that intolerance may thus be indiscriminately applied to old prejudices and an enlightened zeal for great truth; yet it must be admitted that any attempt to interdict a science whose conclusions are based not upon airy speculations, but upon palpable evidence, under the mistaken notion that such conclusions are hostile to the Word of God, must tend to make some men infidels, and furnish with additional weapons those who are so. Let no tolerance be shown to the opinion, prevalent in our day, that religion is a web of the mind's own weaving, that it has no fixed and immutable standard in history, but that it fluctuates with the fluctuation of ages; for that were to act the part of Judas and betray the very truth. But let the simple assurance that the Author of the material and mental constitutions is also the Author of Christianity, for ever stifle all jealousy, and silence all outcry against the steady march of physical and mental science. Natural religion and revealed become the more friendly the better they get acquainted, and the present as well as past times can furnish names alike illustrious for philosophical acquirements and Christian excellence. One of these recently said, amid an illustrious circle of his scientific compeers: "If the God of love is most appropriately worshiped in the Christian temple, the God of nature may be equally honored in the temple of science. Even from its lofty minarets, the philosopher may summon the faithful to prayer; and the priest and the sage may exchange altars without the compromise of faith or of knowledge."[1]

2. The second form of religious intolerance, which we would notice as having an unfavorable bearing on Christianity, is — *the jealousy with which any departure from the common mode of address, and any attempt to accommodate religious discussions to the taste, literature and philosophy of the times, are not unfrequently viewed by some of its professed friends.* It is by no means desirable to make any material change in our usually-adopted style of pulpit preaching. To the poor the Gospel is preached. They form by far the larger portion of almost every religious audience, and to their intelligence and capacities should the teaching of the Church be adapted. In order to secure plainness of speech, however, it is no more necessary to descend to vulgarity than to resort to raving in order to be impressive. Lord Brougham, in his "Dissertation on the Eloquence of the Ancients," says: "The best speakers of all times have never failed to find that they could not speak too well or too carefully to a popular assembly; that if they spoke their best — the best they could address to the most learned and critical assembly — they were sure to succeed." Some of the most popular and useful preachers on both sides of the Tweed are those whose style is level to the comprehension of the feeblest of the flock, while it is characterized by an elegance and strength which render it acceptable to the more refined and intellectual. What is wanting is a greater prevalency of what, in some quarters, extensively prevails,— the style which blends the expository and the sermonizing, the doctrinal and the practical, the stiffness of

[1] Sir D. Brewster's Address at the Meeting of the British Association at Edinburgh, 1850.

the lecture having imparted to it something of the graceful looseness of the sermon, and the declamation of the sermon receiving some of the massiveness of the lecture.

If it be not desirable to lay aside the common mode of address, far less would it be to strip the Gospel of its peculiarities, or to throw them into the shade, in order to remove the offense of the cross. The great preacher who acted, within legitimate bounds, on the principle of becoming all things to all men, acted always, too, on his noble determination to know nothing among men save Jesus Christ and Him crucified. The field of divine truth is extensive in itself, and richly diversified in its objects, but Christ is the sun which clothes the whole with light as with a garment, and the cross is the seat whence He sheds abroad the brightness of his glory. Over this wide field it behoves the Christian teacher to conduct his disciples, and to make them acquainted with every flower and tree that grows on its surface; but all his lessons should be given from under the shadow of the cross, and, on whatever subject he touches, there should be a constant reference to this, as the tree of life, whose leaves are for the healing of the nations.

But it is of the want of Paul's principle of accommodation, acted on in consistency with due prominence being given to the doctrines of the cross, that we complain. He accommodated himself to the prejudices of the synagogue and of the market-place. He closed with the philosophers in the Areopagus, and with the more unlearned among the people. He pursued one train of thought, and adopted one style, while reasoning with the Jews; and another and different one when addressing the Gentiles. And yet, while thus becoming all things to all men, he made it manifest that he counted all things but loss for the excellency of the knowledge of Christ. It is the greater prevalency of branching off from the cardinal doctrine of the Gospel while holding fast by it; and of throwing the sanctity of religion over philosophical researches on the one hand, and of making science minister to the illustrations of religious truth on the other, that we desiderate in much of our religious teaching. The pulpit, being designed for the instruction of men in every age in the things of God, should be prepared to meet the various forms of error which are ever and anon thrown up from the heart of society, to dissipate the illusions which have been thrown around them, and to show how nature, when interpreted aright, yields an unbiased and spontaneous testimony to revelation. Far be it that the lessons of the pulpit should ever be turned into philosophical discussions, into learned disquisitions, or into a mere baptized lifeless morality. Of the former there has been more than enough in past ages, and of the latter there may be in some quarters too much still. But let it not be forgotten that nature teaches many useful and pious lessons, and that the Bible appeals to them; that in the same record we are admonished to behold the Lamb of God that taketh away the sins of the world, and to consider the lilies of the field, how they grow; that the inspired canon contains the Proverbs of Solomon as well as the Psalms of David, the philosophical epistle of James as well as the doctrinal epistles of Paul. Let not God's Book of Nature be treated as if its inscriptions had grown dim and effete before the clearer light of revelation, and, while irreligious men would make the stars in their courses fight against the prophets and apostles, and adduce the great "stone book" as a witness against the Word of Life; let those who are set to teach in the church show that the records of the material creation, of the heavens above and of the earth beneath, are in perfect harmony with the statements of the scriptural page. There is the leaven of a secularist infidelity diffusing itself among the masses, and of a philosophical unbelief making its way among the educated classes, to the existence and influence of which many who wait upon the ministrations of the sanctuary are not entire strangers; and this surely warrants an occasional departure from the usual mode of address, in order to strip false systems of their pretensions, and to exhibit by contrast the glory of the true. Paul, if we mistake not, would have acted thus, had he lived in an age like ours, so widely different in many points from his own; and in doing so, would have manifested the harmony of his two grand principles — determining to know nothing among men save Jesus Christ and Him crucified, and becoming all things to all men in order that he might win some.

Now, it is in the jealousy with which some devoted teachers of religion view any such accommodation to the tastes and prejudices of the times, and in the, perhaps, still stronger jealousy with which such an occasional departure from the old course would be received by multitudes of simple-minded hearers, that we discover an influence really injurious to Christianity. We are not, let it be remembered, advocating a trimming mode of preaching, the substitution of a sort of religious philosophy for the Gospel itself, or mere displays of literary tastes, in order to captivate literary men. No. This, besides proving, as it ever has done, a wretched failure, would be an abandonment or an unworthy compromise of the one great principle of Paul to which we have adverted. But it is the greater prevalency of the system which has been partially adopted by some distinguished teachers, of making occasional excursions to other topics, while habitually expounding, and enforcing the great doctrines of the cross, and of linking even these other topics with the truth of the Gospel for which we plead. It is undeniable that Christianity in the teaching of by far the greater number of its devoted ministers, wears a more contracted and exclusive aspect than really belongs to it; and that the stern refusal to adapt the pulpit to the age, has led some intelligent minds to cherish unfavorable opinions of the great truths of the Gospel. The jealous exclusion of almost every topic from the sacred teaching which is not directly included within the system of evangelical doctrine, or the intolerance shown when an occasional excursion is made beyond the prescribed boundary, has induced many to associate the grand themes of the pulpit with a narrow and illiberal exclusiveness to which in themselves these themes are strangers. "If the priesthood of the sanctuary," remarks Dr. Vaughan,[1] "is to be a match for the priesthood of letters, the path of its labor must become wider and more diversified every day. Men who see this must give little heed to those who see it not."

Dr. Chalmers, in the introduction to his celebrated Astronomical Discourses, which we consider a good exemplification of the two principles of Paul formerly adverted to, makes a remark in some measure still applicable. He is speaking of "those narrow and intolerant professors who take an alarm at the very sound and semblance of philosophy; and feel as if there was an utter irreconcilable antipathy between its lessons on the one hand and the soundness and piety of the Bible on the other," and adds, "it were well, I conceive, for our cause that such persons could become a little more indulgent on the subject; that they give up a portion of those ancient and hereditary prepossessions which go so far to cramp and enthrall them; that they would suffer theology to take that wide range of argument and of illustration which belongs to her; and that, less sensitively jealous of any desecration being

[1] Letter and Spirit, p. 78.

brought upon the Sabbath or the pulpit, they would suffer her freely to announce all those truths which either serve to protect Christianity from the contempt of science; or to protect the teachers of Christianity from those invasions which are practiced both on the sacredness of the office and on the solitude of its devotional and intellectual labors."

It is unfortunate that theology, the grandest of all the sciences, should have been kept so much aloof from the others, as it is unfortunate that the others have been kept so much aloof from theology; unfortunate it is that theology has often been made to look strangely and jealously on natural science, as it is that natural science has often looked strangely and jealously on theology. The two real friends have been made to cherish silent or open contempt for each other; and while the contempt of science has often occasioned the contempt of theology, the contempt of theology has often occasioned the contempt of science.

3. The most common species of religious intolerance, and one that has given to Christianity a more repulsive aspect than any other, remains to be noticed — the *intolerance of different forms, rites and ceremonies.* The form of godliness, in the present state, is necessary to the manifestation and maintenance of its power. But men in every age have been prone to attach that importance to the external shape which only belongs to the inner life. And in proportion to the exclusiveness of attachment to any particular form has been the intolerance shown to those who differ from it. Christianity is the ministration of the spirit. Its Divine Founder frowned upon the formalism and consequent intolerance of his day. The New Testament, while giving no countenance to the neglect of the outward institutions of religion, places them in complete subordination to piety itself; and, by the utter absence of

minute regulations as to external ceremonies, indicates not only that they are of inferior importance compared with the weightier matters of the law, but that professing Christians should show much indulgence toward one another in reference to them. The several sections of the church have often acted as if the New Testament had its book of Leviticus, and their individual interpretation could not possibly be otherwise than the right one; and as if they had been commanded to punish or stand aloof from those who denied there was any such book in the New Testament, or who ventured to adopt another interpretation of its meaning. From the beginning until now, some men, pent up within their own sacred inclosure, and being unable to see any good beyond, have been crying, "the temple of the Lord, the temple of the Lord are we." Their own Zion has filled up so largely the sphere of their vision as to be looked upon as exclusively *the* church, and they say, with an implied disparagement of all other hills, "our fathers worshiped in this mountain." The line of genealogy — the chain of succession — has become so exclusively sacred in their estimation as the channel of grace, as to have blinded their eyes to an illustrious ancestral piety elsewhere, and to lead them to say with ineffable complacency, "we have Abraham to our father." And while intolerance has been manifesting itself in this way, under a pretended zeal for the honor of Christianity itself, that very Christianity, in the life of its great Author, and in the pages of inspiration, has been rebuking the foul and wicked spirit, and calling upon it to come out of the church.

Men who have no inclination to examine the evidences of Christianity, and to contemplate its native grandeur disconnected from the weakness and intolerance of its professed friends, confound the one with the other. Or they are something like individuals prevented from entering into a magnificent castle, and surveying its beautiful grounds, by the surly looks of the porters that stand at the gate. This intolerance, like an evil genius, has so often accompanied Christianity in its descent down the stream of ages, and in its progress through the world, leading to the formation of conventicle acts, and acts of uniformity, unchurching, anathematizing, imprisoning and burning those who were of a different way, that it would not be wonderful were thousands to rise up in judgment, and say to the demon of intolerance, "You made us infidels." Vast multitudes, in every age, will, in spite of all remonstrance, estimate Christianity by the spirit and conduct of its professed followers. And, while they see much in the past, and not a little in the present, of that temper which, under the plea of religion, would bring down fire from heaven and consume the Samaritans; or which manifests itself in a conceited piety, saying, "Stand by yourself, come not near to me, for I am holier than you;" their prejudices against Christianity will strengthen, and they will be apt to confound the darkness and the light. No one, at all acquainted with the writings of infidels, more especially with those which have been popularized and diffused through the masses, but must know that this species of religious intolerance is handled and held up as if it were the natural fruit of religion itself. And how often, in the walks of social intercourse, do we meet with intelligent and liberal-minded men who cannot conceal their disaffection to Christianity on account of what may be called the church intolerance of many of its professors.

Coleridge has said, "I will be tolerant of everything else but every other man's intolerance." Religious intolerance is the most odious and insufferable of all. The spirit of humanity, if it be not enslaved, rises up against it; and on many minds who have not learned to distinguish between the gentleness of Christ and the bitterness of some professing Christians, such is its influence as to involve in one feeling of disgust everything in the shape and name of Christianity. What an inconceivably paltry, troublesome, intolerant thing must Christianity be in the eyes of some men, who form their notions of it from some portions of church history, or from those who stickle for caste, vestments and ceremonies, as if the life of genuine religion was bound up in them. And so much fiery zeal has been manifested by large bodies of professing Christians in every age for the mere wood, hay and stubble, that it is not to be wondered at if those who were indisposed to appeal to the Bible should have come to the conclusion that there was nothing else in religion worth contending for. The church in every age has had its Hamans who could not bear to see Mordecai sitting at the gate. There have been multitudes of great and petty Lauds who would rather have had the plague in their parishes than religious dissent, and who would sooner have tolerated drunkenness and uncleanness than the unpardonable sin of Puritanism and Nonconformity. The imprisonment of a John Bunyan and thousands of men of less note, because they would pray without a common prayer-book; the outrage of refusing Christian burial to men who had not been baptized within the pale of a particular communion; the denial of the validity of any ordination but this particular one or that particular one; the jealousy sometimes shown toward lay preaching, not lest error should be propagated, but lest the priest's office should be invaded; and the many ways in which the old proposition is openly expressed, or half concealed, "out of our church no salvation;" these, which are but the intolerancies of erring, deluded, or proud men, have done incalculable injuries to that benignant work which is of God. "The prevalence of so intolerant a theory," says Isaac Taylor, when speaking of Tractarianism, "and the bold avowal of it by those who are regarded as the best-informed expounders of Christianity, silently but extensively operates to drive cultured and ingenuous minds into deism or atheism. What is this Christianity, say such, which, while professing to be a religion, not of bondage and forms, but of truth and love, nevertheless impels its adherents to violate all charity on the precarious ground of an elaborate hypothesis!"[1]

The disciples may forbid a man to cast out demons in the name of Jesus, because he follows not with them. But the Lord, instead of sanctioning their conduct, rebukes them. It is enough for Him that the man is doing his work, and doing it in his name. "Such a church, or such a community," says Vinet, "believes that to follow Jesus Christ, it is necessary to be with it, form a part of its organization, join the society of which it is composed, espouse its interests, and hang out its banner."[2] The Lord rebukes such a spirit. He looks over all the hedgework of forms and ceremonies within which his professed followers have too often inclosed themselves, and says, "he that is not against us is for us." Let not Christianity, then, be made responsible for what it repudiates; but let it not be denied that an intolerance of different external forms and rites, on the part of churches, has been prejudicial to the Gospel and strengthening to infidelity.

[1] Spiritual Christianity, p. 99. [2] Vinet's Vital Christianity, p. 223.

# CHAPTER VI.

## DISUNION OF THE CHURCH.

Christ's Church really one — Scriptural illustrations of this — A truth often lost sight of — Disjointed state of the Church a Common refuge of infidelity — An argument easily applied — Its influence on a man whose religious knowledge is merely superficial, and who has but a very lingering attachment to Christianity — The sophism repelled by a man of an opposite character—The refuge, however, remains — Deistical writers used it — A source of perplexity to the weak and inquiring, and an auxiliary to the hostile — Remark of Robert Hall — Unity not to be confounded with uniformity — Romish unity a huge fiction — Remark of Whately — Scriptural unity consistent with minor differences — Remark of Sir James Stephen — Mr. Ruskin's "Notes" — Difference between moral and mathematical certainty — Voltaire — Macaulay's remarks on Gladstone — Visible unanimity to be aimed at — Savior's Prayer — Twofold influence of Christian unity — The exhibition of unity would tell mightily as a proof of the divinity of Christianity — Instanced in the early Church — The consequent unity of action would tell powerfully on successful propagation of Christianity — Primitive Church had unity of action so long as it had unity of exhibition — Noble things done since by combined Christian effort — God, in the signs of the times, is calling upon Christians to manifest their unity.

THE Church of Christ, amid all outward diversities and conflicting interests, is really one. What Cyprian, one of the most illustrious of the Fathers, said, with a too partial, if not an exclusive reference to *the* existing church, is true of the great company of the faithful, composed of men in all ages and lands, who hold the Head, even Christ: "The church is one, which, by reason of its fecundity, is extended into a multitude, in the same manner as the rays of the sun, however numerous, constitute but one light; and the branches of a tree, however many, are attached to one trunk, which is supported by its tenacious root; and when various rivers flow from the same fountain, though number is diffused by the redundant supply of waters, unity is preserved in their origin."[1] This essential

[1] Hall's Terms of Communion.

characteristic of the Christian community is illustrated by several comparisons in Scripture. The church is represented as a building of which the Lord Jesus is the foundation, and believers in every place and age are living stones united to Him and to each other, and built up a spiritual house.' It is spoken of as one fold under the care of the one Shepherd, as a whole family or brotherhood named after the Father of our Lord Jesus Christ, and, not to multiply illustrations, it is described as one body, all genuine believers holding the same Head, and every one members one of another. Yet the church, in many of its branches, has often lost sight of this delightful truth, and acted a part directly contrary to its influence. The harmony has been broken, brethren have set brethren at nought, schisms have been made in the body, and member has been saying unto member, "I have no need of thee." The faithful have been ranging themselves under different leaders, some saying we are of Paul, others, we are of Apollos, others, we are of Cephas; while their common Lord and Savior has been saying unto them, "One is your Master, even Christ, and all ye are brethren."

The disjointed and disorderly state of the church has been notoriously one of the most common refuges of infidelity. At the beginning, the lovely manifestation of its inward unity often drew the unwilling homage from the world, "Behold how these Christians love one another!" And we may easily conceive how influential must have been the exhibition of Christian unity in disarming the prejudices and overcoming the hostility of those without. To see vast multitudes of individuals, men of every kindred and tongue, and nation, and people, separated from each other by country and language, by a diversity of station and interests, all glorying in the same cross, bound by the bands of love into one Christian brotherhood, and harmoniously engaged in doing the greatest good to the world, must, in many cases, have been instrumental in producing the conviction that Christianity is of God. "It was this, indeed," remarks Neander, "which, in a cold and selfish age, struck the pagans with wonder." But the picture has been reversed. Modern Christendom has too often presented the unseemly spectacle of the several companies of the Prince of Peace contending against each other, instead of uniting their strength and advancing against the common foe. The unbelieving world has meanwhile looked on, and said with a more deeply-rooted prejudice, "See how these Christians are divided, how they hate and oppose each other. This is your boasted Christianity, and these are the followers of Him whom they call meek and lowly of heart!"

The argument against the Gospel, derived from the divisions and discords of the Christian community, is a very popular one. It lies upon the surface of things, requiring no great grasp of comprehension either on the part of him who takes it up and applies it, or on the part of him who receives it. There are multitudes, whose natural aversion to Christianity would fail to manifest itself openly under the pressure of abstract reasoning, who will be drawn out to an avowed unbelief, by the use of popular sophisms, and an appeal to those palpable facts which are unhappily furnished by the divided state of the Christian world. Disunion among the adherents of any system is a weapon put into the hands of opponents, which they readily point against the system itself. And the weapon flies the swifter toward the mark, according as the pretensions of the system and the conduct of its professors are at variance. With what a degree of self-elation, then, must many an infidel, who had neither the honesty nor the inclination to examine Christianity, have looked upon the sectarianism and contention of the church. And how impregnable must he have felt his position, when encountering a man somewhat like-minded with himself, only retaining the shadow of a hereditary reverence for Christianity, but as little disposed to imitate the noble Bereans in searching the Scriptures to see whether or not these things are so. He would have at hand a number of texts in which the character and pretensions of the Gospel are expressed or implied, and, with a view of falsifying these, he would appeal to the temper and conduct of the adherents of the Gospel, place the one in conflict with the other; and, as if it were indisputable that the temper was the genuine influence of Christianity, endeavor to fix upon the system the brand of imposture. He would need only to lay hold of the song, so descriptive of the Gospel, which was sung by the angels over the plains of Bethlehem, and then making his appeal to the history of the church, and to the actual state of some portions of the Christian world, complacently ask, "Where is glory to God in the highest, and on earth peace, good will toward men?" The appeal would not be without its influence on the mind of a man who had no experimental knowledge of the peaceful tendency of the Gospel, whose acquaintance with the state of the Christian world was of the most superficial character, and whose lingering attachment to Christianity was like the last sear leaf on a tree, ready to be carried off by the next wind that blew.

An individual whose acquaintance with Christian truth was enlightened, deep and experimental, and whose knowledge of the Christian community extended to other facts than external divisions and imperfections, could withstand the appeal and repel the sophism. He could say to the infidel pleader, These are not all the facts of the case. Your argument is a one-sided one. You have gone to the bleak and wintry side of the hill, and have come away with the notion that all around is gloomy and sterile, whereas the other slope is clothed to the top with verdure, and on it the sun is brightly shining. You have raked up the divisions and contentions of the church, but you have not told us of the times of her unity and valiant contendings for the truth. And not only so, but you have confounded the corruptions of Christianity with Christianity itself, the accidental with the essential, the work of man with the work of God. The divisions, of which you make so much, are to be deplored, but they are not unforeseen obstacles thwarting the march of Christianity; on the contrary, the Christian record foretold them, Christianity itself overcomes them, and eventually makes them swell the train of her triumph. The church, amid all outward diversities, is verily one; and when the storms have been hushed, and the dark clouds have passed away, the world will see the true vine, and, clustering on either side of it—united by a common bond, pervaded by a common principle of life, and bearing the same manner of fruits—a goodly array of living branches.

But this mode of stating the case, however just and true, and whatever might be its weight on the mind of an anxious inquirer, would not prevail with the man whose tendencies were in an opposite direction. There is the palpable fact of a disjointed and divided church standing before him, there are schisms in the kingdom that is declared to be one, there is the sound of discordant voices and conflicting interests among the followers of the Prince of Peace. And so long as these excrescences of the religious life are manifested, and men are to be found who will persist in forming their notions of Christianity, not from the New Testament, but from the imperfections and inconsistencies of its followers, so long will indifference and infidelity have a refuge in the sectarianism and contentions of the Christian world. We may get behind the refuge and endeavor to push the man from it, we may tell him that he has mistaken a mud shed for a strong tower, we may cry out against his unfairness and little-mindedness in confounding what is accidental with what is essential, and in suffering himself to be prejudiced against a revelation from heaven because of the contendings of its professed friends. We may carry the point farther, and charge his hostility, as the Savior himself has done, on a deep-rooted aversion of mind and heart to the high and holy principles, the strict and uncompromising requirements of the Gospel itself. But, after having done all this, the refuge, such as it is, remains; and the man still resorts to it in the way of justifying and confirming his aversion to the Gospel truth. We might be almost sure, too, that, in the case of many, were this refuge taken away, others would be resorted to, and their prejudices against Christianity be not a whit lessened. But this does not affect the fact, that the visible disunion of the Christian church has been a stumbling-block to the world, and has strengthened the hands of the infidel.

The deistical writers, from Lord Herbert downwards, have availed themselves, with much disingenuousness indeed, of this weapon against the Christian cause; and have fallaciously, yet with some plausibility, argued, that a system which admitted of such conflicting opinions among its adherents, could possess nothing like certainty; and that a church professedly one and yet split into a number of isolated or opposing sects, must be a contradiction. Herbert, Bolingbroke, and other writers of a lower grade in the same school, may have become unbelievers, independent altogether of the subordinate cause which we are now considering, and might have retained their unbelief had that cause been removed out of the way: but it was among the auxiliaries that strengthened their prejudices against Christianity, furnished them with weapons of attack, and gave their infidel sentiments a readier access into the minds of other men. The world has, in these conflicting sects and divisions, a hold which it had not in the primitive age of Christianity; and, without assigning to the unity of the church that efficiency as a cause which some (with a view of precluding a higher agency) have done,[1] we cannot doubt that its visible unity, short though its continuance was, had a strong subordinate influence in recommending the Christian cause, any more than we can doubt that the return of peace and unity will be powerfully instrumental in the conversions of the latter day. "Nothing," says Lord Bacon, "doth so much keep men out of the church, and drive men out of the church, as breach of unity." And, as Isaac Taylor remarks, "If we could only bring to view the secret causes of that infidelity which, it is to be feared, prevails among the educated classes, this now named — the scandal arising from religious dissensions — would probably appear to be one of the most frequent and determinative."[2]

The most powerful arguments in favor of Christianity have been repelled and thrown upon its advocates by the infidel sarcasm, "Agree among yourselves first; and then, manifesting yourselves, what you profess to be, the disciples of one Master, come and ask us to join you." And, it has been felt, when advocating the Christian cause before those who are indifferent or opposed to it, that however shallow the sophisms by which they endeavor to defend their hostility, and however much that hostility is to be traced to an ulterior and more powerful cause, a stumbling-block, an occasion of offense, would be destroyed, were the breaches in Zion healed; and the church would then look forth "as the morning," on a world destined to be her

[1] Gibbon. [2] Spiritual Christianity, p. 149.

inheritance, "fair as the moon, clear as the sun, and terrible as an army with banners." The divisions and conflicting opinions of the Christian world have been a source of painful perplexity to the weak and inquiring on the one hand, and have operated as a flattering unction to the indifferent, and an auxiliary force to the decidedly hostile on the other. Some of the former, with great want of manliness, have sought refuge from the embarrassment in the infallibility and uniformity of Rome; thus renouncing the right of private judgment, after having exercised it in choosing their new mother, and rolling their responsibility ever afterwards upon the back of a self-styled infallibility; while the latter, seeing division to be the weakness of the church, have, with much unfairness, ascribed it to the weakness of Christianity itself. Robert Hall, in allusion to the controversies and factions which distracted the church subsequent to the Reformation, arising out of the *abuse* of the right of private judgment then nobly vindicated, says, "In this disjointed and disordered state of the Christian church, they who never looked into the interior of Christianity were apt to suspect, that to a subject so fruitful in particular disputes must attach a general uncertainty; and that a religion founded on revelation could never have occasioned such discordancy of principle and practice among its disciples. Thus infidelity is the joint offspring of an irreligious temper and unholy speculation, employed, not in examining the evidences of Christianity, but in detecting the vices and imperfections of professing Christians." [1]

Unity is not to be confounded with uniformity. The distinction between the two, however, has often been lost sight of, both by the enemies and friends of Christianity. The church has had many an extensive scheme of uni-

[1] Modern Infidelity.

formity, while within it there has been anything but unity. Popery glories in her undivided empire, but it is only the oneness of an external ceremonial, which shelters men of no opinions about religion, and men of almost every diversity of opinion. It is the unity of millions yielding an external homage to one man, and scrupulously observing the same outward ceremonies, while between multitudes of them there are few or no other points of contact. It is a huge fiction to maintain that Rome is, in the proper sense of the expression, a united church, while within the uniform pale are all kinds of doctrines, from supralapsarianism to atheism. "It is not true," remarks Archbishop Whately, "that the church of Rome is, even in their own sense of the word, exempt from *divisions* and dissensions. The great means of unity, according to most of them, is the authority of the Pope; yet they are not agreed among themselves about the extent of the Pope's authority; some thinking the Pope infallible, others denying that he is; some making him superior to a general council, others inferior, etc. Nay, learned men have reckoned up at least twenty-four fierce schisms and dissensions (some of them very bloody) about *who* was Pope; when several rivals, each claimed to be the true Pope, and condemned all others as impostors. Again, they are divided among themselves about many of the same things as Protestants are divided about — as free will, predestination, etc.; besides many disputes which have no place among *us*." [1]

Protestantism, too, in aping the imposing system of Rome, has had its schemes of uniformity, but these schemes have failed of exhibiting Christian unity. The unity for which the Savior prayed was a oneness of heart and soul among his people — manifested in loving each other, in seeking the salvation of men, and in promoting the exten-

[1] Cautions for the Times, p. 28.

sion of his kingdom. The unity is perfectly consistent with minor differences. It is not necessary to its exhibition, and in order to secure its good results, that all be bound up in one and the same system of ecclesiastical organization.[1] This we regard as altogether utopian. On such points, for example, as church government and the subjects of baptism, Scripture is not so full and explicit as to preclude diversity of sentiment among sincerely good men. And the grand reason, we doubt not, is, that the disciples of Christ may be taught to forbear one another in love. Uniformity is never enjoined in Scripture, but unity, times and ways without number, is. It is according as Christians have already attained, that they are to walk by the same rule and to mind the same thing. Besides, who does not see that the unanimity of the church would be more strikingly manifested, and present a more persuasive spectacle to the world, did it exist along with minor diversities, than under a smoothly-shaven system of uniformity? In the latter case, there might be a danger of ecclesiastical despotism, which would excite the jealousy of the world;

[1] Mr. Ruskin, in concluding his "Notes on the Construction of Sheepfolds," thus speaks: "But how to unite the two great sects of paralyzed Protestants? By keeping simply to Scripture. The members of the Scottish church have not a shadow of excuse for refusing episcopacy; it has indeed been abused among them; grievously abused; but it is in the Bible; and that is all they have a right to ask. They have also no shadow of excuse for refusing to employ a written form of prayer. It may not be to their taste — it may not be the way in which they like to pray; but it is no question, at present, of likes or dislikes, but of duties" (p. 49.). Suppose another author, in *his* "Notes on the Construction of Sheepfolds," were to say: "The members of the episcopal church have not a shadow of excuse for refusing presbyterianism; it has indeed been abused among them; but it is in the Bible; and that is all they have a right to ask;" would not the one statement, even in the estimation of many episcopalians — not to speak of thousands of Christian men who are neither episcopalians nor presbyterians — be as good as the other? In truth, no section of the Christian church, in making proposals for union, is entitled to speak in this strain to any other section. It is an aping of Romish airs; it is a setting at defiance Christian men's conscientious convictions, and it throws a stumbling-block not only in the way of incorporation but of co-operation. "Christ *has* ordered us to be at peace one with another." But *these* are not the terms.

in the former case, there would be the working of a powerful common principle, making it manifest that the religion which produced such benignant harmony amid such diversity must be not of man but of God. "There is," says Sir James Stephen, "an essential unity in that 'Kingdom which is not of this world.' But within the provinces of that mighty state there is room for endless varieties of administration, and for local laws and customs widely differing from each other. The unity consists in the one object of worship — the one object of affiance — the one source of virtue — the one cementing principle of mutual love, which pervade and animate the whole. The diversities are, and must be, as numerous and intractable as are the essential distinctions which nature, habit and circumstances have created among men. Uniformity of creeds, of discipline, of ritual, and of ceremonies, in such a world as ours! — a world where no two men are not as distinguishable in their mental as in their physical aspect; where every petty community has its separate system of civil government; where all that meets the eye, and all that arrests the ear, has a stamp of boundless and infinite variety!"[1]

If many of the professed friends of Christianity have erred in their zeal for uniformity of religious opinions and ceremonies, its avowed enemies have unfairly argued as if the absence of uniformity indicated the want of certitude. In "Voltaire's Dictionary," under the article "Sect," it is said, "There is no sect in geometry, mathematics, or experimental philosophy. When truth is evident, it is impossible to divide people into parties and factions. Nobody disputes that it is broad day at noon." In this way it is attempted to preclude all inquiry into the evidences of Christianity, and to lead men to conclude that religion has

[1] Essays in Ecclesiastical Biography, vol. i, p. 518.

no fixed data, because there have been so many conflicting opinions and divisions within its province. It is surely a miserable ungenerous charge against the Christian religion, that it has not the evidence of the mathematical sciences —an evidence that arises out of their very nature, but which is altogether foreign to a system of moral truth. The argument amounts to this, that because the Gospel cannot be shown to be as demonstrably true as that the three angles of a triangle are equal to two right angles, therefore it cannot be proved to be true at all. In other words, no evidence is to be relied on but that which belongs to what are called the accurate sciences. By such a course of reasoning as this, political economy, for example, might be denounced as a baseless science, because the greatest politicians have embraced the most conflicting theories in legislation; and all philosophical investigations that are not of a strictly mathematical character, might be interdicted as useless, because they have given rise to much opposing speculations. Moral subjects can admit of no evidence that is incompatible with human responsibility. So that to object that Christianity has no certainty because it has not mathematical certainty, is the same thing as saying that it cannot be true because it wants the evidence which would deprive men of the liberty of rejecting it. Besides, there are no inducements for a sane man to deny that two and two make four, or that it is broad day at noon; but there are strong mental tendencies which lead multitudes to darken the luster of Christianity, and to deny that it is true. As a system of pure moral truth, it thwarts depraved human propensities; and that accounts for its being corrupted or rejected by men, though its evidences stand before them as clear and majestic as the sun.

But it is too much to grant that there are no sects in experimental philosophy. Astronomy and geology belong to the inductive sciences, and very opposite theories in both have been held by the most eminent philosophers. But who would conclude, on the ground of these conflicting theories, that there is not a true system of astronomy or geology? And where is the fairness of denouncing Christianity as the most uncertain of all things, because its adherents, on some points, have held very different opinions? The objection we are noticing, is not unlike that which is urged against the Gospel on account of the mysterious nature of its truths. The sciences which admit of demonstration, pursued to a certain length, land the mind in a region of mysteries, as well as do the truths of revelation. So that, if the attribute of mysteriousness is sufficient to falsify a system, it would falsify the higher branches of mathematical science. And if the circumstance of a diversity of opinion having scope within a system be an argument against the system itself, it must sweep away from the region of the true many other commonly received systems of truth besides the religion of Christ.

Mr. Gladstone, in his zeal for high-church principles, has asserted that the state of the exact sciences proves, that, as respects religion, "the association of these two ideas, activity of inquiry and variety of conclusion, is a fallacious one." His brilliant reviewer, Mr. Macaulay, says, in reply, "Our way of ascertaining the tendency of free inquiry is simply to open our eyes and look at the world in which we live; and there we see that free inquiry on mathematical subjects produces unity, and that free inquiry on moral subjects produces discrepancy. . . . Discrepancy there will be among the most diligent and candid, as long as the constitution of the human mind, and the nature of moral evidence, continue unchanged. That we have not freedom and unity together is a very sad thing; and so it is that we have not wings. But we are just as likely to see the one defect removed as the other. It is not only in religion that this discrepancy is found. It is the same with all matters which depend on moral evidence, with judicial questions, for example, and with political questions. All the judges will work a sum in the rule-of-three on the same principle, and bring out the same conclusion. But it does not follow that, however honest and laborious they may be, they will all be of one mind on the Douglas case."[1]

But if it is vain to think of securing union in the church by a visible uniformity, or by amalgamating all denominations into one, it is not vain to seek after visible unanimity among the several sections of the church holding those fundamental doctrines which we mentioned, in the beginning of this essay, as emphatically constituting THE truth of God. We may, and will, continue to have diversities of forms, but let these be seen to be animated by an all-pervading unity of spirit. It is obviously implied in the Savior's intercessory prayer, that the world must be confirmed in its infidelity by the visible disunion of the Christian community; and that the world's conversion depends, in a great measure, on the palpable unanimity of his professed followers. He prayed for their union, in order that the world might *believe* that the Father had sent Him. This consummation, so devoutly to be wished, would have a favorable bearing on mankind in two ways at least, just as the divided state of the church has an unfavorable influence in two opposite ways.

In the first place, the exhibition of unity would tell mightily as a demonstration of the divinity of Christianity. "Our thoughts," remarks the author of the Essay on the Port-Royalists, "are steeped in imagery; and where the palpable form is not, the impalpable spirit escapes the

[1] Review of Gladstone on Church and State. (Edinburgh Review, April, 1839.)

notice of the unreflecting multitude. In common hands, analysis stops at the species or the genus, and cannot rise to the order or the class. To distinguish birds from fishes, beasts from insects, limits the efforts of the vulgar observer of the face of animated nature. But Cuvier could trace the sublime unity, the universal type, the fontal Idea, existing in the creative intelligence, which connects as one the mammoth and the snail. So, common observers can distinguish from each other the different varieties of religious society, and can rise no higher. Where one assembly worships with harmonies of music, fumes of incense, ancient liturgies, and a gorgeous ceremonial, and another listens to the unaided voice of a single pastor, they can perceive and record the differences; but the hidden ties which unite them both escape such observation. All appears as contrast, and all ministers to antipathy and discord."[1] The sublime unity of the church of Christ, the hidden ties which link one member with another, and all with the Head, escape the notice of the world. They are spiritually discerned. Hence the necessity of a visible outward expression of the real hidden unity. The prayer of the God-man Mediator demands palpable unanimity. Mere unanimity among the adherents of any system does not of itself prove the truth of that system. Men have often combined for the propagation of error. But the unity may be of such a kind, displaying such purity, disinterestedness and benevolence, as to carry along with it a convincing evidence that it is of God. It may be seen to be such an effect as no known motive power among men could produce, and which must be ascribed to a divine interposition.

Such was the visible union manifested by the primitive Christians which was attended with such remarkable triumphs. It was such a union of heart and hand for bring-

[1] Sir James Stephen's Essays in Eccles. Biog. vol. i, pp. 519, 520.

ing the greatest glory to God, and effecting the greatest good among men, as the world never saw. It was a lovely, persuasive spectacle, as free from selfish elements on the one hand as from fanaticism on the other. The world beheld men of every diversity of character, separated naturally from each other by different habits and stations, and by the most conflicting interests, coming under the transforming influence of the Christian faith, losing thereby their mutual repulsions and enmities, moving in the same element of love, bound sweetly and strongly to a common crucified Lord and to each other, and looking on that world with something of the benevolent yearnings of Him who came to seek and to save that which was lost. It was not a union of men who had agreed to merge their differing tastes and sentiments in a common impulse, and to combine for the purpose of furthering a cause which would get them a name on the earth, or secure some worldly interests. In such a case, the heterogeneous elements might have been driven asunder, mutual jealousies and rivalries would have arisen, and the bonds of union would have been broken amid the tumult of passions and conflicting gains. Such were the disastrous results of the introduction of worldly elements afterwards into the church. But it was a union of materials, which, though originally discordant, underwent a radical change; and while each reflected the image of their common Lord, all were bound in love to one another, and in the most disinterested effort to regenerate and bless the world. Multitudes beheld the astonishing spectacle. It was a new and lovely creation, which could not be accounted for on natural principles. The purity, love, and benevolence of the Gospel were impressively exhibited in the community of its professed followers; and, in that exhibition, the world saw and felt an evidence that Christianity is divine, and that the Father had sent the Son.

So will it be again. The evidence derived from the palpable unanimity of the Christian church is emerging forth anew. To this result the leagued assaults of infidelity and superstition are contributing. The Redeemer, with his fan in his hand, is purging his floor, making more manifest the broad distinction between his friends and his foes. And when the faithful of every name have ceased to make matters, confessedly subordinate, rallying points for a party; and are made willing to acknowledge, and co-operate with, all those who hold by the Head; when those jealousies and discords are banished from the kingdom of God which, however natural in the empires of earth, are uncongenial to the kingdom of heaven; and when the church looks forth again as one united force on the world, at war with nothing but all the powers of evil, and manifestly the greatest instrument of good; all, but the willfully blinded and irrecoverably depraved, will be constrained to acknowledge the hand of the Invisible, and to receive Christianity as of God. "Fain would I," says Calvin, "that all the churches of Christ were so united, that the angels might look down from heaven, and add to our glory with their harmony." He might have added, as no doubt he felt, that the unreasonableness of unbelief might be driven from one of its refuges of lies.

We are led to remark secondly, that the unity of action, consequent on the unity of exhibition, would tell powerfully on the successful propagation of Christianity. Sectarianism has been the bane of the church. Multiplied divisions have weakened her energies. A vast amount of zeal and power, which should have been brought to bear on the conversion of the world, has been expended in assailing and defending the several points on which the

Christian community has been split into fragments. Christendom has often resembled a battle-field, in which the several detachments of the same army, instead of combining in one aggressive movement against the common foe, have raised the shout of war against each other. The enemy, meanwhile, has exulted at the sight, and not only been fortified in the belief that Christianity is a profession under which men drive low and selfish designs, but has strengthened his position in defying the armies of the living God. The storms of controversy may have been overruled for purifying the atmosphere of the church, and preserving in vigor the faith once delivered to the saints; but although good has come out of the evil, the evil has been manifested in the consumption of so much intellectual energy and effort on internal disputes, which might have been bestowed on the infinitely nobler object of converting the world to God.

There have been great questions of principle involved in many of the divisions of the church; and better is it to have divisions, than that important principles should be sacrificed; but the rent has not unfrequently been made on the most unjustifiable pretexts; and even when the denominational distinctions have been called for, the zeal in aiding the common object of evangelizing the world has been wofully disproportionate to that bestowed on lengthening the cords and strengthening the stakes of party interests. The primitive church, so long as it had the unity of exhibition, had the unity of action also. It not only presented one undivided front to the world, but it brought the full tide of its heavenly energy to bear on the point of the world's conversion. In the palpable unanimity of the Christian community was not only exhibited a lovely persuasive spectacle; but, out of that unanimity, arose a might of benevolence which, like a noble river, enriched by a thousand streamlets, fertilized and gladdened every region through which it flowed. The force which was afterwards spent on internal strifes and party interests, was exerted in executing the Lord's commission to go into all the world, and preach the Gospel to every creature: and it ran speedily, and vast multitudes everywhere became obedient to the faith. The church stood out from the world, one in its interests and aims, and the world felt the power of its instrumentality, and acknowledged that it was of God. If ever there was a period when Christianity seemed on the eve of making the world all her own, it was within the century after the effusion of Pentecost, when, under an united impulse, and endued with power from on high, she traveled onward in the greatness of her strength. The victories of Imperial Rome were eclipsed by the bloodless conquests of the "kingdom not of this world." The standard of the cross was planted beyond the bounds where stood the standard of Cæsar. And the angel, having the everlasting Gospel, flew farther than the Roman eagles. A united church, in the face of the most powerful obstacles, spread itself, within a century after the ascension of Christ, more rapidly and extensively than it has done in any single century since. And, as already hinted, without assigning this as exclusively the cause of the rapid progress of the Gospel; or, with Gibbon, accounting it one of a number of natural causes that produced the unparalleled effect—(for the question occurs, whence that union?)—we cannot, with the Savior's intercessory prayer before us, hesitate to acknowledge it as a powerfully subordinate source of the church's strength. Ichabod might almost have been written upon her—for her glory had nearly departed—when men of worldly policy tampered with her purity, and strifes and divisions brake her in pieces.

But there have been noble things done since, by the combined efforts of large portions of the Christian community, which indicate what a mighty influence for good a thoroughly united church would exert on the mass of mankind. The reformation from Popery, the most glorious event since the introduction of Christianity, was, to a considerable degree, the united work of the children of God that were scattered abroad. The London Missionary Society, the British and Foreign Bible Society, the Tract Society, and some other kindred institutions, have, by the catholicity of their constitution, opened up common channels, into which the several sections of the church might bring their enlightened efforts, and thereby diffuse the river of the water of life over our own and other lands. But these have been but earnests, and indications of what that unity which the Savior prayed for would effect. It is no utopian dream — a thing to be desired rather than expected — to believe that the time will come when the church will possess that unity of exhibition and of action of which we have been speaking, that then infidelity will be driven from one of its refuges, and the world, now unbelieving without a cause, will have a clear palpable proof that the Father has sent the Son, and that Christianity is divine. The old sarcasm of the unbeliever, derived from the disjointed and disorderly state of the church, will be silenced; the repulsive aspect, which divisions have given to Christianity, will be effaced, and her native loveliness be restored; a mighty stumbling-block, in the way of the diffusion of the Gospel, will be removed; and Christians, being united to each other in heart and hand, will come, with a moral might such as the world has not experienced for ages, to the help of the Lord, to the help of the Lord against the mighty. The brief but bright description of the churches given by James Montgomery, will then be realized: "Distinct as the billows, but one as the sea." Meanwhile God, in the signs of the times, is calling upon all the friends of the pure gospel truth to make it manifest that they are one. The religion of Christ, in our land, is powerfully beset by a bold reviving Romanism on the one hand, and by a subtile, busy, well-organized infidelity on the other. Both would, in a great measure, be disarmed and driven back, were the ranks of evangelical Protestantism to re-unite and move forward under the impulse of an all-pervading spirit of unity. Let the churches hear the words of the Genevese Reformer, whose love of union was as the love of life: "Keep your smaller differences, let us have no discord on that account; but let us march in one solid column, under the banners of the Captain of our salvation, and with undivided counsels form the legions of the cross upon the territories of darkness and of death."

www.ingramcontent.com/pod-product-compliance
Lightning Source LLC
LaVergne TN
LVHW020119110826

845151LV00001B/206

* 9 7 8 1 4 2 5 5 4 2 3 8 2 *